War In Peace

Volume 3

War In Peace

The Marshall Cavendish Illustrated Encyclopedia of Postwar Conflict.

Editor-in-Chief
Ashley Brown

Editorial Board
Brig-Gen. James Collins Jr (USA Retd.)
Vice-Admiral Sir Louis Le Bailly KBE CB
Ian V Hogg; David Floyd
Professor Laurence Martin
Air-Vice Marshal SWB Menaul CB CBE DFC AFC

MARSHALL CAVENDISH
NEW YORK, LONDON, TORONTO

Reference Edition Published 1985

Published by Marshall Cavendish Corporation
147 West Merrick Road
Freeport, Long Island
N.Y. 11520

Printed and Bound in Italy by L.E.G.O. S.p.a. Vicenza.

British Library Cataloguing in Publication Data

Brown, Ashley
   War in peace : the Marshall Cavendish
   illustrated encyclopaedia of post-war conflict.
   1. History, Modern—1945-   2. War—History
   —20th century
   I. Title   II. Dartford, Mark
   909.82   D842

   ISBN 0-86307-293-3
         0 86307 296 8   vol. 3

Library of Congress Cataloging in Publication Data

Main entry under title:

War in peace.

   Includes bibliographies and index.
   1. Military history, Modern—20th century.   2. Military
art and science—History—20th century.   3. World politics—1945-
I. Marshall Cavendish Corporation.
U42.W373 1984   355'.009'04   84-19386
ISBN 0-86307-293-3
         0 86307 296 8   vol. 3

Editorial Staff

Editor	Ashley Brown
Editorial Director	Brian Innes
Editorial Manager	Clare Byatt
Editorial Editors	Sam Elder
	Adrian Gilbert
Sub Editors	Sue Leonard
	Simon Innes
Artwork Editor	Jonathan Reed
Artwork Buyer	Jean Morley
Picture Editor	Carina Dvorak
Picture Consultant	Robert Hunt
Design	EDC

Reference Edition Staff

Editor	Mark Dartford
Designer	Graham Beehag
Consultant	Robert Paulley
Indexers	F & K Gill
Creation	DPM Services

Editorial Board

Contributors

David Blue served with the CIA in various countries of Southeast Asia, including Laos, and is a writer on and a student of small wars.

Gordon Brook-Shepherd spent 15 years in Vienna, first as lieutenant-colonel on the staff of the British High Commission and then as a foreign correspondent for the *Daily Telegraph*. A graduate in history from Cambridge, he is currently Chief Assistant Editor of the *Sunday Telegraph*.

Jeffrey J. Clarke is an expert on recent military history, particularly the Vietnam War, and has written for the American Center of Military History.

Major-General Richard Clutterbuck OBE has been Senior Lecturer in politics at Exeter University since his retirement from the army in 1972. His works include *Protest and the Urban Guerrilla, Guerrillas and Terrorists* and *Kidnap and Ransom*.

Alexander S. Cochran Jr is a historian whose area of research is modern Indochinese affairs with particular reference to the war in Vietnam since 1945. He is at present working in the Southeast Asia Branch of the Center of Military History, Department of the Army.

Colonel Peter M. Dunn is a serving officer in the USAF. His doctoral thesis is on the history of Indochina during the mid-1940s.

John B. Dwyer served both with the infantry and with armoured units in Vietnam. He was editor and publisher of the Vietnam veteran's newsletter *Perimeter* and has been a writer and correspondent for *National Vietnam Veteran's Review* for the past few years. His particular interest are Special Forces and Special Operations.

Brenda Ralph Lewis has specialised in political and military history since 1964. She s a regular contributor to military and historical magazines in both Britain and the United States.

Hugh Lunghi served in Moscow in the British Military Mission and the British Embassy for six years during and after World War II. He was interpreter for the British Chiefs of Staff at the Teheran, Yalta and Potsdam conferences, and also interpreted for Churchill and Anthony Eden. He subsequently worked in the BBC External Services and is a former editor of *Index on Censorship*.

Charles Messenger retired from the army in 1980 to become a fulltime military writer after 21 years service in the Royal Tank Regiment. Over the past 10 years he has written several books on 20th century warfare, as well as contributing articles to a number of defence and historical journals. He is currently a Research Associate at the Royal United Services Institute for Defence Studies in London.

Billy C. Mossman is a well-known American writer and historian. He is currently working on a volume on the Korean War for the US Army Center of Military History.

Bryan Perrett served in the Royal Armoured Corps from 1952 to 1971. He contributes regularly to a number of established military journals and acted as Defence Correspondent to the *Liverpool Echo* during the Falklands War. His recent books include *Weapons of the Falklands Conflict* and *A History of Blitzkrieg*.

Chapman Pincher is one of England's leading authorities on international espionage and counter-intelligence. He is the author of political novels and books on spying, the most recent of which is *Their Trade is Treachery*, which deals with the penetration of Britain's secret services by the Russian secret police.

Yehoshua Porath is a noted scholar at the Hebrew University in Jerusalem. He has made a special study of the Palestinian problem and is the author of two books on the subject, the most recent of which is *The Palestinian Arab National Movement 1929—39*, which was published in Britain in 1977.

Contributors

Antony Preston is Naval Editor of the military magazine *Defence* and author of numerous publications including *Battleships, Aircraft Carriers* and *Submarines*.

Brigadier-General Edwin H. Simmons, US Marine Corps, Retired, is the Director of Marine Corps History and Museums. At the time of the Inchon operation and the Chosin Reservoir campaign, he, as a major, commanded Weapons Company, 3rd Battalion, 1st Marines. Widely published, he is the author of *The United States Marines*.

Ronald Spector is an expert on Vietnam and has recently completed a book on that subject for the Center of Military History in the United States.

Andres Suarez served in the Cuban ministry of education from 1948—1951, took part in the Cuban revolution, and served in the ministry of housing from 1959. From 1965, he has been Professor of Latin American Studies at the University of Florida. Other publications include *Cuba and the Sino—Soviet Rift*.

Sir Robert Thompson KBE, CMG, DSO, MC is a world authority on guerrilla warfare, on which he has written extensively. He was directly involved in the Emergency in Malaya in the 1950s and rose to become permanent Secretary for Defence. From 1961 to 1965 he headed the British Advisory Mission to Vietnam and since then he has advised several governments, including the United States, on counter-insurgency operations Sir Robert Thompson is a Council member of the Institute for the Study of Conflict, London. His books include *Defeating Communist Insurgency and Revolutionary War in World Strategy, 1945—69.*

Patrick Turnbull commanded 'D' Force, Burma during World War II. His 29 published works include a history of the Foreign Legion.

Contents of Volume

War at Sea

Naval developments 1945-55

The decade from 1945 to 1955 saw the navies that had won the crucial sea battles of World War II cut down and modified for peacetime. The administrators of the navies of the Western powers faced a number of problems, however. The two most important were how to cope with technological advances that were affecting all levels of combat, and what role to adopt in the confrontation of the Cold War against a Soviet empire that had very few large naval units.

Soon after World War II ended it became apparent that there were two schools of thought in naval strategy. One held that, although striking power in the form of the battleship had certainly been superseded, the far-reaching power of the aircraft carrier and her aircraft made this the new form of capital ship. On the other hand, extreme exponents of air power claimed that nuclear weapons had made sea power totally obsolete. Both sides claimed that the two nuclear tests at Bikini Atoll in 1946 supported their argument – one because neither the air burst nor the underwater burst had wiped out the target ships, the other because the ships which had been damaged were totally unfit for combat.

For a while it seemed that the air power school of thought had prevailed, in spite of its failure to clear up the detailed points about just how bombers were to

achieve the sort of pinpoint delivery needed. Ship-designers moved very cautiously, and there was no rush to build 'atom age' warships. In 1949, for example, an inter-service wrangle resulted in the US Navy losing its fight to build a new aircraft carrier, the *United States*. The air force argued that its B-36 bomber could do the job more effectively than the Navy's twin-engined carrier-borne bombers, where-as the navy maintained that its widely dispersed carriers would be able to hit the Soviet heartland without sacrificing any of its other roles.

The US Navy lost that round, for the prevailing political wisdom was that the Russians would attack without warning. The memory of Pearl Harbor was still fresh in American minds in the late 1940s, and when the Soviet Union detonated its first nuclear device in 1949 this view was reinforced. The 'four-minute war' threatened by the intercontinental ballistic missile was not yet part of strategic folklore, but through the postwar period there was an assumption by many politicians and air force and army planners that the navy would have little or no role to play if war broke out.

These theories did not affect the fact that Western powers still had very powerful fleets. The navies which eventually made up the main strength of Nato

Launching a Short Seacat shipborne SAM. Seacat is one of the world's most widely deployed shipborne weapons and is operated by a total of 15 navies. Its initial development began in 1951 and in July 1962 it finally entered service with the Royal Navy.

Above: The main naval armament of the USS *Missouri* blasts away at targets in the Chonjin area during the early part of the Korean War.

Below: Jet and piston-engined aircraft line the decks of the USS *Antietam* off the east coast of Korea.

South Korean ground forces and the first American reinforcements were quickly overrun by the North Koreans, and had it not been for immediate intervention air strikes from carriers, the vital port of Pusan might have had to be abandoned.

Korea gave the allied navies a chance to show their solidarity, and Australian, Canadian and British aircraft carriers all took part in operations between 1950 and 1953, supported by cruisers, destroyers and escorts. The war was, of course, misleading in some respects, for the United Nations' warships enjoyed a degree of immunity from North Korean (and later, Chinese) counteraction. Apart from occasional duels with shore artillery, the warships lying offshore were in a sort of 'sanctuary' which was in stark contrast to the tough fighting conditions suffered by the ground forces.

The most alarming lesson to be learned in Korea was that the Soviet Union was much more advanced in mine warfare than any Western intelligence agencies had predicted. Therefore, as the shallow harbours in Europe were known to be particularly vulnerable to large-scale mining the Royal Navy was immediately given the task of developing designs for coastal and inshore minesweepers to deal with the threat. Large numbers of wooden-hulled minesweepers were built, either in British shipyards or to British designs in Europe, and several navies were given American funds for this purpose, under the Mutual Defense Assistance Program. Several hundred minesweepers were built, and many of them have survived into the 1980s.

had an enormous preponderance of numbers over the Soviet Fleet, particularly in the new techniques of carrier warfare. In 1947 the US Navy could boast more than 20 *Essex* class carriers, as well as nine light fleet carriers and three of the new 45,000-tonne Midway class. Backing up these front-line units were large numbers of escort carriers. The British could muster another five fleet carriers, and were completing two 45,000-tonners, *Eagle* and *Ark Royal;* they also had eight light fleet carriers completed and another 10 hulls in various stages of construction.

The early postwar theories were considerably modified by the practical test of the Korean War. Any doubts about the value of carrier air power, for example, were rapidly dispelled by experience there.

If the mine was an old weapon, there was also a new weapon that affected naval thinking in the decade after 1945; the missile. During the Korean War the air threat to ships was negligible, but this did not mean that navies were unmindful of the threat from the Soviet Union's shore-based air forces. The knowledge of what had been achieved by primitive German anti-ship guided missiles in the Bay of Biscay and the Mediterranean led directly to the first American guided missile developments. In December 1944 the Applied Physics Laboratory of Johns Hopkins University answered a request for proposals for anti-aircraft guided missiles, and out of this came Project Bumblebee.

The first workable surface-to-air guided weapon, Terrier, flew in 1950, and although the trials were disappointing the design was 'frozen' because of the Korean War. After many teething troubles Terrier was finally passed for operational service in 1955, in two converted heavy cruisers. The Bumblebee programme envisaged two additional missiles, for it was soon recognised that Terrier was far too bulky to be fitted into destroyers, and also lacked range. The Talos system answered the need for range, but could only be fitted in cruisers, leaving the 16km (10-mile) Tartar to be developed for destroyers.

The British, with equally bitter memories of losses to air attack, had started development of their own surface-to-air missile. The Seaslug, which first flew in 1951, became operational in 1961, while the French Masurca took even longer to develop. No other European or Nato navy could afford the development of these expensive systems, but in the early 1950s there was general acceptance that the British and the Americans would provide air-defence from their aircraft carriers, backed up by the Canadians, French and Dutch. The British, however, went a step further and developed a successful close-range (4600m or 5000-yard) missile, Seacat. The first test vehicle flew in 1955 but the missile did not reach the fleet for another six years.

It was generally agreed that gunfire by itself would not provide defence against high-speed aircraft, but a stop-gap role was seen for guns until the missiles were ready, and as a back-up to missile defence. A number of late World War II gun-systems continued to be

developed, emphasising high rates of fire and automatic radar-controlled tracking.

The large sums being spent on naval aviation and air defence paled into insignificance beside the research and development budgets for defence against submarines. The realisation that Germany had nearly turned the tables as late as 1945 with the outstanding Type XXI U-boat caused an immediate rush to extract as many ideas as possible from German designers. The Russians went so far as to load the incomplete carrier *Graf Zeppelin* with U-boat sections, while the British and Americans each recommissioned a Type XVIIB boat to test the Walter hydrogen peroxide turbine. Other U-boats were tested to destruction and copies of German homing torpedoes appeared in the British, French and American navies within a short space of time.

Speed and silence

What made the Type XXI so deadly was its combination of a streamlined hull-form and large-capacity batteries, which gave her a high 'burst' speed. At a stroke this made the majority of the corvettes, frigates and destroyer-escorts built to fight the Battle of the Atlantic obsolete, for at 16 to 20 knots they could not catch a Type XXI. By 1949 intelligence sources knew that 'XXI technology' had been incorporated into the latest Russian submarines, and as Josef Stalin was known to have plans to build over 200 hulls there was justifiable alarm.

The Americans and British had a large number of war-built destroyers and many of these were re-armed as anti-submarine escorts and frigates. The British went further and designed a fast frigate capable of pursuing a submerged submarine at high speed. Armed with the latest weaponry and sonars, the Type 12, as it was designated, was probably the finest escort in the world, and variants of it are still being built in the 1980s. Relying totally on sea trade, the British felt justified in devoting a large percentage of their resources to anti-submarine research and in the

Below: The devastating effects of a sea mine on a South Korean minesweeper in Wonsan harbour in October 1950. Inset: The USS *England* firing Terrier missiles. The Terrier nuclear-option missile is a beam-rider and is effective against both surface targets and formations of aircraft or missiles.

early 1950s were the acknowledged leaders in sonar design.

Western submarines also benefited from the Type XXI and other German ideas. In the late 1940s the US Navy began a large-scale modernisation of its fleet submarines, streamlining the hulls and lengthening them to enable the batteries to be enlarged. Known as 'Guppies' from the acronym for 'greater underwater propulsive power', these rebuilt submarines were intended principally to counter Soviet submarines, for postwar experiments revealed that submarines could fight submarines. It was not a new idea, for the British had built submarine-hunting submarines in 1918 and a few submarine-versus-submarine encounters had taken place in World War II, but with improved sonars it became a major feature of anti-submarine warfare from the early 1950s.

The 'Guppy' features proved so successful that they were copied by other navies, not only for older submarines but for new vessels as well. The biggest revolution of all, however, was just beginning. In 1952 the United States Congress authorised funds for building the world's first nuclear-powered submarine. This was the USS *Nautilus*, which was commissioned on 30 September 1954. Paradoxically, in one respect nuclear power looked back to the past and reintroduced steam turbine propulsion to submarines for the first time in 40 years, the reactor-core merely generating heat to provide steam. The choice of a submarine as the nuclear prototype was particularly appropriate, for eliminating the need for atmospheric oxygen freed the submarine from the need to come to the surface to recharge batteries.

Less than a year before *Nautilus* entered service another historic submarine joined the US Fleet. The USS *Albacore*'s unique whale-shaped hull offered a remarkable improvement in handling and speed under water, and after lengthy trials the 'teardrop' form was adopted for future construction. The combination of the 'teardrop' hull and nuclear propulsion pointed the way to an enormous improvement in the effectiveness of submarines in naval warfare.

Although nuclear propulsion was clearly superior, experiments with hydrogen peroxide turbines continued in Great Britain and the Soviet Union. The British built *Explorer* and *Excalibur* in an attempt to cure the faults of the original German Walter turbine, and the Russians installed Walter turbines in several submarines, but although some impressive speeds were recorded – 27 knots by the British pair – the system was inherently unreliable and did not justify the expense.

All the victorious navies had a large number of new war-built ships, so the 10 years following 1945 did not see a large amount of new construction. Instead there was a concentration of effort on increasing the effectiveness of existing designs to meet any future threat. It was clear to naval aviators that the high landing speeds of turbojet aircraft were too much for existing carriers to handle, and the late 1940s and early 1950s saw a large crop of experiments and ideas.

Below: The Soviet cruiser *Sverdlov,* natural successor to the war-built Chapaev class. Although some of this class carry surface-to-air missiles, they are mostly retained for offshore bombardment. Bottom: Convair Terrier missiles in their launchers aboard the USS *Boston.*

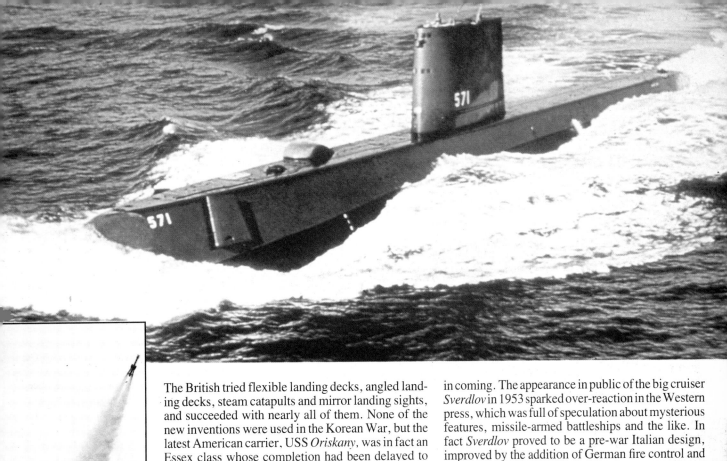

The British tried flexible landing decks, angled landing decks, steam catapults and mirror landing sights, and succeeded with nearly all of them. None of the new inventions were used in the Korean War, but the latest American carrier, USS *Oriskany*, was in fact an Essex class whose completion had been delayed to permit the incorporation of new ideas.

In line with American perceptions of a massive Soviet air assault on the North American continent using the polar route, great emphasis was placed on chains of land radar stations, notably the Distant Early Warning (DEW) line across northern Canada and Alaska. To extend the coverage of the DEW line destroyer escorts were fitted as radar pickets, and even submarines were pressed into service.

The Soviet surface navy did not figure largely in these plans, for the simple reason that it did not yet pose a threat. The ravages of World War II had not yet been repaired fully and, although Stalin still nurtured a belief in big surface ships, the new ships were slow in coming. The appearance in public of the big cruiser *Sverdlov* in 1953 sparked over-reaction in the Western press, which was full of speculation about mysterious features, missile-armed battleships and the like. In fact *Sverdlov* proved to be a pre-war Italian design, improved by the addition of German fire control and copies of British wartime radars; but as the first of Stalin's new navy to be seen in public the impression she created swamped objective analysis.

Looking back on the decade from 1945 it is easy to criticise the fears of Western naval planners. Time was to show that balanced naval forces still had a role to play, and that World War III was not imminent. But equally, credit must be given for those same planners' foresight. Most of the new equipment and designs which were generated proved valid 20 years later. Virtually all the naval technology in use up to 1980 existed or was in embryo by 1955, and only in the 1980s has replacement become an urgent necessity.

Antony Preston

Top: USS *Nautilus,* the world's first nuclear-powered submarine. She put to sea for the first time in January 1955 but has since been used for experiments in submarine communication. Above: A Whitworth Gloster Seaslug arrows skyward. Development of this type of beam-riding missile began in 1944 and the first successful flight took place in January 1951.

The naval balance 1955

navies	aircraft carriers	post WW II patrol submarines displacing 700 tonnes or more	coastal submarines displacing less than 700 tonnes	major surface warships – missile armed	major surface warships conventionally armed	patrol boats, torpedo boats and gunboats
USA	33 fleet 66 escort*	1 nuclear 190 conventional	0	2	835	120
Royal Navy (UK)	15	55 conventional	2	0	304	97
other Nato countries	7	54 conventional	1	0	278	170
Nato total	55 attack 66 escort	1 nuclear 299 conventional	3	2	1417	387
USSR	0	215 conventional	269	0	256	516
other Warsaw Pact countries	0	0	0	0	7	54
Warsaw Pact total	0	215 conventional	269	0	263	570

*the 66 escort carriers were unable to deploy jet aircraft and had no attack capability

Disaster in the Mediterranean

When two Royal Navy vessels were lost to mines

On 22 October 1946 two British destroyers – *Saumarez* and *Volage* – were blasted by mines while passing through the northern channel of the Corfu Straits, close to the coast of Albania. As a result 44 sailors were killed and a further 40 injured.

The incident arose over the status of the Corfu Straits as an international waterway. Comprising a narrow strip of sea between Albania and the Greek island of Corfu, the central channel of the straits traditionally offered free passage for all peaceful ships, but in 1946 newly-communist Albania disputed this, claiming the entire area as territorial water and demanding the right to control all traffic. The situation was complicated by the fact that the straits had been mined during World War II, and although a narrow channel had been left clear, it passed within 1.5km (½ mile) of the Albanian port of Saranda. Ships therefore had to enter undisputed Albanian waters, leaving the question of free passage extremely blurred. The British government gave the Royal Navy the task of clarifying matters by using the straits, thus hoping to establish by precedent the rule of international maritime law.

When the cruisers *Orion* and *Superb* entered the area on 15 May 1946 they came under fire from Albanian shore batteries near Saranda. Britain accused the Albanians of unwarranted aggression and demanded an apology. When none was forthcoming the decision was taken to send a special naval force through the straits with the apparent intention of provoking an attack which could then be used to condemn Albania before the world.

In late October the force, comprising the cruisers *Mauritius* and *Leander* with destroyers *Saumarez* and *Volage* in attendance, gathered at Corfu harbour. Commanded by Rear Admiral H.R.G. Kinahan, the ships set out at 1330 hours on the 22nd in two pairs – *Mauritius* and *Saumarez* in the lead, with *Leander* and *Volage* 3km (2 miles) astern. Some 80km (50 miles) to the north the aircraft carrier *Ocean*, with her escort destroyer *Raider*, provided support in case of an attack. Kinahan's orders were to react with force to any Albanian aggression.

At first all went quietly. At 1447 hours, in an atmosphere of anticlimax, *Mauritius* cleared the potential flashpoint close to Saranda and turned for the open sea. Six minutes later a huge explosion rocked *Saumarez*, sending a brilliant yellow flash high into the air on both sides of her hull. Captain W. H. Selby signalled Kinahan that he had been mined. On board *Mauritius* the squadron navigating officer fixed the destroyer's position – almost exactly in the centre of the supposedly mine-free channel.

Damage to *Saumarez* was crippling. The explosion ripped through Number One boiler room, fractured five of the fuel tanks and opened the forward part of the ship to the sea. Her power gone, she wallowed bow-down in the water and; as leaking oil ignited, fires swept through her shattered compartments. With 36 of her crewmen dead or dying, she began drifting helplessly towards uncleared minefields, shallow waters and a hostile shore.

Kinahan reacted quickly. Lacking sea-room in mine-infested waters, he sent *Leander* around the island of Corfu so as to be available in the south, called for assistance from *Ocean* and *Raider* and ordered Commander Reginald Paul in *Volage* to take *Saumarez* in tow. Paul approached the crippled destroyer with caution. He attached a line to her stern but this first attempt failed. As he manoeuvred for a second attempt the two ships collided, tearing a 2.5m (8 foot) gash in *Volage*'s bow. Although this was above the water-line, Paul ordered a party forward to plug the hole. Eight men were still working there when another mine exploded, killing them instantly

Above: The Corfu Straits, looking out from Corfu itself with Albania in the distance. Below: Difficult moments requiring expert seamanship as *Volage* manoeuvres in order to take *Saumarez* in tow.

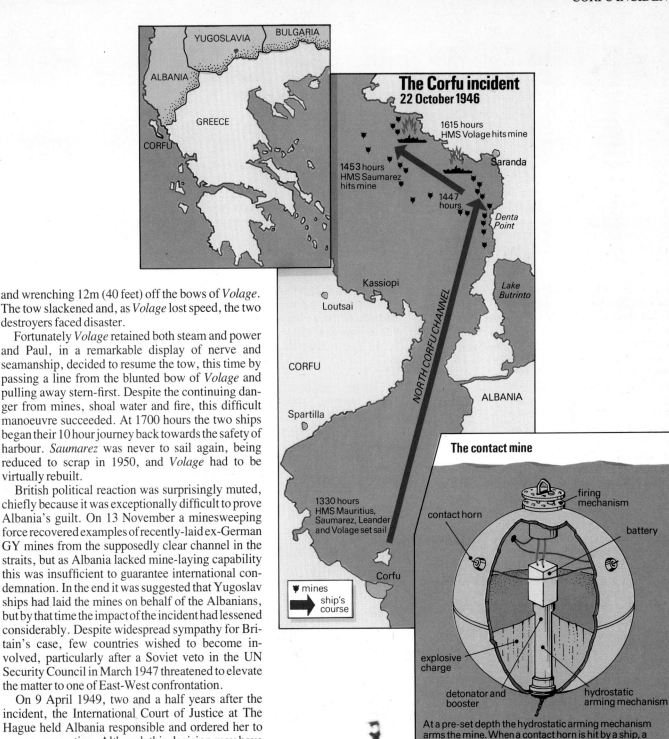

The Corfu incident
22 October 1946

1615 hours
HMS Volage hits mine

Saranda

1453 hours
HMS Saumarez
hits mine

1447
hours

Denta
Point

Kassiopi

Loutsai

Lake
Butrinto

NORTH CORFU CHANNEL

CORFU

ALBANIA

Spartilla

1330 hours
HMS Mauritius,
Saumarez, Leander
and Volage set sail

Corfu

mines
ship's
course

YUGOSLAVIA   BULGARIA

ALBANIA

GREECE

CORFU

The contact mine

firing
mechanism

contact horn

battery

explosive
charge

detonator and
booster

hydrostatic
arming mechanism

At a pre-set depth the hydrostatic arming mechanism
arms the mine. When a contact horn is hit by a ship, a
current runs to the firing mechanism which turns on the
battery. The battery then fires the detonator and booster
which explode the main charge.

and wrenching 12m (40 feet) off the bows of *Volage*.
The tow slackened and, as *Volage* lost speed, the two
destroyers faced disaster.

Fortunately *Volage* retained both steam and power
and Paul, in a remarkable display of nerve and
seamanship, decided to resume the tow, this time by
passing a line from the blunted bow of *Volage* and
pulling away stern-first. Despite the continuing danger from mines, shoal water and fire, this difficult
manoeuvre succeeded. At 1700 hours the two ships
began their 10 hour journey back towards the safety of
harbour. *Saumarez* was never to sail again, being
reduced to scrap in 1950, and *Volage* had to be
virtually rebuilt.

British political reaction was surprisingly muted,
chiefly because it was exceptionally difficult to prove
Albania's guilt. On 13 November a minesweeping
force recovered examples of recently-laid ex-German
GY mines from the supposedly clear channel in the
straits, but as Albania lacked mine-laying capability
this was insufficient to guarantee international condemnation. In the end it was suggested that Yugoslav
ships had laid the mines on behalf of the Albanians,
but by that time the impact of the incident had lessened
considerably. Despite widespread sympathy for Britain's case, few countries wished to become involved, particularly after a Soviet veto in the UN
Security Council in March 1947 threatened to elevate
the matter to one of East-West confrontation.

On 9 April 1949, two and a half years after the
incident, the International Court of Justice at The
Hague held Albania responsible and ordered her to
pay compensation. Although this decision may have
vindicated British actions, with 44 dead the cost was
extremely high. The compensation has never been
paid.   **John Pimlott**

Running the gauntlet

The desperate escape of HMS Amethyst

On 19 April 1949 the frigate HMS *Amethyst* left the Chinese port of Shanghai under orders to sail up the Yangtse River (now called the Chang Jiang) to relieve the destroyer *Consort* as guardian of the British Embassy at Nanking (Nanjing). It was a delicate task. China was in the throes of civil war and the Yangtse acted as boundary between communist forces in the north and Nationalists in the south. Indeed, a communist assault across the river was imminent.

Amethyst never completed her journey. At 0920 hours on 20 April she came under sustained and highly accurate communist artillery fire while passing between the northern village of San-chiang-ying and Rose Island, 200km (125 miles) from Nanking. Motives for the attack are still not clear – communist gunners may have mistaken *Amethyst* for a Nationalist warship – but the results were devastating. In a barrage lasting over an hour, 53 shells hammered into the frigate, leaving 22 of her crew dead or dying and 31 wounded. The bridge was destroyed, incapacitating all upon it including the captain, Lieutenant-Commander B. M. Skinner. The wheelhouse was hit, causing the ship to veer violently to port and, after the 'low power room' was wrecked, coordinated control of the guns failed. A few shots were fired from X-gun in the stern, but communist machine guns silenced the courageous crew. Her gyro-compass smashed and command structure disrupted, *Amethyst* ran aground on the mud of Rose Island, helpless under the hostile guns.

Home at last. After more than three months aground in the Yangtse River, and continually harassed as she lay between the advancing communist forces and the retreating Nationalists, the *Amethyst* finally escaped, making an epic 140-mile dash down the river to rejoin the fleet at Woosung. She was then escorted to safety. Here she lies at anchor in Hong Kong harbour.

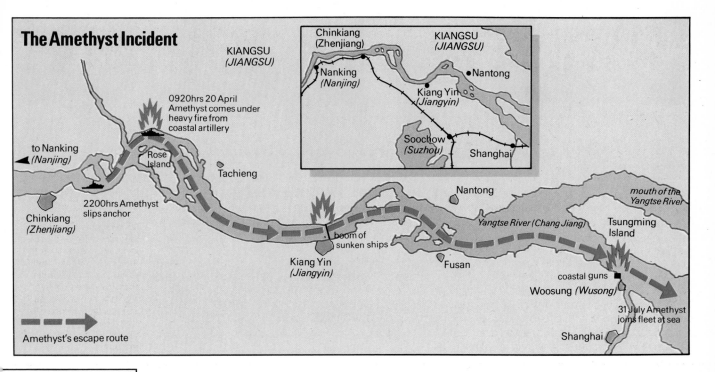

The Amethyst Incident

0920hrs 20 April
Amethyst comes under
heavy fire from
coastal artillery

to Nanking
(Nanjing)

Rose Island

Tachieng

2200hrs Amethyst
slips anchor

Chinkiang
(Zhenjiang)

KIANGSU
(JIANGSU)

Chinkiang
(Zhenjiang)

Nanking
(Nanjing)

KIANGSU
(JIANGSU)

Nantong

Kiang Yin
(Jiangyin)

Soochow
(Suzhou)

Shanghai

Nantong

Yangtse River (Chang Jiang)

mouth of the
Yangtse River

Tsungming
Island

boom of
sunken ships

Kiang Yin
(Jiangyin)

Fusan

coastal guns
Woosung (Wusong)

31 July Amethyst
joins fleet at sea

Shanghai

Amethyst's escape route

Command devolved onto First Lieutenant G. L. Weston, himself badly injured. His first thought was for the safety of his crew. With the ship's doctor dead the wounded desperately needed help, so Weston ordered the evacuation of all but a small 'steaming party' to the relative security of Nationalist positions on the south bank. But not all the crew received the order, and confusion reigned as 60 men went over the side. That left just over 100 still on board.

By now *Amethyst*'s plight was known elsewhere. A distress message had been acknowledged by Nanking, so rescue seemed possible. Weston countermanded his evacuation order and prepared to take a tow from *Consort*, which had been waiting 65km (40 miles) upstream under cover of darkness. But when she appeared, with all guns blazing, at 1430 hours, she too came under communist fire and was forced to escape alone.

Further rescue attempts fared no better. On the morning of the 21st, by which time Weston had managed to refloat and move his ship 2.5km (1½ miles) upstream, the cruiser *London*, accompanied by the frigate *Black Swan,* failed to break through from Shanghai. In the late afternoon a Sunderland flying-boat, sent from Hong Kong with medical aid, barely touched down close to *Amethyst* before departing hastily under communist fire. Nevertheless, one of the doctors on board, Flight Lieutenant M. E. Fearnley, RAF, managed to jump out and reach *Amethyst*, where he organised a further evacuation of wounded. Weston, typically, refused to leave.

This second group of wounded, once on the south bank, made contact with an overland rescue party from Nanking, led by the embassy's assistant naval attaché, Lieutenant-Commander J. S. Kerans. He supervised their evacuation to Shanghai, where they joined the men who had left the ship two days earlier, and then boarded *Amethyst* to take command. Weston was evacuated and Kerans prepared the ship for destruction. By this time the frigate had been moved a further 16km (10 miles) upriver, but on 23 April the long-awaited communist offensive isolated and surrounded her. With overland escape routes blocked,

Kerans was forced to keep the crew on board and await events.

The communists first made contact with *Amethyst* on 26 April, demanding talks on shore. This set the pattern for the next three months, with communist representatives promising free passage for the ship if Kerans would admit that she had fired first on 20 April in a deliberate 'invasion' of communist territory. This he naturally refused to do, but as the days dragged into weeks he came under mounting pressure. Although the morale of his 80-man crew did not weaken significantly, conditions on board deteriorated. Food rationing had to be introduced and power cuts were imposed as fuel stocks dwindled, despite an unexpected communist delivery of 54 tons of oil from a captured dump at Nanking on 10 July. In fact, oil was the crucial factor. If Kerans was to attempt an escape he needed a minimum of 47 tons. When it was reported to him on 30 July that stocks were down to 53 tons, he made his decision.

The escape was set for 2200 hours that night, to take full advantage of a favourable moon. *Amethyst* would have to travel 240km (150 miles) down the Yangtse at night, between river banks manned by hostile troops. It was a hair-raising journey, characterised by more than a fair share of luck. Just as *Amethyst* was about to weigh anchor, a Chinese merchant ship appeared, moving downstream, so Kerans decided to follow. This ploy worked until the ships reached Tachieng 15 minutes later, when flares and artillery fire challenged their progress. In the ensuing confusion the merchant ship acted as both decoy and shield, allowing *Amethyst* to slip through unnoticed. At high speed she swept past Rose Island and approached the next obstacle, a boom of sunken ships across the river at Kiang Yin (Jiangyin). Quite by chance, Kerans took her through the only gap, under cover of smoke. By 0242 hours on 31 July, 160km (100 miles) had been covered, but *Amethyst* had still to face the coastal guns at Woosung (Wusong), at the mouth of the river. As the first streaks of dawn appeared, she succeeded in avoiding the probing searchlights and reached the open sea. Her ordeal was over at last. **John Pimlott**

Hitting the beach

Amphibious warfare in the modern world

Top: US troops go ashore at Iwo Jima in February 1945 and begin to unload rations and supplies as a prelude to the main offensive. Left: A fleet of US LVTP-7s advance against the beach near Beirut, 1982. Right: Hitting the beach at speed, these troops break to left and right in order to split enemy fire as they move to take up positions on a beach-head.

nes

World War II saw the emergence of the United States as a superpower of acknowledged military might. Although industry and finance provided the basis of American strength, sea power was the chief means by which this strength was brought to battlefields around the globe. In the course of the war the United States provided her allies with enough equipment to supply 2000 infantry divisions. Her industry produced 41 billion smallarms rounds, 296,000 aircraft, 102,000 tanks and 76,000 ships. It was this latter strength, which included more than 5200 combat units, that enabled the United States to deploy her power.

No better illustration of American capabilities exists than 6 June 1944. On that day American forces landed on the Normandy coast; and on the very same day, combat forces left Majuro Atoll in the Marshalls in order to support the landings on Saipan, nine days and 2800km (1500 miles) away in the southern Marianas. The coincidence of these two operations makes June 1944 a pinnacle of American achievement. Certainly that month represented a peak in the history of amphibious warfare, even though many more assault landings were carried out in the Pacific before Japan's final surrender in August 1945.

So it was that World War II ended with the United States indisputably the strongest nation in the world. Her air forces were immensely powerful and her ground forces extremely large, well-equipped and supplied, but it was her fleets and her amphibious capabilities that were the means by which American power was projected across the world. It was this power that so alarmed the Soviet Union. The Soviets had no means of opposing the mighty amphibious forces that the Americans (and British) could deploy, any more than they had the means to challenge their strategic bomber forces.

Yet, since the end of World War II, there has been endless argument concerning the validity of the amphibious assault in modern warfare. This might seem strange, as most nations have a coastline and some 70 per cent of the surface of the globe is covered by water. Furthermore, one-sixth of the world's coastlines is vulnerable to a seaborne assault. These factors would seem to ensure the continued importance and relevance of sea power in general and amphibious power in particular, but this has not been the case.

Fight for the beaches

American success in amphibious warfare in the Pacific was based on the ability of the Americans to surround and isolate a target before overwhelming it with massive superiority of firepower. In the European theatre American (and British) success had to have a slightly different basis. Amphibious warfare is one of the most hazardous forms of combat. The approach to the objective must be correct, and the assault forces must be organised so that they arrive on the target in the correct and most effective order possible. Beaches must be selected with a view to assault forces being able to fight their way onto them, and then off them. Specialist engineer and armour support proved their value on numerous occasions in World War II while, of course, artillery, rocket and air support were indispensable to the success of the assault phase. But in the European theatre, where the British and Americans were opposed by an enemy with a good road and rail system at his disposal, the main problem for any seaborne invasion lay in building up forces within a confined beachhead at a faster rate than the enemy could bring up reinforcements.

Invariably, there was a period following every Allied invasion in Europe when the two sides built up at roughly equal rates, but in nearly every instance the amphibious attacker was able to secure the upper hand because his forces ashore had two advantages. First, they had fire support from the fleet which could be used to shatter a counter-attack, as was the case in

opportunities for strategic and tactical surprise. The concentration of force for the assault presents a defender with a massive target and, of course, the sheer volume of firepower from warships and aircraft is now a thing of the past.

For these reasons amphibious operations of the kind that took place at Salerno, Leyte, Iwo Jima and Okinawa are never likely to be repeated by any Western power, and since 1945 there have been only two major assault landings of the World War II type. These were the American landings at Inchon, Korea, in September 1950 and the Anglo-French landings at Port Said (Suez Canal), Egypt, in November 1956. In both cases the amphibious option was available because of the legacy of World War II: the Americans in the first instance and the British and French in the second had sufficient fire support, and landing ships and craft remaining from World War II to carry out this type of operation. At Suez, for example, the British and French between them deployed seven carriers and enjoyed the support of aircraft based on Cyprus. But within three years of Suez all of Britain's battleships had gone, and the heavy and light cruisers were similarly being phased out of service.

With the phasing out of old ships and the introduction of new technology that has reduced the fire support available to amphibious forces, there has

Salerno in 1943. Second, interdiction of the enemy's lines of communication was certain to weaken him in the long-term to the extent that his successful defence could not be sustained. At Anzio in 1944, for example, Allied sea communications were able to maintain and increase the forces ashore while air power, in conjunction with offensive action on the ground, wore down German resistance until it broke.

The strength of amphibious warfare lies in its ability to draw on far-flung resources and to land in a place of one's own choice. Through feints and deception, the key to success lies in a last-minute concentration of overwhelming superiority at a point of enemy weakness. But in the postwar world the question marks that have been placed against amphibious warfare have arisen for obvious reasons. Increasingly sophisticated means of surveillance have lessened the

Above: A US Navy air-cushioned patrol vehicle. Below: Soviet PT-76 light amphibious tanks go ashore. Bottom: The aftermath of a landing on Tarawa in 1943. Right top: The wide landing zone at Wonsan in 1950.

been a need to recast amphibious doctrine on the part of Western powers – and for the Soviet Union to devise one. The devising of Soviet doctrine had to go hand in hand with reviving a marine force. The Soviets deactivated their naval infantry at the end of the war, and not until 1964 did it reappear as a separate branch of the Soviet Navy.

Since that time the Soviet amphibious capacity has grown considerably and in the early 1980s there were five Marine brigades. Two were with the Pacific Fleet while the Black Sea, Baltic and Northern Fleets each had a single formation. As befits a service that has more ships than any other navy, the Soviets have the capacity to lift all their Marines, but the role of Soviet amphibious forces has reflected the evolution of the Soviet Navy as a whole from a coastal defence force to a 'blue water' navy. In the Baltic and Black Seas, and to a lesser extent in northern waters, the role of the Marines and the navy remains the same as the role of the navy since the 1930s, namely the defence of the homeland, the protection of the flanks of the army, and support of any offensive operation by the ground forces.

Hovercraft threat

In the two enclosed seas, the Black Sea and the Baltic, the nearness of Soviet air bases, the availability of Pact support, the presence of shipping that can be requisitioned, and the existence of very powerful purpose-built amphibious forces gives the Soviet Union an amphibious capability not dissimilar to that of the British and Americans in World War II. But whereas many Soviet landing vessels could be readily identified in a 1944 context, modern technology has allowed the development of hovercraft. Twelve of the enormous 156m (512 foot) long *Aist* hovercraft, able to move five main battle tanks (or four MBTs plus 150 men, or 350 men) at 65 knots, serve in the Baltic Fleet. As Exercise Soyuz-81 clearly showed, the Russians intend to use the hovercraft in conjunction with their other amphibious forces in assault landings. Backed by land-based air power and helicopter gunships, they see their Marines either seizing coastal objectives in front of advancing ground forces or moving directly to secure the straits that control the exits of these seas.

To date the Soviet deployment of hovercraft has been local, but whereas some 17 per cent of the world's coastline is vulnerable to seaborne assault by ships, about 70 per cent is vulnerable to assault by the much faster hovercraft. With its capacity to move directly inland and its extremely high speed in comparison to most ships, the hovercraft may well cause the whole concept of amphibious operations to be revised. The development by the Soviet Union of a local amphibious capability has been matched in recent years by a build-up of oceanic forces, particularly in the Pacific. Whereas in the past Soviet amphibious forces have had to work with small landing ships such as the *Polnocny* class and the 4500-tonne *Ropucha* and *Alligator* classes, the development of a series of high-cost amphibious and major combat units foreshadows a Soviet drive for an amphibious capability on the world's oceans.

The most obvious manifestation of this is the development of the first units of the 12,500-tonne *Ivan Rogov* class, ships roughly equivalent to the British *Fearless* or the American *Ogden* class. The *Rogov* can carry a battalion of either infantry or armour, and she has operated on the Vietnam station

Landing at San Carlos

'As we passed Fanning Head we prepared to go below. Eventually our boat numbers were called to assemble in the main lounge where there was a scene like a street market. Sergeants were handing round rubber contraceptives to cover the muzzles of the rifles to keep out mud and water....We seemed to wait for eternity in our rows for embarkation, and later we were told the delay had been due to an accident with the first boat. A man had slipped between the landing craft and the *Norland*, crushing his pelvis....Suddenly the order to move was given, and we pushed forward, stumbling in the dark, grabbing the pack of the man in front, now stopping abruptly and now moving forward with a jerk....

'The landing craft swung sharply to the east, and moved into the beach. The red light had appeared from the SBS and the order to haul on bergens was given. 'What was that?' Chris Keeble asked sharply. 'I am sure I heard a shot.' I had not heard anything, but later we discovered that a rifle had gone off when the order was given to release safety catches and a para had shot the edge of his neighbour's boot accidentally.

'I had been muttering into my tape-recorder, but such commentaries are always too long for broadcast. As soon as the ramp went down, I made the simple statement: "This is the moment we have been waiting for ...the ramp is down...we are going forward...I'm in the water" ...We had landed on the Falklands.'

Robert Fox, who reported for BBC Radio during the Falklands conflict, 1982.

Below: Paras alight from landing craft in a dawn assault on East Falkland.

in the company of *Kiev*-class carriers whose Forger VTOL (vertical take-off and landing) aircraft can provide close air support for landings. Given the Soviet weakness in terms of fixed-wing aviation at sea, the development of the nuclear-powered *Kirov* class of battle cruiser could provide the means of air defence for an amphibious task force since these ships are equipped with a powerful array of surface-to-air missiles. The construction of such support ships as the four-strong *Magnitogorsk* class, the oiler *Berezina* and the hospital ships *Ob* and *Yenisei* indicates the Soviet desire to match America's amphibious capability. For a nation whose Pacific Fleet a decade ago was little more than a force primarily concerned with mine warfare, the Soviet development of an amphibious capability in the Pacific represents a remarkable achievement.

US deployment

The Americans possess roughly the same lift capacity as the Russians, and over half of their Marine Corps strength is assigned to Europe. But given the nature of the Soviet submarine and air threat to the North Atlantic theatre and the fact that it is hazardous to try and use the sea for amphibious operations before it is commanded or controlled, American amphibious forces are forced to rely on prepositioning in an effort to deter or defend, since this must be more credible an effect than undertaking either the offensive or a counter-offensive. The US Marines are powerfully supported by their own air groups and helicopters. They use helicopter lift in order to bring forces ashore so that they may be concentrated while the risks to the ships are minimised. In this sense the *Tarawa* and *Iwo Jima* classes of assault carriers bestow upon the Americans a strength and flexibility that the Russians cannot match. It is an ability critical to the exercise of power in any situation short of war.

Between 1946 and 1963 the Americans deployed their armed forces as a means of achieving political objectives on no fewer than 134 occasions. Many involved either an initial amphibious commitment or the maintenance of forces by sea. Perhaps the most famous single incident, apart from the 1961 Bay of Pigs episode in Cuba, was the intervention in Lebanon in July 1958. On that occasion the Americans put a token force of 1500 men ashore at Beirut at one day's notice and followed this with another 8000 over the

Above: A Marine landing operation during Soviet Army training exercises. Right: An AMX30, the French main battle tank, displays its amphibious capability. The snorkel fitted to the loaders hatch enables the AMX30 to operate in water to a depth of 4m (13ft 2in). Bottom: A US Marine LVTP-7 amphibious assault vehicle goes ashore near Beirut in 1982.

next four days. In such a peacekeeping role, or as a means of demonstrating force, will and commitment, or threatening an unfriendly power, an amphibious capability is a useful aid to diplomacy. In war, however, it is essential, as was shown in the Falklands in 1982. Britain took the Argentinians by surprise when she put forces ashore at San Carlos in May. In the course of the war the British mounted a series of relatively small landings and were able to sustain them without fully securing control of the skies or of the seas, but such operations would be extremely hazardous if carried out in wartime in northwest Europe. Nevertheless, there is no doubt that the ability to put Marines ashore (if need be in the face of an enemy), to secure a choke point, to bring support to threatened allies or to cover withdrawals remain the key functions of American amphibious operations and are vital to a maritime alliance that depends upon the sea for its survival and capacity to fight.

H. P. Willmott

Key Weapons

The GENERAL DYNAMICS

F-111

Few modern combat aircraft have had such a stormy and controversial development history as the USAF's General Dynamics F-111 tactical fighter. The root of its problems lay in the TFX (tactical fighter experimental) requirement issued at the behest of Secretary of Defense Robert S. McNamara in 1961. This requirement sought to produce an aircraft that would meet the demands of the USAF's interdiction mission and the US Navy's requirement for a fleet defence interceptor, as well as carrying out close air-support missions at the request of ground forces. Clearly, if a single aircraft could be produced to undertake all three missions there would be considerable savings in development and procurement costs, with the additional benefit of commonality of equipment between the two services.

There was nothing inherently implausible in the idea of a multi-role fighter which could be operated by both the USAF and the US Navy. The McDonnell-Douglas F-4 Phantom was just such an aircraft and has since enjoyed a long and successful career with both services. However, the TFX project did not result in a successful USAF/US Navy fighter aircraft, largely because the highly-specialised requirements for a fleet air defence fighter (eventually to be met by the Grumman F-14 Tomcat) and a long-range interdiction aircraft, proved to be incompatible. The decision was therefore taken to build two separate aircraft, the F-111A and the F-111B. The F-111B naval fighter was to be built under subcontract by the Grumman Aircraft Corporation, because of its wide experience in the design and manufacture of naval aircraft, but production problems, unplanned weight increases (which would have severely curtailed operations from aircraft carriers) and powerplant malfunctions led Congress to cancel the naval fighters.

There remained the USAF's F-111A interdiction/ strike fighter, which was intended to replace the Republic F-105 Thunderchief. The F-111A first flew in December 1964 and entered service with Tactical Air Command's 474th TFW (Tactical Fighter Wing) at Canon air force base, New Mexico, in October 1967. Early in 1968 the 474th TFW moved to Nellis air force base, Nevada, and began to prepare a small detachment of F-111As for service in Southeast Asia. Six F-111As left Nellis for Thailand in March 1968 under project Combat Lancer. Yet controversy was still to dog the F-111. Before the month was out two Combat Lancer aircraft were lost on sorties over North Vietnam. Replacement F-111s were despatched from Nellis, but in April a third aircraft was lost and thereafter the detachment saw little action, being recalled to the United States in November. Even then misfortune continued to follow the F-111 and in December 1969, following the loss of 15 aircraft, the type was grounded pending the resolution of its problems.

The F-111 design was not, as may be supposed, a disastrous failure. Indeed the aircraft has matured into one of the most effective combat aircraft in the USAF's operational inventory. Its early problems were largely due to the fact that it was a very advanced aircraft, which incorporated a considerable amount of then-unproven new technology. At the time of the Combat Lancer deployment, the F-111 had not completed its operational test programme and so its commitment to combat was premature.

The most obvious of the F-111's advanced features was its variable-geometry wing, with a sweepback angle that could be varied between 16 degrees (fully forward) and 72.5 degrees (fully aft). This allows the aircraft to operate from relatively short runways, yet it can reach supersonic speed at low altitude and Mach 2.5 above 18,300m (60,000ft). Its two Pratt & Whitney TF30-P-3 powerplants each develop some 8390kg (18,500lb) of thrust with reheat (increased to

Previous page: An unusual view of the F-111 with wings swept back for supersonic flight. Although its early career was marred by extensive teething troubles, the F-111 is now recognised as an extremely effective strike aircraft. Above: An early model of the F-111, one of the first variable geometry warplanes to come into service in the West, and in its day one of the most advanced. Until the arrival of the Panavia Tornado the F-111 had no real rival as a Nato strike aircraft.

11,340kg, or 24,000lb, with the F-111F's TF30-P-100) and were the first turbofan engines to be fitted with an afterburner, thus combining fuel economy for cruising flight with high engine thrust when required. The F-111 carries a pilot and weapons system officer seated side by side in a pressurised crew escape module, which can be blasted away from the aircraft in an emergency and descends to earth under its own parachute.

The F-111 can carry a 20mm Vulcan rotary cannon mounted in the internal weapons bay, or two 428kg (750lb) bombs. Up to 14,300kg (31,500lb) of bombs can be carried on the underwing pylons, but as only four of the six pylons swivel to remain aligned with the airflow if the wings are swept back, this load is usually reduced on operational missions. Typically the F-111 will lift a 2720kg (6000lb) bomb load over a combat radius of 1850km (1000 nautical miles). The F-111's armament can include tactical nuclear weapons.

When flying an interdiction mission the F-111 will operate at high-subsonic speed (around Mach 0.9) at heights down to 61m (200ft) above ground level. It can achieve this in all weathers by day or night thanks to its advanced avionics, which include terrain-following radar able to maintain a preselected height-clearance above ground. Navigation is carried out by

Above left: An F-111 pilot carries out his pre-flight checks from his seat in the tandem cockpit of the aircraft. Above: A US F-111 takes-off from an RAF airbase in Germany, its afterburner fully activated.

Right: A ground crew man disconnects the extended electrical charging system from the wing of an F-111.

Left: F-111s are prepared for a mission at their air-base in Germany. In the foreground are ammunition trailers with Mk 82 Snakeye high-drag bombs on board.

an inertial system, which is self-contained and independent of external sources of reference once the aircraft's starting position has been fed into the set. An attack radar can be used for ground mapping and to pick up the aircraft's target. Some aircraft are now being fitted with the Pave Tack system, which comprises a forward-looking infra-red sensor for target acquisition by day or night and a laser rangefinder and designator for use with guided weapons such as the Maverick air-to-surface missile or GBU-15 glide bomb.

Although the F-111 has a fighter designation, its only concession to that is the presence of the 20mm cannon. It carries no other armament common to modern-day fighters and is, in effect, a single-purpose bomber with a high capability in the recon-

Above: An F-111 unloads a stick of 12 500lb bombs over a practice target in the desert. Above right: A mid-flight refuelling operation on an F-111 as seen from a KC-135 tanker. The side-by-side seating of the F-111 is unusual in a supersonic aircraft, though it does allow easy communication between the two aircrew.

naissance role. Its main advantage over a conventional bomber, however, is that it is a true all-weather delivery system which, with the aid of such things as terrain-following radar and inertial navigation, can fly at treetop level at night and place a heavy bombload directly onto its target. Furthermore, the advanced technology within the weapons system enables an F-111 to bomb point targets with maximum accuracy from a standoff position. The computer calculates the entire manoeuvre.

In USAF service there are four tactical fighter versions of the F-111 which, although it has no official name, is universally known as the Aardvark. The F-111A is the initial production aircraft and these serve with the 366th TFW at Mountain Home air force base, Idaho. The F-111D, which equips the 27th TFW in New Mexico, has an improved nav/attack system and uprated engines. The F-111E has further improvements to its avionics and powerplant, plus redesigned engine inlets and a new stores management system. It serves with the 20th TFW at Upper Heyford, Oxfordshire. The F-111Fs are also UK-based. equipping the 48th TFW at Lakenheath in Suffolk. This version is the most advanced F-111 and is currently being equipped with the Pave Tack system.

It was not until September 1972 that the F-111 returned to combat in Southeast Asia, the 474th TFW detaching aircraft to Tahkli in Thailand. From then until the signing of the Paris Peace Accords in January 1973, which ended American involvement in the Vietnam War, F-111s flew more than 3000 combat missions. A single F-111 could deliver the same bombload as five F-4 Phantoms and it needed none of the supporting tanker aircraft, fighter escorts, ECM

and defence suppression aircraft that had to accompany an F-4 strike force. Furthermore, as it could operate in all weathers, it was not grounded in the monsoon season. However, if the weather could not stop the F-111s flying, technical problems and spares shortages often did so. Unscheduled maintenance requirements still ground an unacceptably high proportion of the F-111 force to this day.

Apart from the F-111 tactical fighters, the USAF operates two wings of FB-111A strategic bombers. It was originally intended to buy a total of 263 FB-111s, which were to replace the Convair B-58 Hustler and early model B-52s with 14 of Strategic Air Command's bombardment squadrons. But escalating costs and early technical problems with the F-111 led to this order being drastically cut back, and only 76 FB-111As were built in the period from 1966 to 1971. Compared to its tactical counterpart, the FB-111 has a wingspan extended by 2.1m (7ft) to 21m (70ft), a strengthened undercarriage, extra fuel tanks and im-

Above: An F-111 takes on fuel from a KC-135 tanker. Even without refuelling the F-111 has an extraordinary maximum range in excess of 5000km (3100 miles).

Below: An F-111 comes into land. By operating a reverse thrust to brake its landing speed the F-111 can eliminate the need for a cumbersome brake parachute.

proved avionics. It can carry up to six AGM-69A SRAM (short range attack missiles) on four wing pylons and in the internal weapons bay, which can also house free-fall nuclear weapons.

The FB-111As serve with the 380th BW (Bombardment Wing) at Plattsburgh air force base, New York, and the 509th BW at Pease, New Hampshire. The bomber's 6297km (3400 nautical mile) range classes it as a medium rather than a heavy bomber, for although the FB-111A is equipped for inflight refuelling, crew fatigue is a problem with only a pilot and navigator aboard. Consequently the FB-111As are assigned to targets on the periphery of Soviet territory rather than those requiring deep penetration. There have been proposals to modernise the FB-111A force by re-engining and 'stretching' the existing airframes to produce a more capable bomber. These plans have been dropped, however, in favour of the new B-1B design.

The Royal Australian Air Force is the only foreign operator of the F-111, having taken delivery of 24 F-111Cs between 1963 and 1969. This version has the extended wingtips of the F-111B and the strengthened undercarriage of the FB-111A. The aircraft are operated in the long-range attack and maritime strike roles by Nos 1 and 6 Squadrons RAAF, based at Amberley, Queensland. Four aircraft have been modified as RF-111Cs for all-weather reconnaissance and they carry infra-red linescan and cameras in a weapons bay sensor pack. In order to replace aircraft lost in accidents, four ex-USAF F-111As have been purchased and they will be modified to F-111C standard. Future plans call for the fitting of Pave Tack to the Australian aircraft, which are also to be fitted with Harpoon anti-shipping missiles. Another foreign order for the F-111 was never fulfilled. This was the United Kingdom's proposed purchase of 50 F-111Ks as a replacement for the cancelled TSR-2. The F-111 order was itself cancelled in 1968.

The latest F-111 variant to enter service with the USAF is the EF-111A Electric Fox. This is a tactical ECM jamming aircraft, which is to be produced by modifying 42 standard F-111As. It is fitted with the same ALQ-99 jamming system that is used by the US Navy's EA-6B Prowler and can remain on station for up to eight hours, operating 160km (100 miles) from base, when used as a stand-off jamming aircraft. Alternatively, its Mach 2.2 performance allows it to accompany a strike force as ECM escort.

F-111A

Type Interdiction/strike aircraft
Dimensions Span (fully spread) 19.2m (63ft); fully swept 9.74m (31ft 11in); length 22.4m (73ft 6in); height 5.18m (17ft)
Weight Empty 20,943kg (46,172lb); loaded 41,500kg (91,500lb)
Powerplant Two 8390kg (18,500lb) thrust Pratt & Whitney TF30-P-3 afterburning turbofans

Performance Maximum speed at 11,000m (36,000ft) Mach 2.2; cruising speed 919km/h (571mph)
Range With maximum internal fuel 5093km (3165 miles)
Ceiling 15,500m (51,000ft) service ceiling at combat weight

Armament One M61 Vulcan 20mm cannon in internal weapons bay, or two 428kg (750lb) bombs carried internally; up to 14,300kg (31,500lb) of ordnance carried on wing pylons

Top: An F-111 banks over to port revealing its four tandem triplet bomb mountings holding a total of 24 500lb bombs. The FB variant is capable of delivering up to 17,010kg (37,500lb). Above: An F-111 flies above a British training range with its wings fully spread, indicating a relatively low airspeed. Right: An F-111 prepares to land, its ECM pod visible underneath its port wing.

Emergency in Kenya

Bloody rebellion in a crown colony

In September 1952 there erupted in Kenya a remarkable uprising that was to require four years of hard campaigning to counter. The uprising, known as Mau Mau, ended the colonial order in its classic form in Kenya, though the legacy of that order was to survive for a number of years after independence was granted in 1963.

In the colony of Kenya white settlers held a virtual monopoly of commercial agriculture. They also possessed and controlled some of the country's secondary light industry; the balance of this secondary industry and most tertiary industry, wholesale and retail distribution, was in the hands of Kenya's second settler community, the Asians. In this colonial order the Africans supplied the labour. Urban labour was rewarded with a wage barely adequate for survival in a 'bed-space' in an overcrowded slum building. Labour was also supplied for the white farmers either

Below: The beautiful Kenyan highlands which were the scenes of terrible carnage during the Mau Mau uprising. Jomo Kenyatta (inset) was among the early leaders of Kenyan nationalism and in later years ascended to the presidency. His involvement in, or responsibility for, Mau Mau's excesses has never been effectively investigated.

on monthly terms or, more usually, on a manorial villeinage system under which the labourers, known as 'resident labourers' or 'squatters', worked for a farmer for some 200 days each year in return for a sub-economic wage and the use of land for their own crops and stock. The rest of the African population engaged in subsistence agriculture in ethnic 'reserves' and grew cheap food for the urban workers. This order had been established in the early 1900s at a time when Kenya's population was some 2.5 million. By 1952 the population was 5.25 million.

The pressure of population on land was the prime cause of Mau Mau, a movement which often called itself the Kenya Land Freedom Army. From the 1930s discontent had been building up in three areas: on the white man's farms, where squatter families grew in size but had nowhere else to go and, in

addition, were subject to increasingly strict stock and acreage regulations; in the towns, where wage levels and conditions of life became increasingly inhuman; and in the ethnic reserves, especially that of the largest of Kenya's peoples, the Kikuyu, where land was totally inadequate to accommodate a growing population let alone the return of any surplus squatters.

Political pressures for change were inadequate. The Kenyan political system provided generous representation for white settlers in the legislature but only very limited representation for Africans, the first of whom took his seat as late as 1944 and by 1952 had been joined by only four more. Government, although overall in the hands of colonial service officials (many of whom were conscientious if paternal), generally operated 'by agreement' with the white settlers. It was not oppressive – there were only a few prisoners that could be called 'political' in the years immediately prior to September 1952 – but it was careless and it was badly out of tune with the post-1945 world.

Tactics of terror

The revolt that followed was, then, a peasant revolt with all the cruelty and absence of clear authority of a preliterate rural rebellion. It was not a national uprising, as only the Kikuyu and two other ethnic groups closely related to them, the Embu and the Meru, were involved. Despite subsequent protestations, the other Kenyan African peoples were either indifferent or firmly opposed to Mau Mau. Among the Kikuyu the majority of educated men were genuinely opposed to the strategy and tactics of the movement, even if they sympathised with its political aim of changing the colonial order. Nor was Mau Mau the return to atavistic savagery that was frequently portrayed at the time by the white officials and most churchmen. (The horrors, it was argued, were a justification for the reassertion of authority by all means, even if these were sometimes almost as repulsive as those of Mau Mau.)

But rather than treat the movement as the 'night side of the African soul' (the only explanation the white colonial regime found credible), Mau Mau can now be put more clearly into context by comparing it with later revolts against colonial authority – that of the FLN in Algeria, for example – in which the terror was more rigidly controlled and the political aims more sharply defined.

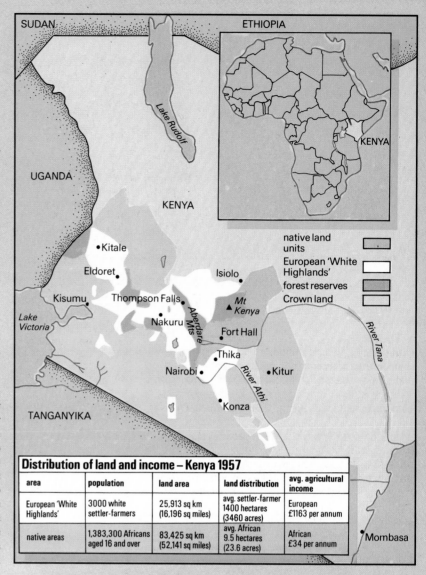

Distribution of land and income – Kenya 1957				
area	population	land area	land distribution	avg. agricultural income
European 'White Highlands'	3000 white settler-farmers	25,913 sq km (16,196 sq miles)	avg. settler-farmer 1400 hectares (3460 acres)	European £1163 per annum
native areas	1,383,300 Africans aged 16 and over	83,425 sq km (52,141 sq miles)	avg. African 9.5 hectares (23.6 acres)	African £34 per annum

Frustrated after the early successful attacks on isolated Europeans, Mau Mau began attacks on those Kikuyu who had income – in, for example, government service – or property, especially those who owned land. Many of these began to move towards the side of law and order, though obviously not necessarily approving of government policy. As the campaign worsened from the rebels' point of view the

Below: In an attempt to remove local support from the Mau Mau a Home Guard was raised from among the Kikuyu. Here an assistant district officer talks to potential recruits.

numbers of 'loyalists' increased. The village defence force, the Kikuyu Guard, was its military expression, one decisive to the success of the government's entire campaign.

The actual origins of Mau Mau, the first political oath-takings, occurred among badly managed government resettlement schemes for surplus squatters and surplus reserve dwellers in the early 1940s. More militant oathing occurred from 1942 onwards. To this oathing was added a feeling of discontent when, after World War II, it seemed that the white settlers were trying to put the political clock back. It was aggravated by the fact that large numbers of new white settlers began to arrive in Kenya. A few of the Kikuyu discontented had gained military experience during the war. Generally, however, the Kikuyu were not regarded as a martial race and no-one foresaw the possibility of a tough, determined military insurrection. Yet, despite the small numbers of firearms available to them and the absence of any adjoining friendly country which could be used as a refuge, the insurgents were to strike a remarkable blow which was to have significant repercussions.

Britain's response

The campaign itself involved military and police security operations in the white settled areas and towns near Kikuyuland, patrols and mass sweeps in the Aberdare Range and on Mount Kenya, and a vast 'rehabilitation' programme in which some 90,000 people were put through a detention programme of screening, a dose of 'psychological purification' and an elementary civics course. Rural public works, agricultural development and resettlement schemes followed. The military commitment was heavy and expensive. At its height, the campaign involved five British infantry battalions, six King's African Rifles battalions, two RAF bomber squadrons and a greatly expanded police force. In addition, huge sums of money were necessary to fund urgent political social and economic reforms. All this was far beyond Kenya's resources. Britain having to pay, Britain called the tune. The local Europeans, part frightened by Mau Mau and part dazzled by Kenya's rapid economic expansion, acquiesced. 'Government by agreement' with the settler community was replaced initially by the concept of 'multiracialism' with participation of all races, and then by the acceptance of the principle of majority rule.

While the campaign was being won by the military,

Above: A mixed patrol, weapons at the ready, goes in to search a hut. This patrol was part of the force involved in Operation Longstop, an operation designed to clear 162sq km (100sq miles) of the Aberdare forests of terrorist gangs.

Below: Two worlds meet. A. Swann (District Commissioner, Kiambu) and Sir Evelyn Baring, Governor of Kenya (far right), address members of the Kikuyu Home Guard.

the police and the Kikuyu Guard, the initial overwhelming support from the Kikuyu people enjoyed by Mau Mau was being steadily eroded, and the stability of Kenya's other peoples retained, by a programme of radical reform. It is a mistake to view the success of counter-insurgency in Kenya in purely military terms. Without the reforms only a military stalemate would have resulted.

The major reforms were the formal political ones that culminated in the 1960 Lancaster House conference. There, agreement was reached on providing an African majority in the legislature as well as economic measures involving vast injections of money into African agriculture for the opening up of new areas and for the consolidation into viable plots of scattered 'strips' of land in the Kikuyu Reserve. Wages for urban workers were improved and social reforms began to break down social colour bars. This process was accelerated by greatly expanded educational facilities for Africans. The final elements of reform dated from the early 1960s, when the White Highlands were opened up to African purchase, the segregated school system was abolished and Africans were rapidly promoted in the public service. In 1963, formal independence was granted. Without Mau Mau, these reforms might have taken decades to accomplish.

The ripples from Mau Mau extended beyond the ending of the Emergency in 1960, and beyond Kenya itself. Some of the reasons for the stability enjoyed by Kenya in the two decades since independence have clear origins in the Mau Mau period. The basis for this was the start made, in commercial agriculture, in converting white settler estates to African smallholdings in the mid-1950s. The release from prison in 1962 of Jomo Kenyatta was also of enormous significance. He emerged with a martyr's crown which gave him a stature none could challenge and enabled him to impose his conservative style of nationalism upon the country. The Mau Mau troubles influenced the ultimate break-up of the Federation of Rhodesia and Nyasaland and encouraged South Africa in its commitment to apartheid. They also encouraged a revolution in Conservative Party thinking in Britain, resulting in rapid decolonisation. The 12,000 Kikuyu who took to the hills after Kenyatta's arrest in October 1952 may never have read Harold Macmillan's 'wind of change' speech in 1960, but they certainly helped him write it.   **Anthony Clayton**

Mau Mau methods

The organisation and tactics of terror

Although initial interpretations of the Mau Mau uprising of the early 1950s explained the acts of hostility as merely a regression from civilisation, more recent views see the uprising for what it intrinsically was – an unusual form of anti-colonial revolt, in which peasant land hunger and Kikuyu tribalism played an important part.

The Mau Mau organisation was formed within the framework of the 'legal' Kenya African Union (KAU), but membership was distinguished from that of the KAU by the taking of oaths. While the oath-taking may superficially seem to be of little consequence, it was considered to be sufficiently serious to be declared illegal. All Kikuyu tribesmen discovered, or suspected of, taking the oath were liable to be imprisoned or detained indefinitely.

The reason for the oath-taking was that the Kikuyu were deeply superstitious, after years of attempting to defend themselves from attacks by both the warlike Masai and Arab slave-traders through the use of magic. Mau Mau leaders therefore contrived awesome oaths designed to cover all contingencies and to ensure that all members would remain both loyal to the movement and anti-white. The oath itself consisted of two parts, the first being a series of magic actions designed to convince the person that he was invoking a supernatural power, and the second part being the actual undertaking in which he would call

Above: Two young Kikuyu slaughtered by Mau Mau terrorists. The white European farmer for whom they worked, and whose farm was on Kikuyu lands, was murdered in his bath during the same raid.
Right: The administration fights fire with fire. A witch doctor (right) 'cleanses' two members of the Mau Mau of the oaths which they made to the society.

upon the supernatural power to support him. By these means the Mau Mau gained some sort of hold, albeit often involuntary, over much of the Kikuyu population.

The expansion of the Kikuyu under the protection of the British administration had led to severe over-crowding within the tribal lands. Not only did this cause a great deal of tension within Kikuyu society, but it also meant that the Kikuyu looked outside at the vast acreages of land being farmed by a few white farmers. Educated Kikuyu, returning from European universities and looking for political and social

Taking the oath

Through oathing ceremonies, members of the Kikuyu were recruited to the Mau Mau cause. One initiate, Karari Njama, has described how he was taken to the house of an oath administrator who 'dipped some herb leaves in a Kikuyu gourd containing a mixture of goat's blood, its abdominal dung [i.e. the undigested stomach contents of the goat] and water, then sprayed us with it uttering words of cleansing and blessing. Each at his own time, we were initiated. Naked, I stood facing Mount Kenya, holding high a dampened ball of soil (damped by milk, animal fat and blood) in my right hand and the other ball against my navel by my left hand. There were five two-foot pieces of the goat's small intestines laying on the ground about a foot and a half apart and I was instructed to step over these one at a time when completing the set of vows I was about to take.' He made seven vows, including a commitment to 'obey the orders of my leaders at all times,' to 'never sell land to any white man' and to 'fight the real fight for the land and freedom of our country till we get it or till my last drop of blood'.

'I dropped the two balls of soil in a Kikuyu gourd which contained a Kikuyu knife and a Kikuyu needle. I then sat down on a stool. He [the administrator of the oath] gave me the well stripped chest of a billy goat, from the neck to the testicles. It had a hole in the bottom and he told me to put my penis in that hole and hold the goat's chest upright with both my arms. I then repeated the vows for a second time, each time biting the goat's chest....

'He then picked up the Kikuyu sword, knife and needle. Swinging these over me seven times, each time banging them down on my head, he uttered the blacksmith's curse, condemning me to death if I violated the vows I had sworn. He then brought a very small Kikuyu gourd that contained a mixture of lion and leopard fat. He dipped a reed in it and with the fat made a cross on my forehead wishing me to be as brave as a lion or a leopard and to have their personality which would frighten my enemies. He then asked me to lick the remainder of the fat off the reed. The ceremony was over.'

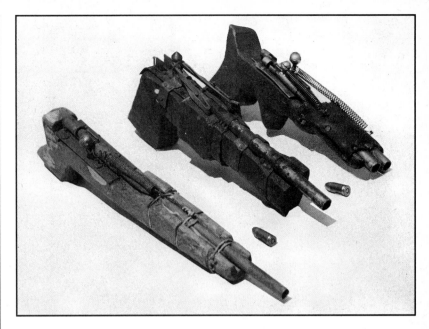

Above: As Mau Mau activities escalated and the perpetration of atrocities became a common practice, support diminished for the movement, among the Kikuyu themselves as well as internationally. Supplies of arms and ammunition tailed off, forcing the Mau Mau to rely upon home-made weapons such as those shown in the photograph.

change in Kenya, combined the move for agrarian reform with sacred oath-taking to bind Kikuyu inexorably to the Mau Mau movement.

Gradually the Mau Mau became organised for war and its members were divided into two groups, a militant wing and a passive wing. The passive wing was supposed to maintain forces in the field and was made up mostly of people who provided money, supplies, shelter, recruits and intelligence information. Although claiming to be directed by a group known as the 'Kenya Parliament' and by a central committee in Nairobi, in fact it was only in Nairobi itself that any real organisation and direction was to be found. The militant wing lived mostly in the Aberdare forests and consisted of gang members. It purported to be organised into sections of up to 35 men, platoons of up to 100 men and companies of up to 250 men.

Initially, orders from the passive wing were related to field operations feasibility, and the supplies of both arms and ammunition were far from abundant. Furthermore, there was little contact between individual Mau Mau groups. They were held together by an awed respect for the unit leaders, the fear of breaking oaths and the possibility of punishment.

Although initially conceived in the early 1940s, it was not until 1951 that the Mau Mau really began to take the offensive with attacks on white farmers. By the time the State of Emergency had been declared in October 1952, there were perhaps 12,000 guerrillas in the field.

During Operation Jock Scott on 20/21 October 1952, the suspected Mau Mau activists Jomo Kenyatta, Fred Kubai and Achieng Onako were arrested, but the organisation of Mau Mau was so loose that the effects of these arrests were hardly noticeable. Such was the nature of Mau Mau that the administration could not necessarily pinpoint leaders and this, in the future, led to the detention of thousands of suspects.

On 26 March 1953 two Mau Mau raids took place which proved to be of profound significance. At Naivasha, insurgents stormed the police station, killed two constables, released 173 prisoners and stole a large amount of weapons. At Lari, insurgents killed 74 people (mostly women and children), wounded 50 more and left 50 people missing – probably dismembered. The Lari massacre did much damage to the prestige of Mau Mau. Lari had been a settlement forced upon the Kikuyu by the government, yet despite the reluctance of the tribesmen to go, those who accepted the land (which had been claimed by other Kikuyu) were considered by the Mau Mau to be traitors and were subsequently killed. The massacre removed support for Mau Mau both within Kenya and internationally.

Operation Anvil in 1954 and the detention of some 20,000 Kikuyu destroyed the Mau Mau hierarchy and cells in Nairobi, severed lines of communication from the city and isolated the forest groups. As the security forces measures began to bite, lack of organisation, loss of support and extremely limited supplies of arms and ammunition forced Mau Mau into isolation, leaving them to fight as loosely-based armed gangs relying upon sabotage and terror as their key weapons. **Alexander McNair-Wilson**

Combing the Aberdares

Above: A captain leads a mixed patrol through a jungle clearing. Below: A fusilier checks the blade of his jungle knife.

British security operations in Kenya

In the years immediately following World War II the British colony of Kenya was prosperous and peaceful. The future looked full of promise. Yet, on 21 October 1952, a State of Emergency was declared after a secret organisation calling itself Mau Mau had embarked upon a campaign of frightening violence. To this day no-one knows exactly what the words Mau Mau mean, but it was recognised from the outset that the organisation was almost exclusively confined to members of the Kikuyu tribe. The Kikuyu lived in Central Province, which encompassed Nairobi, and it was there that Mau Mau violence was enacted, the rest of the country remaining relatively undisturbed. Although many acts of violence were perpetrated against whites, the great majority were committed by Mau Mau Kikuyu against others of their own tribe.

From 1948 attempts were made through the courts to reduce the influence of the Mau Mau leadership, but they met with little success. In 1950 the organisation was banned, yet it prospered underground and slowly built up its strength and influence. In 1951 warnings of growing unrest arrived in Nairobi from district officers and police officers in the Kikuyu Reserve and the White Highlands where the settlers' farms were increasingly disturbed. But the govern-ment, either through inertia or because it saw no concrete evidence on which to act, allowed valuable time to slip past and did nothing.

The leading political figure among the Kikuyu was Jomo Kenyatta, who had returned to Kenya in 1946 after many years spent in England. He was regarded by government officials as the inspiration for Mau Mau, and as the crisis developed he was frequently pressured to denounce the organisation in the speaches he made throughout the country. He never did so. Even though Kenyatta and others continued whipping up their followers into a frenzy of anti-government and white settler feeling in 1952, the authorities refused to act forcefully to contain the growing unrest. Then in September a senior Kikuyu chief, Waruhiu, was shot and killed. He had been totally loyal to the government and so, at last, author-ity was sought from Britain to declare a State of Emergency.

The order decreeing the Emergency was signed on 20 October 1952 and announced the following morn-ing. Concurrently with the announcement a battalion of British troops (1st Battalion, The Lancashire Fusi-liers) began arriving by air from Egypt to reinforce the six King's African Rifles battalions already in the

The disaffected area

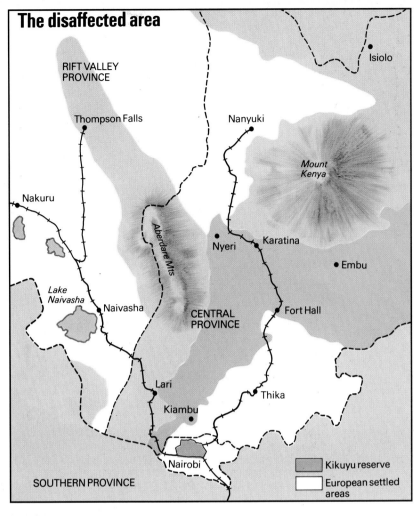

RIFT VALLEY PROVINCE

Isiolo

Thompson Falls

Nanyuki

Mount Kenya

Nakuru

Aberdare Mts

Nyeri

Karatina

Embu

Lake Naivasha

Naivasha

CENTRAL PROVINCE

Fort Hall

Lari

Thika

Kiambu

Nairobi

SOUTHERN PROVINCE

Kikuyu reserve

European settled areas

crucial, also, to the eradication of Mau Mau.

All of these measures took time to organise and were essentially long term in aim. Accordingly, the escalating violence continued unchecked for many months after the State of Emergency had been declared. The security forces were inevitably to remain for some time on the defensive and, as a result, discontent grew among the settler population (which numbered 40,000 at the start of the Emergency).

In an effort to curb Mau Mau freedom of action the vast forest lands of the Aberdare Range and Mount Kenya, where it was known that Mau Mau gangs had gathered, were declared prohibited areas in which anyone might be shot on sight. The Kikuyu Reserve in Central Province was designated as a Special Area where anyone could be shot who failed to respond to a challenge. Such developments did much to improve the operational efficiency of the security forces.

Following the example of Malaya, the next step was to create a joint operational organisation to deal with internal security. At colony level a committee, later to be known as the War Council, was formed on which civil, military and police officers sat to coordinate policy and allocate resources. Similar committees were instituted at province and district level. In January 1953 a senior army officer, Major-General W. R. N. Hinde was appointed to advise the governor (Sir Evelyn Baring) on internal security matters. His appointment was soon changed to that of Director of Operations and he became responsible for the coordination of overall strategy.

On 26 March 1953, two events occurred which were to be of great significance in the battle to destroy Mau Mau. At the time they appeared to be major disasters for the government and the security forces. The first was a brutal attack on the Kikuyu settlement

colony. At the same time parties of police descended on the homes of dissident Kikuyu leaders and took into detention all those suspected of engaging in Mau Mau activities. Jomo Kenyatta was among those arrested. Lastly, police reservists were called up and the Kenya Regiment, the colony's Territorial Army force, was mobilised.

The army found itself dispersed over vast distances which made communication and administration extremely difficult. What was more, it was almost impossible to get to grips with the enemy. There was no information about the Mau Mau gangs that had gone into hiding: their numbers, their whereabouts and their intentions were totally unknown. All that could be done was to react to any act of violence in the hope of being able to follow up and bring the enemy to battle.

This clearly unsatisfactory situation had to be remedied, so steps were taken to build up a viable police Special Branch which could begin to acquire information and construct a detailed picture of Mau Mau so that the security forces could move onto the offensive. The head of MI5 in London was despatched to Kenya to create this organisation and it was, as in Malaya and elsewhere, eventually to be one of the keys to success.

Another measure was the formation of the Kikuyu Home Guard, later called the Kikuyu Guard. This body was built up by recruiting, arming and training loyal Kikuyu with the aim of directly combatting the attempts by Mau Mau to gain control over the whole of the Kikuyu population. This scheme was to be

Massacre at Lari

'Kenya has been shocked and horrified by the massacre of loyal Kikuyu in the Lari location .... The latest official statement says that at least 150 persons are dead, including a large number of children. The police believe that three Mau Mau gangs, each numbering 30 or 40, struck simultaneously at the same place. About 500 arrests have been made.... One group fastened the doors of huts belonging to "home guards" and government employees; another group, carrying torches, set fire to the grass roofs; and a third, armed with *pangas*, swords, and hatchets, struck down men, women and children as they made desperate attempts to escape from the burning huts. All were terribly mutilated, and some who were unable to get out of their burning homes died in the flames. Chief Makimei, who was one of the intended victims, fought off the attackers with the aid of his bodyguard and shot and killed a terrorist. But the elderly Chief Luka, who had escaped Mau Mau attacks on several occasions, was hacked to death. His limbs were severed and his skull smashed. His whole family, including his eight wives, was wiped out. Most of the "home guards" on their return from patrol found their families murdered and their homes destroyed.'

Report in The Times, *28 March 1953.*

of Lari, some 40km (25 miles) from Nairobi. Many women and children were killed, some in the most violent manner; in all, 74 people lost their lives as homes, farm huts and shelters were set ablaze by a large force of Mau Mau. The attackers excelled themselves in their ferocity. In the aftermath of the massacre the view was widely held that Mau Mau had effectively destroyed their own chances of eventual success by a display of such depravity that potential adherents to their cause were filled with revulsion.

The second incident was at Naivasha, a settlement in the Rift Valley. Here Mau Mau carried out a well-organised attack on a small police post. They killed two policemen, stole a large number of guns and a quantity of ammunition. They also released some 173 detainees held in a nearby compound. The whole affair was deeply humiliating for the Kenya police, but it produced a strong determination to prevent similar disasters in the future.

Change of command

Further measures were now implemented. In April, two more British battalions were flown in from Britain; and in June, General Sir George Erskine arrived to take over as Commander-in-Chief in East Africa and effectively as Director of Operations in Kenya.

Another important development at this time was the decision to arm the Kikuyu Guard with guns in place of their more primitive weapons. This was a clear sign of government confidence, despite the fact that at the time clear evidence existed that large numbers of Mau Mau supporters were leaving Nairobi and the Kikuyu Reserve to join the armed bands in the forests.

Soon after his arrival, Erskine decided that the time was ripe to put the army onto the offensive, to extricate them from the eternal round of guards and patrols in defence of the population. Such duties could now fall on the Kikuyu Guard and the police who were better armed and recruited and capable of taking on the task.

The forests of the Aberdare Range and Mount Kenya provided excellent hiding places for Mau Mau, and so the commander-in-chief determined to deploy the army inside the forest to hunt the terrorists down. Even getting to the forest was, however, a long and tiring job; and besides, the necessary movement in vehicles announced to everyone for miles around what was happening. To overcome these problems

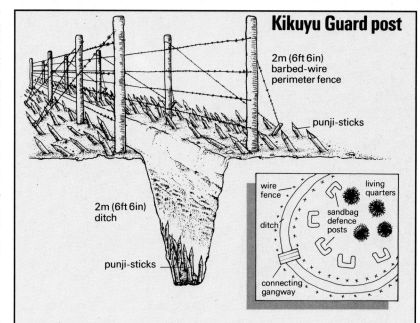

Kikuyu Guard post

2m (6ft 6in) barbed-wire perimeter fence

punji-sticks

2m (6ft 6in) ditch

punji-sticks

wire fence — living quarters — sandbag defence posts — ditch — connecting gangway

A typical Kikuyu Guard post was manned by about 50 Kikuyu Guard including the headman and a tracker. Apart from traditional African weaponry several .303s and a small number of shotguns were available, and each post had a Verey pistol with red flare cartridges for use in emergencies. The posts were designed to be mutually supporting and were normally sited in an area with a clear field of fire and a good vantage point for lookouts. Since the posts provided an obvious target for Mau Mau surprise attacks, they were fortified with a deep perimeter ditch, barbed-wire fences and punji-sticks. The Kikuyu Guard were quartered in Bashas (thatched huts) inside the perimeter. Throughout the night, when the post was most vulnerable, the Kikuyu Guard posted up to eight sentries on a three-hour shift system while 18 men were sent out to patrol the surrounding area. To maintain morale and standards of efficiency the posts were in regular contact with police patrols and were periodically inspected.

Below: The need for protection for both European and Kenyan police made it necessary to fortify police stations. This typical station, surrounded by sharpened stakes and barbed wire, illustrates the threat presented by marauding gangs of Mau Mau terrorists.

and to establish a security force dominance in the forest, the decision was made to bulldoze vehicle tracks up into the mountains and set up bases of a permanent nature in the forests themselves.

The morale of the troops improved with this innovation, yet constant patrolling, sweeping and searching led to few contacts and even fewer kills. The forests covered enormous areas and the men of Mau Mau knew them well and managed to stay hidden and alive. Even when a further brigade of troops arrived to build up the government forces in September 1953, there were still insufficient men to wrest the initiative from the enemy.

Early in 1954 it was decided that a large number of troops (withdrawn from operations in the forests) together with the police, should engage in a major series of cordon and search operations in Nairobi itself.

This gigantic operation, code-named Anvil, was undertaken in April 1954. In the course of six weeks the larger part of the city was searched, sector by sector, and tens of thousands of Kikuyu inhabitants were screened. Some 20,000 of them were detained in camps hastily built for the purpose. So successful was this extraordinarily complex operation that the links between the Mau Mau in Nairobi and the armed bands in the forests were almost completely severed, never to be reinstated.

It was in 1954 also that another ruse was employed to hit back at Mau Mau groups in the field. It was

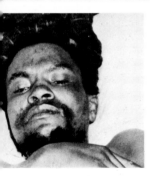

Top: The British, despite the acclaimed loyalty of the Kikuyu Home Guard, were still reluctant to distribute arms among them. Here a patrol armed with spears and bows and arrows prepares to move. Centre: Successful patrolling or security sweeps could mean indeterminate detention for potential Mau Mau recruits or activists. Above: A final blow for the Mau Mau as Dedan Kimathi, one of its most wanted leaders, lies wounded and captive in Nyeri hospital.

found that some members of Mau Mau gangs, when captured, were prepared to work with the security forces against their former comrades. As a result, gangs of these former terrorists were deployed under the control of British Army and police officers.

Two more major operations (Hammer and First Flute) were launched against the Mau Mau in the forests in early 1955. Huge resources were expended and a division's worth of troops were deployed. Once more, in terms of the number of enemy eliminated, these operations were only partially successful but they were later discovered to have dealt a severe blow to Mau Mau morale. These operations continued through to the end of 1956, by which time the power of Mau Mau had virtually evaporated.

The final demise of Mau Mau occurred when their last important leader, Dedan Kimathi, was captured in October 1956. After being shot and wounded, Kimathi escaped from the patrol which attacked him, only to be found three days later on the fringes of the forest by an African policeman who shot him again. Kimathi later stood trial and was executed.

The Emergency gradually subsided as troops were posted out of Kenya and normality returned to area after area. The governor declared the State of Emergency at an end in January 1960. In a little over seven years the Mau Mau had lost more than 10,000 killed as against a total figure for security forces and government sympathisers of just over 2400, of which only 63 were Europeans.   **Major F. A. Godfrey**

Collaborators in the forest

In 1954 Ian Henderson, a Kenyan-born member of the Special Branch, commanded a team assigned to make contact with the Mau Mau rebels with a view to starting negotiations. Henderson, who spoke the Kikuyu language, soon won the terrorists' respect and was given the nickname Kinyanjui, after a venerated former elder statesman of the tribe. By 1955 Mau Mau morale generally was low, but Dedan Kimathi was in no mood to surrender. It was therefore decided to try and capture members of Kimathi's gang, win them over and then use them to bring about Kimathi's capture.

At the end of 1955 three identical letters urging Kimathi's gang to give themselves up were written by a surrendered terrorist and deposited in the forests of the Aberdare mountains. On 26 December Henderson was told that a Mau Mau letter addressed to him had been found in the Aberdares. It read: 'To Sar Kinyanjui of Special Branch. If you find this letter please say so from an aeroplane... wait for me on the Nyeri track and you will find another letter. It is I, Gati.' This later letter told Henderson to return on 1 January.

In his book *The Hunt for Kimathi,* Henderson describes how, at the meeting place, wedged in a cleft bamboo stick, was a government surrender pamphlet on the back of which was written: 'Wait, we are here.' After half an hour two terrorists, Gati and Hungu, suddenly appeared. Both had fallen foul of Kimathi. 'Before he kills us,' they said, 'we thought we had better surrender.'

Henderson takes up the story: 'In the next few days we talked a lot to our two friends, until their fear of us had disappeared, and their outlook on life began to change.... Then we put them back into the Aberdare forest again and met them every few days to test their reliability....

'All the time that Gati and Hungu were in the forest they were afraid that Kimathi would find them. To guard against this happening they kept very much to themselves, and avoided all the places where they knew other gangs had their hideouts. We found them honest about their movements.... and issued them with pistols....

'Once we were certain that our guns were in safe hands we started making them popular with the other terrorists. We sky-shouted a message [via aeroplane] over several parts of the Aberdares claiming that both were badly wanted criminals and offering £600 to anyone who gave information leading to their capture....

'The effect of our hue and cry was dramatic. Within a few days Gati and Hungu became heroes.... Not only had we boosted their reputations to dazzling heights, but we had even provoked Kimathi into changing his opinion about them.... All was well, provided that no one captured them and claimed the reward!'

It proved to be a long and tortuous trail, but by using the collaborators to make contact with terrorists who had direct access to Kimathi, the Mau Mau leader was eventually captured in October 1956.

Chronology 1950–55

EUROPE & NORTH AMERICA

1950
January
31 United States President Harry Truman authorises work to begin on H-bomb.
December
19 Nato General Dwight D. Eisenhower appointed Supreme Allied Commander Europe (SACEUR).

1951
April
18 ANZUS defence pact drawn up by Australia, New Zealand and the United States.

1952
February
18 Nato Greece and Turkey join.
20-25 Nato At Lisbon, members agree on military goals of 50 divisions and 4000 aircraft by end of year; target is not achieved.
May
26 West Germany Occupation statute revoked; Federal Republic of Germany becomes a sovereign state.
27 Western Europe European Defence Community formed by France, West Germany, Italy, Belgium, Luxembourg and the Netherlands.
October
3 Britain tests its first atomic bomb on the Monte Bello Islands off Australia.
November
United States Newspapers report US explosion of hydrogen weapon at Eniwetok in the Pacific.
4 United States Dwight D. Eisenhower elected president.

1953
March
5 Soviet Union Joseph Stalin dies; he is succeeded as premier by Georgi Malenkov.
June
16-17 East Germany Anti-communist riots in East Berlin and East Germany suppressed by Soviet Army.
July
4 Hungary Imre Nagy becomes prime minister.
August
12 Soviet Union tests its first hydrogen bomb.
29-31 Trieste Yugoslavia and Italy involved in border clashes.
September
12 Soviet Union Nikita Khrushchev appointed First Secretary of the Communist Party Central Committee.
26 Spain signs defence agreement with USA.
December
5 Trieste Italy and Yugoslavia agree to withdraw troops.

1954
March
25 East Germany Sovereignty of the German Democratic Republic recognised by the Soviet Union.
August
9 Greece, Turkey and Yugoslavia conclude 20-year treaty of military and political cooperation.
September
30 United States First nuclear-powered submarine, USS *Nautilus*, commissioned.
October
23 West Germany Paris Agreements signed; occupation of West Germany ended, federal republic invited to join Nato, Britain agrees to maintain 55,000 troops in Europe.
December
Nato strategy revised to base planning on immediate use of nuclear weapons (the 'trip-wire' policy).

1955
February
8 Soviet Union Malenkov replaced as premier by Nikolai Bulganin.
April
1 Cyprus Campaign by EOKA (National Organisation of Cypriot Fighters) in favour of union with Greece launched against the British by General Grivas.
18 Hungary Imre Nagy dismissed as premier, replaced by Mátyás Rákosi.
May
5 Nato West Germany becomes member.
14 Warsaw Pact Soviet Union, Poland, Czechoslovakia, Hungary, Romania, Bulgaria, East Germany and Albania conclude 20-year treaty of political and military cooperation, known as the Warsaw Pact. Soviet Marshal Ivan Konev appointed commander-in-chief of combined forces.
15 Austria declares its neutrality; occupying British, French, American and Soviet forces to withdraw.
November
12 West Germany First soldiers receive their commissions in the Bundeswehr.
26 Cyprus State of Emergency proclaimed.

SOUTH ASIA

1950
January
25 India proclaimed a republic.
November
11-20 Nepal Rebels depose king but are later defeated by loyal Gurkha troops.

1953
August
12-19 Ceylon Government suppresses wave of communist-inspired terrorism.

1954
April
29 India signs non-aggression treaty with China, recognising Chinese annexation of Tibet.
May
19 Pakistan Agreement signed with United States for supply of military equipment and technical assistance.
July
Goa Clashes between Indian nationalists and Portuguese.

EAST ASIA

1950
June
25 Korea North Korean forces invade South Korea.
26 United Nations Security Council calls for withdrawal of North Korean troops and for aid to be given to the South.
27 Korea US President Harry Truman orders General Douglas MacArthur, commander of US forces in the Far East, to assist South Korea to resist invasion.
30 Korea US forces begin move to Korea.
July
8 Korea MacArthur appointed Commander-in-Chief, United Nations Command.
August
1 Korea US Eighth Army ordered to withdraw to area around Pusan at southern end of Korean peninsula.
September
15-27 Korea US X Corps lands on beaches at Inchon and retakes Seoul. Eighth Army breaks out of Pusan perimeter.
October
5 Korea UN troops cross 38th parallel into North Korea.
6 Tibet Chinese invade and occupy country.
25 Korea Chinese troops engage UN forces.
December
1-5 Korea X Corps forced to retreat from Chosin reservoir.

1951
January
1-15 Korea Second Chinese offensive crosses 38th parallel, recaptures Seoul and forces US Eighth Army to retreat.
25 Korea UN forces begin northward offensive in Operation Thunderbolt.
March
14 Korea UN forces retake Seoul.
31 Korea South Korean troops cross 38th parallel.
April
11 Korea MacArthur relieved of command of UN and US forces by President Truman and is replaced by General Matthew Ridgway.
22 Korea Communists launch spring offensive; the Glosters engage Chinese forces at the Imjin River.
May
15-20 Korea Second phase of communist offensive.
22-31 Korea UN forces launch counter-offensive and regain 38th parallel.
June
23 United Nations Soviet delegate proposes ceasefire in Korea.
July
8 Korea Initial meeting on armistice talks held at Kaesong.
September
8 Japan signs peace treaty with United States and 4? non-communist nations, and a defence pact with the United States.

1953
April
16-18 Korea Battle for Pork Chop Hill. After initial Chinese success, US forces retake the position.
July
27 Korea Armistice signed at Munsan and Panmunjom.

1954
Spring
Tibet Widespread anti-Chinese revolt, savagely repressed.

MIDDLE EAST

1950
May
19 Egypt closes Suez Canal to Israeli shipping.

1951
April
29 Iran Prime Minister Mohammed Mossadegh nationalises oil industry.
July
20 Jordan King Abdullah assassinated.

1952
January
Egypt Anti-British riots in Cairo.
May
2 Jordan King Hussein succeeds to throne.
July
22 Egypt Military coup d'etat led by General Mohammed Naguib dethrones King Farouk.

1953
August
19 Iran Shah Mohammed Reza Pahlevi removes Mossadegh and takes control.

1954
April
4   Turkey and Pakistan sign mutual assistance treaty.
21   Iraq signs military aid agreement with the United States.
May
20   Pakistan and the United States conclude treaty on military assistance.
October
Egypt Britain agrees to withdraw troops from Suez Canal zone.
November
14   Egypt Colonel Gamal Abdel Nasser replaces General Naguib as president.

1955
February
24   Baghdad Pact signed by Turkey and Iraq; both agree to cooperate in matters of security and defence. Later signatories are Great Britain (5 April), Pakistan (23 September) and Iran (12 October).
March
Egypt, Syria and Saudi Arabia sign treaty in opposition to Baghdad Pact.
September
27   Egypt concludes agreement to receive arms from Czechoslovakia.

CENTRAL AMERICA
1951
May
10   Panama President Arnulfo Arias overthrown in coup d'etat.

1952
March
10   Cuba General Fulgencio Batista seizes power.

1953
July
26-27   Cuba Uprising in Santiago and Bayamo suppressed; Fidel Castro arrested.

1954
June
18-29   Guatemala Anti-communist forces overthrow President Jacobo Guzman.

1955
January
25   Panama Treaty signed with US increasing payment for use of canal zone.

SOUTH AMERICA
1951
May
16   Bolivia General Hugo Balivian seizes power at head of military junta.
September
28   Argentina President Juan Perón defeats military revolt and assumes dictatorial powers.

1952
April
8-11   Bolivia President Balivian ousted by Victor Pas Estenssoro.
December
2   Venezuela Colonel Marcos Perez Jimenez seizes power.

1953
June
13   Colombia General Pinilla seizes power.

October
9   Guyana British use troops to remove left-wing government of Cheddi Jagan to prevent communist takeover.

1954
May
5   Paraguay Army revolt installs General Alfredo Stroessner as president.

1955
September
16-19   Argentina Perón overthrown, flees country; military junta assumes control of government.

SOUTHEAST ASIA
1950
March
29   Philippines Huk rebels launch attacks on towns including San Mateo, San Simon and Los Banos.
April
Malaya Lieutenant-General Sir Harold Briggs takes up post as Director of Operations.
August
17   Indonesia proclaimed a republic.
September
Philippines Ramon Magsaysay appointed Secretary for National Defence.
October
7   Indochina Viet Minh inflict major defeat on French near Dong Khe on the Cao Bang ridge. French forces subsequently abandon most of North Vietnam and dig in at Red River Delta.
December
17   Indochina General Jean de Lattre de Tassigny arrives to take command of French forces in Indochina.

1951
June
18   Indochina French retain hold on Red River Delta as Viet Minh forced to retreat.
October
6   Malaya High Commissioner Sir Henry Gurney assassinated by communist guerrillas.
December
Indochina De Lattre de Tassigny returns to France because of illness and is succeeded as supreme commander of French forces by General Raoul Salan.

1952
February
Malaya General Sir Gerald Templer takes up appointment as High Commissioner and Director of Operations.
22   Indochina French begin withdrawal from Hoa Binh sector.
October
17   Indochina Viet Minh launch attack against French positions on Nghia Lo ridge.
29   Indochina Start of Operation Lorraine, the largest French operation yet in Indochina, directed against Viet Minh supply dumps at Phu Tho and Phu Doan, north of the Red River.
November
14   Indochina Salan orders withdrawal after Operation Lorraine makes little impact.

1953
May
28   Indochina Lieutenant-General Henri Navarre takes over as commander-in-chief of French forces.
August
12   Indochina Garrison at Na San evacuated by French.
November
20   Indochina First French paratroops are dropped into Dien Bien Phu.
December
10   Indochina French evacuate Lai Chau.

1954
February
8   Malaya Communist high command withdraws to Sumatra.
March
13   Indochina Viet Minh open offensive against Dien Bien Phu.
May
7   Indochina Dien Bien Phu falls to the Viet Minh.
July
21   Geneva Conference Armistice in Indochina agreed. Indochina divided at 17th parallel between North Vietnam (communist) and South Vietnam (anti-communist).
September
8   Seato Southeast Asia Collective Defence Treaty signed in Manila by Australia, France, Great Britain, New Zealand, Pakistan, the Philippines, Thailand and the United States. It is designed to counter communist aggression and subversion in Asia.

1955
January
20   Vietnam Britain and France agree to assist reorganisation of South Vietnamese Army.
April
18-24   Indonesia Conference at Bandung of 29 non-aligned countries from the Third World condemns 'colonialism in all of its manifestations'.

AFRICA
1951
December
24   Libya declares independence.

1952
January
Morocco Hundreds of nationalist supporters arrested by French authorities.
October
21   Kenya State of Emergency proclaimed in response to Mau Mau uprising.

1953
March
26   Kenya Mau Mau massacre 74 people at Lari; the Naivasha police post attacked by Mau Mau.
August
1   Northern Rhodesia, Nyasaland and Southern Rhodesia formed into Central African Federation.
15-20   Morocco French-inspired uprising deposes sultan.
October
20   Kenya Jomo Kenyatta sentenced to prison.

1954
April
Kenya Operation Anvil, large-scale cordon and search initiative, launched against Mau Mau organisation in Nairobi; some 20,000 suspects detained.
November
1   Algeria Start of FLN campaign of violence to secure independence from France.

1955
January
Kenya Operation Hammer launched against Mau Mau bands in Aberdare mountains.
February
Kenya Operation First Flute begins on Mount Kenya.
August
18   Morocco Massacre of French settlers by nationalists at Wadi Zem.
20   Algeria FLN massacre 123 European settlers at Philippeville.
November
5   Morocco France agrees on principle of independence for Morocco.

Civil or military?

The role of police in counter-insurgency

Much of the insurgency experienced since 1945 has been conducted by guerrilla groups for whom political agitation has been as important, if not more so, than military action. Such political subversion is essentially a matter for the police and its Special Branch rather than the armed forces. Indeed, effective policing should prevent subversion from escalating into large-scale military action; it is only when the police have lost control of a situation that military assistance is normally required. Then the question of whether police or armed forces should have overall responsibility for operations – 'primacy' – frequently becomes a matter of controversy.

In theory the police have the great advantage of possessing detailed local knowledge that armed forces do not have. Yet this has not always been the

Above: Japanese police face well-armed student protesters. Crowd control is a major problem for modern police forces and their ability to contain rioters with the minimum application of force is one of their key counter-insurgency roles.

case where the police have been a colonial force and as such have resembled more a para-military gendarmerie than a civilian force. Such police forces have been regarded as agents of colonial government with a duty to protect the administration rather than the citizen. Many post-independence police forces have continued in the pattern set by their colonial predecessors.

The Palestine police, for example, were commanded by British personnel of whom less than 4 per cent spoke Hebrew while the great majority of ordinary constables were Arab. Modelled on the Royal Irish Constabulary (RUC), the Palestine police could have little hope of winning the confidence of the Jewish population. The force was also temperamentally ill-suited to implement the recommendations made by Sir Charles Wickham in December 1946 that it should get back on foot patrol in the streets. The RUC, as a predominantly Protestant force, was unwelcome in many Catholic areas of Northern Ireland when violence began to escalate in the late 1960s, while the Kenya police did not operate at all in Kikuyu areas but left policing to the Kikuyu Tribal Police. Even where the police are more truly representative, a para-military role can alienate the people as occurred in South Vietnam where the police were equated with the collection of taxation and rents and were notorious for their corruption.

Absorption in a para-military role can also lead to the neglect of normal policing which is vital for maintaining the semblance of normality and government control. In Malaya it was argued that too many police were in the para-military Jungle Squads and too few available for manning police posts in towns and villages. Thus, in December 1951, Colonel (later Sir)

Arthur Young of the City of London Police replaced Colonel Nicol Gray of the Royal Marines as Commissioner of Police. Young emphasised a more traditional approach to policing in Operation Service, which was designed to promote greater police 'kindness and help to those in need' as symbolised by the adoption of a new badge showing two clasped hands. In Kenya, however, the Kenya Police Reserve (KPR) not only actively sought a para-military role but formed their own unofficial groups to hunt down the Mau Mau. Young failed to break this prejudice when sent to Kenya in 1954 and soon resigned.

Police victimisation

The problems that police face in trying to combat subversion may be compounded by the fact that insurgency so often begins with a deliberate assault on the police and particularly their intelligence personnel in order to neutralise the latter and generally paralyse the former. The Malayan police suffered twice as many casualties as the army between 1948 and 1951, while in Cyprus EOKA opened its campaign for union with Greece in 1955 with a calculated offensive against Greek Cypriot policemen, forcing many to resign under threat of death. In one particular incident in August 1955 a Greek Cypriot Special Branch man was shot dead in broad daylight in the centre of Nicosia in front of hundreds of onlookers at a political meeting. Similarly in Aden from 1964 onwards, National Liberation Front terrorists systematically eliminated Arab members of the Special Branch.

The result can be highly detrimental to police efficiency and morale. In Cyprus it became difficult to recruit Greek police, in much the same way that Viet Cong terrorism led to a marked unwillingness to join the South Vietnamese police. In Kenya police morale was severely shaken by the attack, on 26 March 1953, by over 80 Mau Mau on the police station at Naivasha in which two constables were killed, 173 prisoners released, 47 weapons seized and a large number of police recruits put to ignominious flight. In Aden the Aden State Police became utterly unreliable while elements of both the South Arabia Police and Federal Armed Police eventually mutinied on 20 June 1967 killing 22 British servicemen.

Where the police have failed to contain violence, the entire conduct of the campaign can be handed over to

Top: Armed with a sub-machine gun and uniformed, a reserve police officer is flanked by two bowmen. Top right: The Palestine Police, an almost paramilitary force, found it impossible to control Jewish terrorism in the 1940s. Above: A Kenya Police officer examines a Kikuyu tribesman for tell-tale Mau Mau razor cuts.

the armed forces or the police themselves can be heavily reinforced. In Malaya the police force was increased from 9000 in July 1948 to 45,000 six months later and to over 60,000 by the end of the Emergency in July 1960. In Cyprus the force was increased from 1700 in 1955 to 4900 by 1957.

The problem with such expansion is that recruits may be deployed with insufficient training. A classic example of this was the expansion of the Royal Irish Constabulary during the 'troubles' of 1919-21 through the recruitment of ex-servicemen in the regular police, the 'Black and Tans', and of ex-officers in

Left: In their secondary role as a paramilitary force, the Royal Ulster Constabulary become a target of hatred which makes their more conventional police duties the more difficult to perform.

Above: The Royal Ulster Constabulary, a mainly Protestant force policing mainly Catholic areas, are placed in an extremely difficult position. Their wide powers of arrest and search in the streets makes them unpopular with the population they are supposed to protect.

the Auxiliary Division, the 'Auxies'. Both enjoyed a certain notoriety. In Palestine there was again a tendency to recruit ex-servicemen while in Malaya the regular police were bolstered by an influx of over 500 former Palestine policemen, the result of which was much internal friction.

In Kenya over 700 men were recruited on short-term contracts from England and the 4800-strong KPR fully mobilised. Some of the newcomers were not always scrupulous about how they achieved results, and the KPR was closely identified with white settler interests. KPR personnel were found guilty of a number of excesses, including burning suspects' eardrums with cigarettes and illegal floggings as well as perjury. A British Parliamentary delegation established that there had been 130 prosecutions of policemen for brutality by February 1954, of which 73 had resulted in conviction; 40 cases were still pending. It remarked that this was 'on a scale which constitutes a threat to public confidence'. A Swahili language newspaper simply branded the KPR as 'undisciplined sadists'. It should be recognised, however, that the rigorous investigation of complaints by the Attorney General was on occasions manipulated by the Mau Mau to place good and efficient police officers under suspicion.

Even in the British experience, however, the involvement of the military has often been necessary to aid the civil power. In a situation such as Aden there was little alternative to the army taking over full responsibility for internal security in January 1967, but elsewhere it has been normal British practise to stress that the army is in support of the police and not

vice-versa. The resulting relationship has not always been a happy one. In Malaya Colonel Gray, as Commissioner of Police, was de facto director of operations from 1948 until the appointment of Lieutenant-General Sir Harold Briggs in March 1950. Thereafter there was considerable friction between the two men over the role of the police. Similarly, there was a very serious disagreement in Northern Ireland between the Chief Constable of the RUC and the General Officer Commanding which culminated in the replacement of both men and the appointment of a Security Coordinator in October 1979.

Such clashes are not unknown elsewhere. In Mozambique there was so much rivalry between the Portuguese Army and the security police by 1974 that at times the police deliberately held back information from the army. In Rhodesia the British South Africa Police (BSAP) had been primarily responsible for the early operations against African guerrillas between 1966 and 1968, but the expansion of the war from December 1972 onwards saw the army taking the dominant role. The BSAP resented the army chairing committees in the Joint Operations Centres and saw the new Military Intelligence Department in 1973 as a rival.

The question of intelligence is often the point that causes the most friction between army and police. The responsibility of Special Branch for intelligence is a keystone of the traditional British approach but it has been forcibly argued by General Sir Frank Kitson (based on his experiences in Malaya, Cyprus and Kenya) that Special Branch is incapable of producing the kind of operational intelligence the army actually requires in order to make contacts in the field. Certainly the British Army has frequently had to help rebuild a police intelligence network after an initial terrorist offensive, but the best solution rests in very close coordination of intelligence services. In Kenya Sir George Erskine had full command over army and operational control of the police and auxiliaries from May 1953 onwards, a joint intelligence staff being quickly established. The situation had improved sufficiently for the police to re-assert their primacy in May 1956. For any armed forces the restoration of police primacy must be the ultimate aim.

Ian Beckett

Key Weapons

AK ASSAULT RIFLES

The man responsible for the famous Soviet AK assault rifle series was Mihael Kalashnikov. Severely wounded as a tank commander during World War II, Kalashnikov was invalided out of the army and during his convalescence he put forward proposals for a sub-machine gun and a carbine, neither of which was accepted. Undeterred he continued working and in 1947 submitted drawings of a new rifle designed around a short 7.62mm cartridge which the Soviet Army had introduced at the end of the war. This time his design was accepted and it was introduced into Soviet service in 1953 as the *Avtomat Kalashnikov Obr 1947*, or AK-47. Since that time it has been estimated that something over 35 million AK series assault rifles have been made, and they are to be found in almost every country of the world; without any doubt the Kalashnikov is the most successful assault rifle ever designed.

What made the AK-47 such a success? Simply that it was sufficiently accurate, reliable, easy to make, easy to maintain and robust enough to stand up to the punishment of the battlefield. There is nothing revolutionary about the design, which is, in truth, a collection of features most of which have been seen on other weapons, (most notably the German MP43/44 assault rifle). But its strength lies in the way these features have been brought together and welded into a near-perfect unity.

The AK-47 is a gas-actuated automatic weapon. Above the barrel lies a cylinder containing a piston; as the bullet is fired and passes up the barrel, a small portion of the propelling gas passes through a port and drives this piston backwards. At the rear end of the piston rod is a carrier which holds the bolt. As the rod and carrier move backwards, a shaped cam track in the carrier engages with a lug on the bolt and revolves

Page 443: Two Kalashnikov-armed Palestinian youths display their weapons for the benefit of a Western news photographer. The boy in the foreground has a conventional AKMS while his companion carries a modified version with a pistol grip attached to the fore-end handgrip. Opposite page: The AK series was adopted by the Soviet Army in 1953 and has been used ever since, whether on active service in Czechoslovakia in 1968 (below) or on manoeuvres in the Soviet Union in 1981 (above), in which infantry are shown advancing in winter conditions supported by MICVs. Above: Troops of the Afghan Army parade in Kabul in 1979 armed with AKMs. Right: A Soviet colour guard of marine infantry pose in typical fashion. Of interest is the difference between the magazines; on the left made from stamped steel while on the right made from plastic.

the bolt, unlocking it from engagement with the rifle breech. Once unlocked the rearward movement of the carrier withdraws the bolt, pulls the empty cartridge case from the chamber and ejects it. At the same time a return spring is compressed, and the firing hammer is cocked by the movement of the carrier. Then the spring forces the carrier and rod back, collecting a fresh cartridge from the magazine and loading it into the chamber. The bolt stops, but the carrier continues forward so that the cam now rotates the bolt in the opposite direction and locks it into the rifle barrel ready for firing. As the soldier pulls the trigger, the hammer springs up and hits the firing pin in the centre of the bolt, and the cartridge is fired, to begin the process over again.

By moving a lever on the right-hand side of the rifle, the soldier can select automatic fire, and in this case the rifle will continue to load, fire, eject and reload so long as the trigger is held down, firing off rounds at a cyclic rate of about 600 rounds per minute, though since the magazine holds only 30 rounds this rate obviously cannot be achieved in practice. In fact, with the fire selector set on 'auto', a rate of 90 rounds per minute would be considered acceptable.

A particular feature of assault rifles – of which the AK-47 is no exception – is the use of a smaller

intermediate cartridge. The M43 7.62mmx39 intermediate round of the AK-47 is lighter than the standard rifle cartridge, and while less powerful it is still capable of carrying out the function assigned to it. In addition, the intermediate round is much more powerful and more accurate than the pistol rounds used in sub-machine guns. The M43 round has a higher trajectory than almost any other ammunition type and as a consequence is ineffective at ranges over 400m (440yds). However, since it is accepted that few soldiers are capable of hitting anything over 200m (220yds), and that most fire-fights occur at much shorter ranges, this lack of long-range effectiveness is not particularly damaging to the rifle's overall performance.

Despite its ruggedness and reliability of operation the AK series does have a few faults, most notably the vulnerability of the rather exposed gas tube, which if damaged will cause operational malfunctions brought about by uneven gas pressure. Also, the rifle has a tendency to overheat during sustained fire, making it difficult to handle and more seriously bringing about the danger of the round spontaneously 'cooking-off' in the chamber.

The AK-47 was manufactured in the traditional manner, the receiver being machined from a block of steel. By modern standards this is uneconomic, and in 1959 a 'modernised' version, the AKM, was produced. This uses stamped steel for the receiver and riveting for the assembly, but otherwise is the same as the earlier model. Both the AK-47 and the AKM can

Above: Moslem street fighters wave aloft a variety of Soviet-made weapons in a lull in the fighting for Beirut during the civil war in Lebanon in 1975. Besides the AK rifles (with folding bayonets attached) are an RPD light machine gun (with bipod) and an RPG7 rocket launcher. Left: A Lebanese militiaman inspects the ground below his position. Note the religious picture stuck onto the stock of his AKM, a traditional custom among Christian troops in Lebanon. Right: This Palestinian soldier follows the practice, made popular in Vietnam, of taping an extra magazine (upside down) to the magazine in the rifle, so that during combat the second magazine can be quickly flipped round, in effect doubling the immediately available ammunition supply.

be found with wooden butts or with folding steel stocks. Motorised and airborne units use the lighter folding stock version which is termed the AKMS. The AKM can be fitted with a NSP-2 infra-red night sight and a knife bayonet that can also function – unlike that of the AK-47 – as an insulated wire cutter and a miniature saw. Additionally, a grenade-launcher attachment can be fitted to the basic model.

As well as outfitting the Soviet Army the Kalashnikov design has been exported to the communist bloc and to a large number of other countries, several of which have begun manufacture themselves, sometimes incorporating minor variations. The Chinese designate it the Type 56 and fit a folding bayonet to the muzzle; the Romanians fit a wooden front pistol grip so that it can be used as a sub-machine gun, while the Hungarians use a perforated metal fore-end and a nylon front grip. Butts of natural wood, laminated plywood and plastic materials are employed by all these nations.

In addition, there are 'Kalashnikov look-alikes'. The Yugoslavian Army is equipped with the M70 rifle, a close copy of the Kalashnikov, and Yugoslavia also produces the M77 which is in 7.62mm Nato calibre for export. The Finns have the Valmet M62/M70; this began as a straight copy of the AK-47 and has since been modified, though in appearance its AK-47 ancestry is quite apparent.

In 1978 the West became aware of a new version, the AK-74, which is essentially an AKM but with a smaller 5.45mm calibre. This development is in line with the adoption of the 5.56mm cartridge by the Americans for their successful M16 rifle. The smaller calibre ensures a lighter cartridge with less recoil force so that automatic fire from the shoulder is more easily controlled and more accurate. While being lighter than the M43 round, the magazine – made of

Top: The AK series has been one of the most exported rifles of the postwar period. This Yemeni guerrilla proudly displays his AK-47, complete with home-made leather casing. Above: Palestinian commandos in Lebanon in 1982. The soldier in the foreground is armed with an AKMS fitted with a rocket-launcher attachment.

plastic – still holds the standard 30 rounds. The most prominent recognition feature of the AK-74 is the muzzle brake and compensator which directs some of the emerging gases up and to the right to counter the rifle's tendency to climb when fired on automatic. It also reduces the recoil force, making the weapon easier to shoot. A further advantage over the 7.62mm version is the AK-74's increased muzzle velocity (900 metres per second as against 715 metres per second) which will provide a flatter trajectory and so greater accuracy and impact force.

The AK series design has also extended to acting in

AKM assault rifle

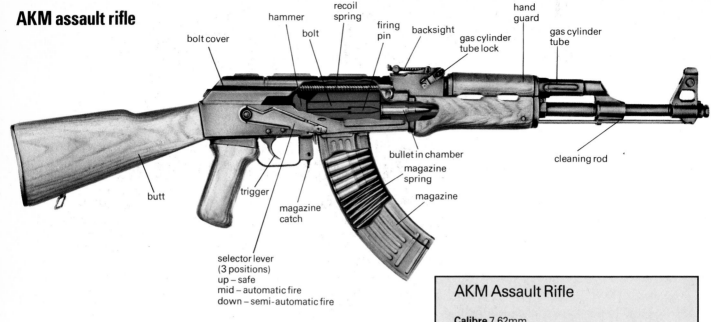

bolt cover
hammer
bolt
recoil spring
firing pin
backsight
gas cylinder tube lock
hand guard
gas cylinder tube

butt
trigger
magazine catch

selector lever
(3 positions)
up – safe
mid – automatic fire
down – semi-automatic fire

bullet in chamber
magazine spring
magazine

cleaning rod

AKM Assault Rifle

Calibre 7.62mm
Length (without bayonet) 88.8cm (35in); AKMS 65.3cm (25.7in) with stock folded
Weight (loaded) 3.80kg (8.38lb); AKMS 3.46kg (7.62lb)
Rate of fire Cyclic 600rpm; practical auto 90rpm; practical semi-auto 40 rpm
Maximum sighted range 1000m (1100yds)
Effective range Auto 200m (220yds); semi-auto 300m (330yds)
Ammunition Ball, tracer, armour piercing, blank, grenade launching
Magazine 30-round box
Cartridge M43 7.62mmx39 intermediate round
Muzzle velocity 715mps (2345fps)

Above left: An RPK light machine gun photographed without its magazine.
Left: The AK-74, which will eventually replace the AKM in the Soviet armed forces. Firing a 5.45mm calibre bullet the AK-74 follows the trend set in the West for small-calibre rifles. Below left: Armed with AKMs and an RPD LMG, Afghan guerrillas engage Soviet troops.

a light machine gun role, namely the RPK and the PK models. Introduced in 1960 the RPK is essentially a bipod-mounted AKM but with a longer, stronger barrel, a different stock and a larger capacity magazine – either a 40-round box or a 75-round drum magazine. Light and very handy to use the RPK is, however, too akin to the AKM to be really effective as a light machine gun: its M43 cartridge is not powerful enough for long range fire and its (unchangeable) barrel overheats rapidly. These problems were largely overcome with the introduction of the PK model which, weighing nearly twice as much as the RPK, fires the full power 7.62mm cartridge and, belt fed, is capable of sustained long-range fire. Highly regarded in the West – following tests by the US Army – this light machine gun can be either bipod or tripod mounted; and in the latter firing position it is termed the PKMB.

The Red menace

Cold War attitudes in the West

The Cold War was the term used to describe the hostility and mistrust between the United States and the Soviet Union, and between the communist world as a whole and the West, which developed in the years immediately after World War II. It was a shorthand way of saying that East-West relations had deteriorated to a point that stopped short only of open warfare between the two superpowers. The mutual hostility has continued into the 1980s at times approaching direct military confrontation, as in the Cuban missile crisis of 1962, and at other times subsiding into a state known as 'detente'; but it is generally accepted that the more intense phases of the Cold War ended in the early 1960s, when both sides more or less accepted the status quo.

At no time during the Cold War did Soviet and American troops confront each other directly, but there were several cases of war by proxy, as in Korea, when US troops fought allies of the Soviet Union, and in the Middle East, where states supported by the United States fought against states supported by the Soviet Union. In the course of the Cold War the Russians used armed force to maintain communist regimes in neighbouring countries, and the Americans used it in their attempts to influence the politics of Latin America. There has been plenty of fighting during the Cold War, but it has all been 'limited', and often small-scale guerrilla warfare.

It was Bernard Baruch, the American financier and adviser to President Roosevelt and Winston Churchill, who first used the term Cold War in a public speech in 1947, when the United States was debating the possibility of extending military and economic aid to countries threatened by the spread of communism. This policy came to be known as the Truman Doctrine, first enunciated on 12 March 1947, and this date is sometimes regarded as marking the beginning of the Cold War. Others regard the starting point as Winston Churchill's speech at Fulton, Missouri, in March 1946 in which he spoke of the 'iron curtain' that had descended between eastern and western Europe. For others the turning point came with the communist takeover in Czechoslovakia in February 1948; and there can be no doubt that the blockade imposed by the Soviet government on West Berlin in 1948 was the 'hottest' point in the early stages of the Cold War. Certainly, the conclusion of the North Atlantic Treaty in 1949 and of the Warsaw Pact in 1955 institutionalised the Cold War as two armed camps faced each other in Europe.

The Cold War did not just 'begin' at one point, however. It had its origins in the hostility between the democratic regimes of western Europe and America and the communist regimes installed in the Soviet Union by the revolution of 1917 and in the countries of eastern Europe after World War II. There was an essential, and undeniable, conflict between states based upon the theory of class conflict and inevitable revolution and those that were supposed to succumb to that revolution.

In World War II, of course, Great Britain, the United States and the Soviet Union were allies in the war against Nazi Germany, which had attacked all of them or their allies. This alliance was at best uneasy because of ideological problems; and suspicions on the Western side were increased by the obvious

The basic Western fear in the Cold War was of a Soviet offensive in Europe. Nato was conceived as the answer to this threat, and since the 1940s has been engaged in a continuous programme of modernisation and training to cope with possible aggression. Here British paras assault 'enemy' positions during a training exercise in a wooded area of West Berlin. The FV432 APC on the right is using its smoke dischargers which are mounted to the left and right of the front hull.

Collier's, August 12, 1950

Soviet Germany's SECRET ARMY

Pursuing her Korean strategy, Russia builds a powerful East German striking force—already 50,000 strong—to invade the Allied-occupied West and unify the country under the Cominform

Left: This extract, taken from *Collier's* magazine in 1950, illustrates Western fears of the communist military build-up. Right: John Foster Dulles, US Secretary of State, addressing a press conference. Dulles was renowned as a determined anti-communist. Below: Soviet Foreign Minister V. M. Molotov and Dulles in 1955 after signing agreements on military withdrawal by both East and West from Austria.

territorial designs of the Russians. Traditional Russian nationalism and communist theorising made for a mix that the British – who had territorial and imperial fears and ambitions of their own at stake – found very worrying.

In December 1941, when British Foreign Secretary Anthony Eden visited Moscow, Stalin had recovered sufficiently from the shock of the German invasion of Russia to suggest that, once Hitler had been disposed of, the Western Allies should agree to legalise the Soviet frontiers as they were when Hitler attacked. That would have meant agreeing, long before the war was over, to the Soviet annexation of the Baltic states (Latvia, Lithuania and Estonia), of parts of Romania and Finland, and of Poland to the Curzon Line. To this proposal Churchill reacted sharply: 'The transfer of the people of the Baltic states to Soviet Russia against their will would be contrary to all the principles for which we are fighting this war and would dishonour our cause,' he told Eden. Nevertheless, he was later forced to accept Stalin's demands.

At the conferences at Tehran and Yalta, at which the shape of the postwar world was decided, Soviet ambitions went far beyond the restoration of the 1941 frontier. Stalin wanted the Western governments to recognise Russia's right to a 'sphere of influence' in Europe – a sort of cordon sanitaire of friendly states which would act as a defensive glacis to strengthen Soviet security. Britain and America did not object to this in principle; in fact, when he met Stalin in Moscow in October 1944, Churchill proposed that Russia should be given a 90 per cent interest in Romania, 75 per cent in Bulgaria, and 50 per cent in Yugoslavia and Hungary. It was at least partial acknowledgement of the justice of Stalin's demands.

Soviet strongholds

There were people in influential positions both in London and Washington who believed that recognition of Soviet domination of eastern Europe provided the only hope for a secure peace. One of these was the American diplomat George Kennan, then serving in the US embassy in Moscow, who argued that there was nothing the West could do to alter the course of events in eastern Europe and that it should abandon the area to the Russians, while taking steps to prevent further Soviet inroads into Europe. He recommended 'a prompt and clear recognition of the division of Europe into spheres of influence and of a policy based on the fact of such division'.

What Western statesmen soon came to appreciate, however, was that Stalin's understanding of what was meant by a 'sphere of influence' was very different from theirs. Their understanding of the arrangement was set out in the Declaration on Liberated Europe, which Stalin had agreed to at Yalta and which committed him to the establishment of 'democratic regimes' in eastern Europe through 'free elections'. But, as Averell Harriman, the American ambassador in Moscow, told Washington: 'Words have a different connotation to the Soviets than they have to us. When they speak of insisting on "friendly governments" in their neighbouring countries they have in mind something quite different from what we would mean.' Stalin himself once revealed to Anthony Eden how little importance he attached to declarations of general principle. 'A declaration I regard as algebra, but an agreement as practical arithmetic,' he said. 'I do not wish to decry algebra but I prefer practical arithmetic.' He later made it clear that he considered that the 'arithmetical' agreement he reached with Churchill over eastern Europe gave him the all-clear to establish

Soviet control throughout the whole area.

George Kennan was the first to question whether Stalin would be satisfied with eastern Europe alone. 'If initially successful, will it [the Soviet Union] know where to stop?' he asked in May 1944. 'Will it not be inexorably carried forward, by its very nature, in a struggle to reach the whole – to attain complete mastery of the shores of the Atlantic and the Pacific?' Harriman expressed a similar point of view: 'If the policy is accepted that the Soviet Union has a right to penetrate her immediate neighbours for security, penetration of the next immediate neighbours becomes at a certain time equally logical.'

'We can't do business with Stalin'

Disillusionment with Stalin and fears that he might not be satisfied with possession of eastern Europe were the real foundations of the Cold War from the Western point of view. Before he died in April 1945 Roosevelt admitted he no longer trusted Stalin. 'Averell is right: we can't do business with Stalin. He has broken every one of the promises he made at Yalta,' he said. His successor, Harry Truman, more or less accepted the Soviet domination of eastern Europe. The attempt to collaborate with the Soviet Union in eastern Europe was replaced by a policy of 'containment' which took the form of the Truman Doctrine and the Marshall Plan.

In the aftermath of World War II, with the Red Army in firm occupation of most of eastern Europe, there seemed little that the West could do about the establishment of communist regimes. The ugly stories filtering out about the suppression of opposition and the creation of police states were disturbing enough, however; and the remorseless drive to power of the communist party in Czechoslovakia was, in this context, sufficient to send shivers down many spines, particularly as the communist parties of France and Italy were enjoying considerable electoral success and there was open civil war in Greece between the government and communist rebels.

The spectre of a centrally directed, world communist conspiracy was certainly perceived as a real threat in the late 1940s and early 1950s. The Chinese Civil War, the Greek Civil War, the Korean War, the Malayan Emergency and the Viet Minh insurrection in Indochina were all seen as part of the same overall plan for world domination. Nor did this fear diminish as the 1950s continued. Militant nationalism all over the Third World was encouraged by the Soviet Union,

Below: Two staunch anti-communists: President Harry S. Truman, who instituted the Truman Doctrine, and Richard M. Nixon, vice-president from 1952 to 1960, who was eager to combat a threat he saw as 'universal, indivisible and total'.
Below: Senator Joseph McCarthy, who waged a witch-hunt against US communists in high places, reads a hostile article in a communist newspaper.
Above right: A British report of anti-communist measures in the USA.

U.S. ROUND-UP O COMMUNISTS

BRITON IN 13 HELD: 7 MORE SOUGHT

DEPORTATION UNDER NEW ACT

PRESIDENT SETS UP BOARD TO REVIEW CASES

FROM OUR OWN CORRESPONDENT
WASHINGTON, Monday.
The United States Department of Justice announced to-day that it had

and in many quarters the expansion of Soviet influence into Egypt, black Africa or the Middle East seemed a terrifying threat.

In the West there was a range of views of the Soviet Union and its ambitions. There was, first of all, an overwhelming aversion to the communist system. The steady flow of political dissidents who testified to the evils of a totalitarian system; specific examples of the repressive nature of that system, such as the crushing of the Hungarian uprising in 1956; and the mid-1950s revelations of the full horrors of the Stalinist system, of the purges from the 1930s onwards – all made the idea of a Soviet-style system repugnant to the West. The revelations about Stalinism also inevitably raised fears about the possibility of the Soviet leadership taking sudden, almost irrational decisions – such as to attack western Europe.

This quite natural repugnance was, however, embellished and amplified in certain quarters by other factors. In the United States, for example, politicians like Senator Joseph McCarthy initiated witch-hunts against communists which reflected traditional American xenophobia and personal ambition rather than defence against a genuine threat. Then again, in countries such as France and Italy, where communist parties were important minority groups in the electoral system, their opponents (perhaps inevitably) used scare tactics against them. And where Western nations were involved in campaigns against nationalism in the Third World, there was naturally a tendency to paint local nationalists with the communist brush in order to justify such campaigns.

The result of all these factors was that the Cold War became an integral part of the way that the political situation of the world was observed. Men like John Foster Dulles, Secretary of State in the Eisenhower administration, became renowned for their determination to meet any threat from the Soviet Union, while future American presidents Richard Nixon and Ronald Reagan established their careers on stern anti-communism. The world of the 1950s seemed totally split into two camps; it was not until the 1960s, when the Third World began to emerge as a political force, that this view was superseded by one which saw the superpower confrontation as being merely the most important in a series of problems facing a rapidly changing and more complicated world.

David Floyd

Defence and unity

Nato, Seato and Cento:
alliances to contain communism

Article 52 of the Charter of the United Nations, which was signed by 51 states in 1945, specifically allowed for the creation of regional arrangements or agencies to deal with the maintenance of international peace and security in any region of the world. In three regions this opportunity was grasped by states which were all concerned about the danger, as they saw it, of the expansion of communism.

The Europeans and Americans began the process with the establishment of the North Atlantic Treaty Organisation (Nato) in 1949. Certain Southeast Asian countries followed this example with the Manila Pact in 1954, which became the Southeast Asia Treaty Organisation (Seato). Shortly afterwards, in 1955, the Baghdad Pact linked the northern tier of Middle Eastern states to some countries already involved in Nato and Seato to become, by 1959, the Central Treaty Organisation (Cento). The fundamental principle upon which all three alliances were based was the containment of communism, in the belief that collective defence offered the best chance of security. But whereas Nato, facing the threat of Soviet armed forces in Europe, was a firm alliance, both Cento and Seato were much weaker associations of states, often with conflicting interests, in areas where the classic Cold War confrontation was only one of a number of pressures on the countries involved.

An Atlantic alliance

The North Atlantic Treaty, signed in Washington on 4 April 1949, brought together the United States and Canada and 10 European countries so as to provide stability and security through collective defence in the North Atlantic region. The aim was to safeguard the freedom, common heritage and civilisation of the member states founded upon the principles of democracy, individual liberty and the rule of law, in the face of a perceived threat from the Soviet Union. The treaty was quite specific. Article 4 committed the parties to consult together when any one of them was threatened, and Article 5 committed the parties to regard an armed attack against one or more of them in Europe or North America as an attack against them all. This meant that Nato was determined to defend the territory of the member states and the Atlantic Ocean, from the Tropic of Cancer to the North Pole, by collective means.

It was felt necessary to create a peacetime organisation in order to make the alliance credible. As a result the signatories agreed to set up the North Atlantic Council, which is made up of ministers and permanent representatives at ambassadorial level and is the ultimate decision-making body in Nato. Alongside the council a military committee was formed, and this is the highest military authority in Nato. A permanent

Above: Nato delegates meet at their new headquarters in Brussels in October 1967. This, the most important Western alliance against communism, was founded in 1949.

secretariat is headed by the secretary general. A permanent headquarters was established in Paris but later moved to Brussels. Nato has since spawned many specialised committees which develop the details of policy and its implementation. Decisions in the organisation are taken by common consent, emphasising the fact that the members are all sovereign independent states.

The European members of Nato – Belgium, Denmark, France, Iceland, Italy, Luxembourg, the Netherlands, Norway, Portugal and the United Kingdom – were keen to see not only an American commitment of support through the treaty, but the physical presence of American personnel on the ground in Europe. The members therefore created an integrated military structure for the defence of the Nato region. This involved three major commands: Allied Command Europe, Allied Command Atlantic and Allied Command Channel, supplemented by a Canada-US Regional Planning Group. The structure was then sub-divided into subordinate commands.

The aim of the military structure is to enhance the region's security by unifying allied defence plans, strengthening allied forces in peacetime and planning for their best use in war. The integrated military structure, therefore, has led 300,000 US personnel to serve in Allied Command Europe – a boost to the confidence of western Europeans in the firmness of the US commitment to Europe. Nato expanded from 12 member states to 14 on 18 February 1952 when two new members, Greece and Turkey, acceded to the treaty, and from 14 to 15 on 5 May 1955 when West Germany also became a member.

The strategy adopted by Nato in order to achieve the objectives of the alliance combined deterrence and, should deterrence fail, defence. But ever since its creation, Nato has in fact provided an effective deterrent to aggression. Despite problems in both the political and military spheres, events such as the crisis in Hungary in 1956, when Nato was reminded of the Soviet Union's willingness to use force, have kept the

Above: On the day that the Manila Pact was signed, 8 September 1954, John Foster Dulles (left) and the US ambassador to the Philippines (right), drink to the success of the alliance with the President of the Philippines, Ramon Magsaysay (centre). Below: The US Seventh Fleet steams in battle formation through the Pacific. This fleet represented the most powerful striking force at Seato's disposal.

alliance unified and credible. If the success of an alliance can be measured by the fact that not an inch of its territory has been lost since its creation then Nato since 1949 has indeed fulfilled its aims.

Southeast Asian defences

The Southeast Asia Collective Defence Treaty was signed in Manila, the Philippines, on 8 September 1954 by eight participants: Australia, New Zealand, the Philippines, Thailand, Pakistan, France, the United Kingdom and the United States. The so-called Manila Pact, which soon became known as the Southeast Asia Treaty Organisation (Seato), was set up to draw a line against the advance of communism in Southeast Asia just as Nato had done in Europe. In the nine years after 1945, the region had been subjected to many communist insurrections and, with the consolidation of communist power in China, the Korean War and the communist challenge in Indochina, some states in the region and various Western powers were convinced that the provision of collective security for Southeast Asia was essential.

The area to be defended by the treaty included the territories of the Asian members, and the Pacific Ocean area south of a line 21° 30′ North latitude. The area was imprecise, but included Cambodia, Laos and the Republic of Vietnam, which were covered by an additional protocol even though these three states did not sign the treaty.

Seato was designed to counter both aggression and subversion. Individually and collectively, by self-help and mutual aid, the members agreed in Article 2 of the treaty to develop their ability to resist armed attack and counter subversive activities, and in Article 3 to strengthen the economic and social structure of the countries involved to help them combat communism. The resort to military action was by no means automatic, since Article 4 only committed each state to meet the common danger in accordance with its own constitutional processes.

The membership was an extraordinary mix of states. The United Kingdom, with historical connections in Southeast Asia, was soon to find that economics dictated a withdrawal to Europe. France, with recent experience of the area in Indochina but with no serious intention of involving itself militarily in the area ever again, joined for prestige. Both Britain and France were open to the charge of 'imperialist intervention' but both in fact wanted to see the United States take on responsibility for defending the area.

Australia and New Zealand – already linked to the United States by the ANZUS Pact of 1951 – considered Southeast Asia to be their first line of defence. Pakistan, the least involved of all members in the area, was more concerned with rivalry with India. The Philippines was already firmly in the Western camp through a mutual defence treaty with the United States signed in 1951. Thailand, perhaps, stood to gain the most. Never colonised and traditionally neutral, Thailand bordered some of the most troubled areas in Southeast Asia and felt threatened.

Especially after its Korean experience, the United States was keen to counter the threat of communist China, but it was not an unconditional nor a limitless US commitment and very much depended upon the Asian nations themselves contributing to their own defence. US Secretary of State John Foster Dulles, however, believed that the communists intended to dominate all Southeast Asia and that the Geneva Accords of July 1954 which had ended the first war in Indochina had rewarded communist aggression. The alliance, therefore, was directed against communism, and the United States declared that its guarantee applied only to communist aggression.

The real problem for Seato was that it had only three Asian signatories (Pakistan, the Philippines and Thailand). The two largest Asian states that might have become members – India and Indonesia – stood aloof, unwilling to damage their interests by being dragged into the Western camp, however much they might have been worried by a communist threat. And thus the Soviet claim that Seato was merely a bloc of colonial powers trying to maintain their economic and political influence seemed not without substance.

The headquarters of the alliance was established in Bangkok, Thailand. There was no unified command or organised force like that of Nato, though there was military assistance provided and some successful training exercises and defence planning.

Between 1954 and 1961 Seato was modestly successful, with no communist aggression in Pakistan, Thailand or the Philippines. The real deterrent was the power of the United States. However, as the war in Vietnam escalated, and the neighbouring state of Laos became embroiled, both states were entitled to Seato's protection. Seato failed to respond, except to a plea from Thailand in 1962 which led to a commitment of US troops and air support along with small forces from Britain, Australia and New Zealand to Thailand itself. But there was reluctance among some members, in particular the United Kingdom and France, to get involved and the United States increasingly went its own way, leaving Seato to wither away.

Right: British Prime Minister Harold Macmillan opens the fifth conference of the Ministerial Council of the Baghdad Pact, one year prior to the formation of Cento. Above: On 19 August 1959 the Baghdad Pact became Cento. Here Admiral of the Fleet Earl Mountbatten of Burma, UK Chief of Defence Staff (centre back), addresses other defence chiefs at a meeting of the Cento Military Committee.

Below: The French Foreign Legion abandon Bac Ninh in Vietnam in 1954. French defeat by the communist Viet Minh and their subsequent withdrawal from Indochina were major factors behind the formation of Seato.

Setting up Cento

The Central Treaty Organisation (Cento) had no master-plan but grew out of the Baghdad Pact signed on 24 February 1955 by Turkey and Iraq. The Pact of Mutual Cooperation bound the two states to cooperate in matters of security and defence. Both states wanted to ensure stability in the Middle East against aggression and made it clear that they would welcome the accession of other states that were actively concerned with the security and peace of the region. Accordingly, the United Kingdom joined in April 1955, Pakistan followed in September, and finally Iran acceded to the treaty in October. The pact became a defensive partnership of Middle Eastern states working in cooperation with the West.

It would have been surprising if there had been no opposition to the Baghdad Pact, and it came from the Soviet Union and from some Arab states. Egypt under

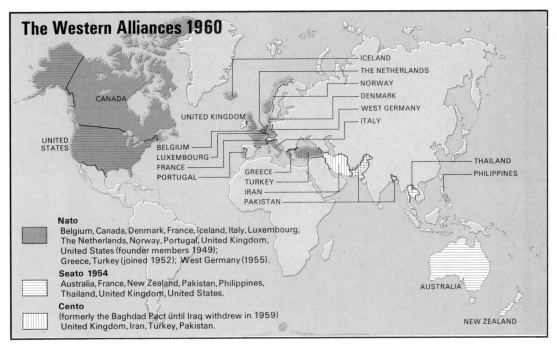

The Western Alliances 1960

ICELAND
THE NETHERLANDS
NORWAY
DENMARK
WEST GERMANY
ITALY

CANADA

UNITED KINGDOM

THAILAND
PHILIPPINES

UNITED
STATES

BELGIUM
LUXEMBOURG
FRANCE
PORTUGAL

GREECE
TURKEY
IRAN
PAKISTAN

AUSTRALIA

NEW ZEALAND

Nato
Belgium, Canada, Denmark, France, Iceland, Italy, Luxembourg, The Netherlands, Norway, Portugal, United Kingdom, United States (founder members 1949); Greece, Turkey (joined 1952); West Germany (1955).

Seato 1954
Australia, France, New Zealand, Pakistan, Philippines, Thailand, United Kingdom, United States.

Cento
(formerly the Baghdad Pact until Iraq withdrew in 1959) United Kingdom, Iran, Turkey, Pakistan.

Below: During the late 1950s and early 1960s, Britain attempted to form a confederation of southern Arabian states in order to stabilise the political situation there. British trained and equipped troops are shown patrolling open country.

Colonel Gamal Abdel Nasser in particular, was very critical, but other Arab states, like Jordan, did contemplate joining. The Soviet Union claimed that the pact was an aggressive military bloc and that the West was only interested in perpetuating the colonial dependence of certain areas. Committees were created to look after military affairs, economic affairs and to coordinate and counter subversive activity. The secretariat was headed by a secretary general. There was, however, no central command, and military and economic assistance was both bilateral and multilateral. The treaty signatories coordinated common plans for regional defence and exercises. But the commitments of the treaty itself were not very specific, speaking only of cooperation for security and defence being based on those measures that the parties could agree to.

America joins the pact

On 23 March 1957 the United States, which had contemplated a Middle East Defence Organisation back in 1951, acceded to the Baghdad Pact as an associate member. The US then took a full part in the work of the pact and its ministerial council. The US also contributed to the international staff and the budget, and provided economic and military assistance. The presence of the United States added significantly to the deterrent value of the treaty, but this fillip was balanced somewhat when Iraq withdrew from the pact on 24 March 1959 following the coup in Baghdad in 1958.

On 19 August 1959 the Baghdad Pact formally became the Central Treaty Organisation. Cento looked impressive on paper but was too widely spread to have any lasting impact. It was deprived of full US membership because of Congressional reluctance and the Jewish lobby; Pakistan was more interested in its confrontation with India; Turkey and Pakistan already had a Treaty of Friendship; Turkey and Iraq had a Treaty of Mutual Defence; and the US had a Mutual Defence Pact with Pakistan. Yet Cento had not had to act and, therefore, might be considered a success.

The collapse of Cento and Seato was an indication of the changes taking place within the Middle East and Asia – the emergence of states that saw themselves and their part of the world as separate from the East-West clash and that found the sharp dividing lines of the Cold War increasingly irrelevant to their own needs. But the very creation of these alliances, and the importance attached to them, also bears witness to the way that the fear of communist expansion was perhaps the major factor influencing the policy of many states in the 1950s. **David Johnson**

Dropping the bomb

Nuclear delivery systems of the 1950s

During the four years from the end of World War II until the first Soviet atomic test in August 1949 the United States possessed a monopoly of nuclear weapons and their delivery systems. However, this seemingly invulnerable position appeared to American planners to be, if not entirely illusory, then at any rate precarious. The reasons for their concern included the small numbers of nuclear weapons available (perhaps as low as 25 in 1947), doubts that America would use these weapons if war broke out, and further doubts that, if used, they would have sufficient effect to halt a Soviet onslaught on western Europe.

There was disquiet also about the efficiency of America's nuclear bombing force. In March 1946 the

US Army Air Force – not to become the US Air Force until July 1947 – formed Strategic Air Command (SAC) as a nuclear-armed air striking force which was to be capable of hitting targets anywhere in the world. On paper its strength seemed impressive enough: six bombardment groups equipped with the Boeing B-29 Superfortress, plus the 509th Composite Group (soon to be redesignated a bombardment group), which was the unit that bombed Hiroshima and Nagasaki in 1945 and carried out the Bikini Atoll atomic test on 1 July 1946. The US services were in the throes of postwar demobilisation, however, and SAC was not spared the effects of budgetary cuts. The 509th Bombardment Wing was, in fact, its only nuclear-capable unit. When that larger-than-life Air Force General Curtis

Above: A Boeing B-47 Stratojet; the first production model flew successfully on 25 June 1950. Below inset: A Boeing B-29 Superfortress. On 6 August 1945, the B-29 Enola Gay dropped the first atomic bomb on Hiroshima. Below: A Boeing B-50, the modified version of the B-29.

LeMay assumed command of SAC in 1948 he claimed that not a single crew in the entire bomber force was capable of efficiently flying a war mission.

Part of the reason for SAC's inadequacies lay with its standard bomber aircraft. The Boeing B-29 Superfortress was the four-engined strategic bomber which had raided Japanese cities from bases in China and the Mariana Islands during 1944-45, but by the late 1940s these ageing aircraft required an increasing number of maintenance man-hours to keep them airborne, a problem exacerbated by serious spares shortages. The 6400km (4000 mile) range of the B-29 was inadequate for the strategic mission, making it necessary to deploy nuclear-armed bombers to forward bases in the United Kingdom, North Africa and the western Pacific in order for them to reach important Soviet targets. During the Berlin blockade crisis in 1948-49 three B-29 groups were deployed to Europe to bring them within range of targets in the western USSR.

Intercontinental offensives

There were two immediate solutions to the problems of short range which would make the unsatisfactory forward basing system unnecessary and enable the American deterrent force to operate from airfields within the United States. One was to build longer-range bombers. This resulted in the massive Convair B-36, an intercontinental-range bomber powered by six 3500hp piston engines and four auxiliary turbojets. The other possibility was to equip the existing force for in-flight refuelling. This too was implemented and the Boeing B-29 and B-50 (an improved Superfortress variant with more powerful engines) were equipped as both tanker and receiver aircraft. However, although these measures produced a long-range bomber force capable of flying intercontinental missions, they relied on piston-engined aircraft which did not have the speed needed to evade jet fighter defences. High speed became vitally important in 1948 when the Soviet Union brought the jet-powered MiG-15 interceptor fighter into service.

In 1951 the Boeing B-47 Stratojet, a swept-wing six-jet bomber, provided SAC with the performance needed to penetrate Soviet airspace, but this was only achieved at the expense of range. The B-47's unrefuelled range of 6400km (4000 miles) made it necessary to retain the forward basing system, with US-based Stratojets being regularly rotated through airfields in Europe, North Africa and the western Pacific. In-flight refuelling was available from SAC's new KC-97 piston-engined tankers, but even with this support the Stratojet lacked true intercontinental range, and the tankers were chiefly used

to provide fuel during the B-47s' overseas deployment flights. One development of the early 1950s which somewhat eased the bombers' payload and range problems was the substantial reduction in weight and size of nuclear weapons from the unwieldy 4500kg (10,000 pound) bombs of the 1940s.

It was not until the late 1950s that SAC achieved a truly global reach with the eight-engined, 16,000km (10,000 mile) range B-52 jet bomber and KC-135A jet tanker aircraft. The first B-52 Stratofortress wing began to form in 1955 and by the end of the decade SAC had become an all-jet bomber force with the retirement of the last of the B-36s. The Stratofortress, as the name implies, was intended to evade enemy interception by operating at high altitudes above the effective ceiling of Soviet surface-to-air missiles and interceptors. However, by 1959 it was believed that the Soviet air defences were capable of engaging high-flying bombers, an assessment confirmed in 1960 when the U-2 reconnaissance aircraft flown by Francis Gary Powers was brought down by an

Above: The Boeing B-52 Stratofortress was the first strategic bomber with the ability to strike at targets anywhere in the world. Below: A flight of Boeing B-47 Stratojets line the runway of an American airbase.

SA-2 missile over Soviet territory. B-52 target penetration tactics were therefore changed to a low-altitude approach to avoid radar detection. This new method of operation made heavy and often unforeseen demands on both the aircraft and its crews, with buffetting at low level imposing severe loads on the airframe and making the bomber difficult to control.

The manned bomber was certainly the most dependable strategic delivery system throughout the 1950s, but at the end of the decade it was joined on alert by SAC's first intercontinental ballistic missile (ICBM). This was the Atlas D, with a range of 9600km (6000 miles). By the end of 1959 only three Atlas ICBMs were in service and it was not until March 1961 that the planned four squadrons of Atlas Ds were operational.

Shorter-range missiles for the delivery of nuclear warheads had also been developed in the 1950s. Parallel US Army and US Air Force development programmes produced the Jupiter and Thor intermediate-range ballistic missiles (IRBMs). These missiles had a range of 2400km (1500 miles) and needed to be based in Europe, being unable to reach Soviet targets from the United States. Jupiter was to be based in Turkey and Italy and Thor was destined for the United Kingdom. The Royal Air Force received its first Thor missile in 1958, but the IRBMs were withdrawn in 1963 with the build-up of the US-based ICBM force and the recognition that fixed missile sites above ground had become vulnerable to pre-emptive attack.

The 1950s also saw the operational deployment of early cruise missiles, essentially pilotless aircraft fitted with a nuclear warhead. Tactical systems included the US Air Force's Matador and Mace, which were based in Germany, and the Navy's Regulus

carried aboard submarines and surface warships. One strategic cruise missile, the 8000km (5000 mile) range Snark, served operationally for four months with SAC's 556th Strategic Missile Squadron at Patrick air force base in Florida. Its short life was due to the unreliability of its guidance system (an inertial and star-tracking hybrid). One early Snark test flight went so far astray as to end up in the wrong hemisphere!

The Regulus cruise missile, which had a range of 800km (500 miles), was not the US Navy's only nuclear-capable system. Ambitious plans for a 65,000 tonne 'super-carrier' able to launch strategic bombing strikes fell foul of defence economies in 1949, thereby precipitating the B-36 controversy. If the admirals could not have their super-carrier, then the USAF had to fight a long and bitter battle in Congress for its new strategic bomber. However, the death of the super-carrier did not signify the end of carrier-based nuclear bombers. In 1949 a P2V Neptune patrol bomber was flown off the carrier USS *Coral Sea* and 11 further Neptunes were modified for the carrier-nuclear-strike mission. They were fol-

Far left: An Atlas intercontinental ballistic missile (ICBM) at Cape Canaveral, USA. Left: A Regulus guided missile is fired from a land-based portable launcher, and (inset) is prepared for launch on the deck of a US submarine. Above: A Jupiter A missile on test. Top right: A Soviet Tupolev Tu-20 Bear long-range reconnaissance aircraft is intercepted by a British Lightning over the North Sea. Above right: A Tupolev Tu-20 Bear-B showing duckbill radar and refuelling probe. Above far right: A GAM-77 Hound Dog missile is locked in position under the wing of a Boeing B-52 bomber.

lowed by the piston-engined AJ-1 Savage in the same year and the turbojet-powered Douglas A3D Skywarrior in 1956.

The Soviet Union lagged behind the United States in both atomic bomb development and delivery systems throughout the 1940s, but by the early 1950s had begun to make up leeway. The first Soviet A-bomb test was in 1949, the same year in which the Tupolev Tu-4 strategic bomber entered service. This was simply a Soviet unlicensed production version of the B-29, several of which had force-landed in Soviet territory after raids on Japan in 1945.

A more advanced medium-range bomber, the turbojet-powered Tu-16 entered service in 1955 as a replacement for the Tu-4. Its range of 6400km (4000 miles) limited it to European strategic targets, but by this time the Soviet Union had two intercontinental-range bombers in service. These were the turboprop-powered Tu-20 Bear and the turbojet-powered Myasishchev Mya-4 Bison, both of which had a maximum range of 17,700km (11,000 miles). Their appearance resulted in something of a scare in the United States, which greatly exaggerated the Soviet threat and led to the expansion of the USAF's Air Defense Command to 40 fighter-interceptor squad-

rons by the end of the decade.

Soviet missile development after World War II was essentially a continuation of German rocket research, as the Soviet armies had captured large stocks of V2 rockets and taken many German technicians as prisoners. The SS-1 and SS-2 short-range missiles were improved versions of the V2, as was the SS-3 medium-range ballistic missile (MRBM). There followed more advanced MRBMs, the 1900km (1200 mile) SS-4 and 3700km (2300 mile) SS-5. None of these new missiles posed any threat to the United States.

Nevertheless, Soviet ICBM development had been proceeding apace and the first test launch of the SS-6 was made in August 1957, two years before the first Atlas launch. Yet operational deployment of the new missile was slow on account of numerous technical problems, and only 10 SS-6s were in service by 1959. These shortcomings did not deter Premier Nikita Khrushchev from claiming that no strategic target in the West was thenceforth immune from attack; and on the strength of this rhetoric the Soviet Strategic Rocket Forces were elevated to the status of an armed service in their own right in May 1960.

Anthony Robinson

The Bundeswehr

A new army for a new Germany

In May 1945 the German Wehrmacht (armed forces) unconditionally surrendered and the victorious allies occupied the whole of Germany. On 2 August 1945 at the Potsdam conference the allied powers unanimously agreed that Germany should be disarmed and demilitarized. It was also decided that all forces and institutions or organisations 'which serve to keep alive the military tradition in Germany shall be completely and finally abolished in such a manner as permanently to prevent the revival or reorganisation of German militarism and Nazism.' Then followed the Nuremberg war trials. Although the German high command and general staff were both acquitted of the charge that they were criminal organisations, individual German officers and soldiers were sentenced to death and imprisonment at Nuremberg and other war crimes trials. Hundreds of thousands of German soldiers were prisoners of war. Those in Anglo-American hands were not all finally released until 1947, while the last major group in Soviet captivity was not released until 1955.

Amongst the German people there was either total hostility or indifference to all that was military. Hardly a German family had gone unscathed during the war, and even Wehrmacht veterans were weary of soldiering and longed to resume some kind of normal life. Yet within a decade of the end of World War II the foundations had been laid not for one, but two German armies, the Bundeswehr in West Germany and the Nationale Volksarmee in East Germany.

The breakdown of the wartime alliance between the Soviet Union and the Western allies (Britain, France and the United States) centred on the future of Germany. The Russians were determined to establish communism in their eastern zone, and any hopes for a unified Germany were dashed by increasing tension between the allied powers and separate developments in both the western and eastern zones. By 1949 the Western allies had agreed to the creation of the Federal Republic of Germany from their old occupation zones and the Russians had reacted by establishing the German Democratic Republic in their eastern zone.

The Basic Law, on which the federal republic was founded in May 1949, prohibited the waging of

Below: From left to right, Lieutenant-General Rottiger, Major-General Müller-Hildebrandt, Franz Josef Strauss and Konrad Adenauer inspect Bundeswehr troops before a military exercise.
Bottom: A soldier of the Bundeswehr scrambles from the back of an infantry combat vehicle during manoeuvres.

aggressive war and permitted citizens to exercise right of conscientious objection to military service. It did not, however, prohibit the raising of armed forces. Even before the establishment of the federal republic there had been discussions among leading West German politicians, including the future first chancellor, Konrad Adenauer, about the possibility of some form of rearmament. As early as 1948 it had been suggested that Germany participate in the collective military defence of western Europe. Western fears increased when the Russians organised East German paramilitary police forces far in excess of the needs of internal security.

Debating defence

After 1949 the United States was anxious to see the formation of West German armed forces, under Nato command, which could help defend the federal republic. The French were alarmed by the proposal, and instead made a counter-proposal in October 1950 for a European Defence Community in which German troop contingents would be employed as part of a European army. Although the plan for a European Defence Community received approval from representatives of Belgium, West Germany, France, Holland, Italy and Luxembourg in May 1952, the French National Assembly rejected the proposal in August 1954.

Britain and the United States took the initiative in the search for a new solution, this time, however, within the existing framework of Nato. In October 1954 the foreign ministers of Britain, France and the USA signed the Paris Agreements, so terminating their occupation of West Germany, which was recognised as a sovereign state and invited to become a member of Nato. This finally occurred in May 1955. West Germany voluntarily agreed to build up an army and to place combat units directly under Nato command. Thus a solution had been found which satisfied Nato requirements for West German rearmament.

Adenauer, meanwhile, had begun to prepare for rearmament. In the spring of 1950 he appointed a former general, Count Gerhard von Schwerin, as his military adviser. Von Schwerin drew up plans for a 10,000-man force of Federal Border Guards and secretly conferred with former senior Wehrmacht officers who concluded that any new armed forces would have to be both politically acceptable and technologically proficient.

On 27 October 1950, Adenauer had appointed Theodor Blank to head a kind of shadow 'defence ministry' which became known as the Blank Office. Although von Schwerin was dismissed because of incautious statements to the press, former officers of the Wehrmacht were absorbed into the Blank Office.

The early Bundeswehr relied on ex-World War II Wehrmacht equipment (top) and on American issue material (above).

Left: Theodor Blank (right), the Minister of Defence, hands out diplomas to General Heusinger to give to the top recruits in the Bundeswehr in 1955.

'For the SS man there is one absolute principle; he must be honest, decent, loyal and friendly to persons of our own blood, and to no one else...I am totally indifferent to what happens to the Russians or the Czechs. If, for instance, an anti-tank ditch has to be dug and 10,000 Russian women die of exhaustion digging it, my only interest is whether the ditch is completed for the benefit of Germany. We will never be savage or heartless where we do not have to be; that is clear. Germans, after all, are the only people in the world who know how to treat animals properly; so we shall know how to treat these human animals properly.'

Reichsführer Heinrich Himmler in a speech at Poznań, October 1943.

'The German soldier must know above all what he is fighting for. The concept of the citizen in uniform implies that a soldier is deeply rooted in the community to which he belongs and is consequently ready to stand up for it. If he is not, then he knows at best *against* what he has to take protective action; against what he must fight; and that is not enough. Only the soldier's full sense of citizenship enables him to experience values, which he has to defend, and only the possibility of democratic participation stimulates in him a sense of responsibility.'

General Wolf von Baudissin, ex-Wehrmacht officer who later became an officer of the Bundeswehr.

These men included Lieutenant-Colonel von Kielmansegg, General Wolf von Baudissin and Lieutenant-General Hans Speidel. They wanted to change the 'Prussian drill-book' image of soldiering to overcome the widespread anti-military feeling then prevalent among German youth. The new image of the German soldier was to be that of the 'citizen in uniform'. Despite this, however, German rearmament was viewed with suspicion in many countries while the Soviet Union was hostile and kept up a barrage of virulent propaganda.

Military limitations

The new armed forces were to be called the Bundeswehr (Federal Defence Force). Under the Paris Agreements of October 1954, West Germany undertook to limit its size to 12 divisions, to refrain from seeking to reunify Germany or alter the boundaries of the federal republic by the use of force, and to abstain from the manufacture of atomic, biological and chemical weapons. Command of the Bundeswehr, which was assigned to Nato, was with the Supreme Allied Commander Europe (SACEUR). Its role was to be strictly limited and controlled by the Bundestag (parliament) so that defence operations could only commence after a State of Defence had been proclaimed by parliamentary vote. German law thus limited the role of the Bundeswehr to obeying the orders of an external commander, SACEUR, except when parliament authorised its employment on national territory for strictly defined purposes.

Control of the Bundeswehr was to be divided between the executive and parliament. Parliament was to be responsible for defence legislation, the military budget, and, when necessary, the declaration of a state of war. The executive's powers were to be divided, with the federal president limited to the appointment and dismissal of civil and military officers, the regulation of the system of ranks and designs of uniforms, and the proclamation of a state of war. In peacetime the minister of defence was to be commander-in-chief of the Bundeswehr, but in wartime this role would be transferred to the chancellor. In order to protect and maintain the concept of the civilian in uniform, legislation, specifically the Soldier's Law of 19 March 1956, was passed facilitating appeal to civil courts by military personnel and the retention of citizens' rights while in uniform. The desire was to exorcise the danger of the Bundeswehr

Top: Despite the somewhat relaxed attitude towards military service, the training programme for the Bundeswehr is rigorous. These troops are practising house clearing techniques. Above: A military service which remains subject to civilian rights has to tread a delicate line where personal freedoms are concerned – and the question of long hair is a particularly interesting area of debate.

becoming a 'state within a state' and thus a danger to democracy.

Recruitment was to be by conscription, and the period of service to be 12 months. The problem of finding experienced officers and NCOs was met by recruiting specially screened military personnel who had previously served in the Wehrmacht. On 12 November 1955 the first 101 soldiers of the Bundeswehr received their commissions, and by the end of 1956 the Bundeswehr had grown to 66,000 men. In 1960 the Bundeswehr had increased to 270,000 personnel and by 1966 to 454,000.

In 1961, the Berlin crisis gave impetus for the Bundeswehr to press for changes in national defence policy, including a successful appeal for conscription to be extended to 18 months. The unilateral decision of France to withdraw from Nato's integrated command structure in 1966 increased the importance of West Germany's contribution to Nato. The image and self-confidence of the Bundeswehr increased accordingly, helped by the careful acquisition of military traditions, the expansion of an independent armaments industry and the emergence of a new generation of regular officers untainted by service in the Wehrmacht.

Keith Simpson

Key Weapons

The AMX30 MBT

In the 1950s the decision was taken by Great Britain, France, West Germany and Italy each to design a main battle tank to submit for possible adoption by Nato. France and West Germany produced designs which both nations were to adopt subsequently – the AMX30 and the Leopard I – although the idea of a Nato tank was soon shelved, and Great Britain went ahead with the design and production of her own MBT, the Chieftain. Design work on the French AMX30 began in 1958 at the Atelier de Construction d'Issy-les-Moulineaux, near Paris, and the first prototype was ready in 1960.

The design priorities were firepower, mobility and protection, in that order and the tank was destined to equip armoured formations of the French Army as a successor to the American M47 Patton medium tank. Adopted in July 1963, the first production models built at the Atelier de Construction Roanne were completed in 1966. Their appearance coincided with the introduction into the French Army of new mechanised brigades and divisions where the mobility of the tank and its long-range main armament would be put to best use. The French currently have over 1000 AMX30s in service and employ 54 in each armoured regiment. Production at Roanne continues at a rate of about 20 tanks a month.

The 105mm CN-105-F1 main armament has its rifled barrel encased in a magnesium alloy thermal sleeve and is mounted in the cast turret. Forty-seven fixed rounds are available for this weapon, 18 in the turret bustle and the remainder in the hull. The special French Obus G HEAT round has a muzzle velocity of 1000m/sec (3280ft/sec) and is of unconventional design. To prevent excessive spin, imparted by the barrel's rifling, which would normally reduce the effectiveness of the HEAT round, the charge is mounted on ball-bearings inside its outer case so that the rate of spin is considerably reduced. This round has a high lethality, a 90 per cent hit probability at 2500m (2735yds) and will penetrate 355mm (14in) of armour. Other ammunition types include high explosive, white phosphorus, illuminating and practice rounds.

The gun will elevate to plus 20 degrees and depress to minus 8 degrees, which ensures good hull-down performance. A co-axial 20mm Modèle F2 cannon with 500 rounds has an anti-aircraft and ground role – it can be elevated independently of the main gun to plus 40 degrees – while the commander has a 7.62mm Modèle F1 machine gun above his cupola which can be remotely fired when the tank is closed down. Two smoke dischargers are fitted to the turret sides.

The SAMM Modèle CH-27-1S hydraulic fire-control system provides stabilisation for the gun while the tank is on the move. The commander directs the fire and is able to over-ride the gunner if necessary.

Previous page: Designed to protect armoured formations against attacks by low-flying aircraft, the AMX30-R mounts the Franco-German Roland surface-to-air missile.

Left: An AMX30 of the French Armoured Corps operating in mountainous terrain. Clearly visible on the commander's cupola are the distinctive periscopes which provide all-round vision when the vehicle is 'closed down'. Above: Powered by the high-performance HS-110 multi-fuelled engine (inset) located at the rear of the hull, an AMX30 grinds steadily up a steep slope. Below: One of the first AMX30 types undergoing field trials. The main armament has yet to be fitted with its thermal sleeves.

The subsequent AMX30-B2 tank variants have a COTAC integrated fire-control system with telescopic sight and computer-controlled graticule which considerably improves accuracy and is being retro-fitted to earlier tanks.

The French place much emphasis on mobility, and the 36-tonne AMX30 with its four-man crew is capable of very rapid deployment, a consequence of its high power-to-weight ratio and low ground pressure. The tank is powered by a Hispano-Suiza HS 110 12-cylinder water-cooled multifuel engine developing 720bhp at 2600rpm. This provides a road speed of 65km/h (40mph) with good acceleration and cross-country performance. The tank has a road range of 600km (373 miles). The tank's width allows it to be transported by rail, which increases its strategic potential.

The hull consists of rolled steel plates welded together to form the usual three compartments namely, driving, fighting and turret, and driving and transmission at the rear. The Hispano-Suiza engine is fitted with a Gravina automatic clutch and combined gearbox and steering unit; five forward and five reverse gears are available to the driver. Torsion-bar suspension is provided and five rubber-clad dual road wheels on each side (with rear drive-sprocket and forward idler) carry steel tracks with rubber inserts to minimise damage to road surfaces. The complete power pack can be removed as a single unit in an hour.

As with the Soviet T54/55 and T62 tanks, two types of snorkel are available for river crossing to a depth of 4m (13ft 1in). The narrow type is used operationally and the wider version for training. The former can be carried on the tank and erected in 10 minutes. Even without the use of a snorkel, the AMX30 can wade through water up to a depth of 2.2m (7ft 3in), with only minimal preparation.

As firepower and mobility were considered more important than armoured protection to the overall design equation, the AMX30 was only lightly armoured in comparison to most other MBTs; for example, an estimated 50mm (1.97in) maximum against the 152mm (6.08in) of the Centurion. Consequently the tank's small size, manoeuvrability and reasonably low silhouette have become all the more important in improving its survival chances on the battlefield. Protection is extended further with the installation of an NBC filtration unit and an automatic fire alarm.

The driver, who sits on the left side, has three

periscopes which are interchangeable with infra-red or passive image-intensification optics. The commander in the right-hand side of the turret has 10 periscopes and a SOPELEM M270 ×10 magnification prism head, plus a SOPELEM M208 rangefinder and an infra-red capability. Near him sits the loader/radio operator who is provided with two periscopes. The gunner, in the left-hand side of the turret, has an M271 day sight with ×8 magnification and infra-red capability. An infra-red searchlight gives a 500m (545yd) range in this mode, or 700m (765yds) with white light. Trial versions have been fitted with radar equipment for target acquisition and tracking. This proliferation of optical devices provides the crew with good all-round observation (always a problem in a closed-down tank) which in turn allows them to exploit the tank's mobility to the full.

The improved AMX30-B2 is in operation and has a hydraulic torque converter, electro-hydraulic gearbox, hydrostatic steering and pressurisation, and a

Above left: The AMX 155mm GCT self-propelled gun with an automatic loading system. Above right: The AMX30 chassis fitted with the S 401A turret mounting the 30mm HS 831A twin-barrel AA cannon and Doppler radar. Right: The AMX30-S, specially adapted for hot climates, is fitted with dust filters and air conditioning. Below right: The improved AMX30-B2 includes the automatic COTAC integrated fire control system. Below: An AMX30, with snorkel attached, can ford water obstacles to a depth of 4m (13ft).

Above left: An AMX30-D armoured recovery vehicle. Designed to carry out repairs and recover damaged vehicles in the forward combat zone, the AMX30-D is fitted with a hydraulic crane, auxiliary winch and dozer blade. Below left: An AMX30-H bridgelaying tank carrying a 22m (71ft 6in) Class 50 scissor bridge. Below: As part of France's nuclear defence force, the AMX30 chassis is fitted with a Pluton tactical nuclear missile with a range of 120km (75 miles).

TV system linked to the elevation of the gun. Older AMX30s are being brought up to this standard. The AMX30-S is a desert version with different gearbox ratios, laser rangefinder and a combined infra-red sight, and a de-rated engine which develops 620bhp at 2400rpm. Other variants include the AMX30-D ARV and scissors bridge and flail versions. The AMX30 chassis is also used to carry Pluton tactical nuclear missiles, and Roland and Javelot anti-aircraft systems. A total of approximately 1000 tanks have been supplied to Greece, Iraq, Lebanon, Peru, Qatar, Saudi Arabia, Spain (which has licence-built 435) and Venezuela. For a tank that has not gained a reputation through combat experience, its sales record on the open export market is impressive indeed.

In June 1979 the first AMX32 prototype appeared. This tank, an improvement on the AMX30-B2, has the COTAC fire control system, a roomier all-welded spaced armour turret, armoured skirts and the ability to accept a 120mm smooth-bore gun.

Above: The French Army on manoeuvres. An infantry unit disembarks from an APC while an AMX30 and an Alouette III helicopter, armed with AS-11 ATGW missiles, provide close support. Below: The new AMX32 incorporates a number of improvements on the AMX30-B2. Designed to accommodate a 120mm smooth-bore main armament, the AMX32 will have the capacity to fire the full range of conventional rounds and a new APFSDS round known as the 105 OFL. Other features include a new transmission and steering system.

AMX30 MBT

Crew 4
Dimensions Length (gun included) 9.48m (31ft 1in); width 3.1m (10ft 2in); height 2.86m (9ft 4½in)
Weight Combat loaded 36,000kg (79,365lb)
Engine Hispano-Suiza HS-110 12-cylinder water-cooled multi-fuel engine developing 720 bhp at 2600rpm

Performance Maximum road speed 65km/h (40mph); range (road) 600km (373 miles); vertical obstacle 0.93m (3ft); trench 2.9m (9ft 6in); gradient 60 per cent; fording 1.3m (4ft 3in), with preparation 2.2m (7ft 3in), with snorkel 4m (13ft 1in)

Armour Conventional cast; details classified but maximum thickness estimated at 50mm (1.97in)
Armament One 105mm gun; one 12.7mm machine gun or 20mm cannon co-axial with main armament, one 7.62mm machine gun on commander's cupola; two smoke dischargers on each side of turret

View from the East

The Cold War seen from behind the Iron Curtain

From the Western point of view, the Cold War was a straightforward reaction to what it saw as the threat of an aggressive, Soviet-inspired communism that aimed to take over the world, by force if necessary. But the eastern bloc – and particularly the Soviet leadership – had, in its turn, its own fears. The Cold War was given its peculiar intensity by the way that the mutual fears of East and West seemed confirmed and were reinforced at every turn by the actions and statements of politicians on both sides of the divide.

The basic Soviet fear was of invasion from the West. Russia had lost 20 million dead during World War II, and the impact of these losses had far-reaching consequences. For the people of the United States and Great Britain, the war was seen as a triumphant, heroic episode in which good triumphed over evil. In eastern Europe, the war was a tragedy of enormous proportions, and the eventual defeat of Nazi Germany was little compensation for the human cost. It was small wonder that the Soviet leadership had firmly-held ideas about the need for security.

At Yalta in 1945, Stalin described to Churchill the Russian attitude towards the postwar reconstruction of Poland. 'The Prime Minister has said that for Great Britain the question of Poland is a question of honour. For Russia it is not only a question of honour but also of security . . . not only because we are on Poland's frontier but also because throughout history Poland has always been a corridor for attack on Russia . . . . During the last 30 years our German enemy has passed through this corridor twice . . . . It is not only a question of honour but of life and death for the Soviet state.'

Western statesmen were inclined to agree that, after a war which had cost them so dear, the Russians were entitled to have a buffer zone of states running the whole length of their western frontiers for the sake of their own security. 'I could sympathise fully with Stalin's desire to protect his western borders from future attack,' said Cordell Hull, the American Secretary of State, 'but I felt that this security could best be obtained through a strong postwar peace organisation.'

It has, indeed, often been argued that security worries did not necessarily mean that the Soviet Union should extend its domination over much of eastern and central Europe; but, on the other hand, the Russian leadership had well-developed grounds for mistrusting any form of international trusteeship that the Western powers might institute. During the 1930s, the democratic governments of Great Britain and France had done very little to stop the expansionary aims of Nazi Germany; they had failed to defend the Spanish Republic against military takeover, and had made only the most feeble gestures when Italy invaded Ethiopia and Japan invaded China in blatant imperial adventures.

The suspicion with which western Europe had regarded the Russian communists ever since they had taken power made the Soviet leadership inherently

T55 tanks, powered by 580hp engines and mounting 100mm guns as main armament and 12.7mm DShKM anti-aircraft machine guns, patrol the Polish countryside.

wary of its World War II allies. Churchill, for example, had been vehemently anti-Bolshevik and had been a prime mover in the sending of British troops to Russia to aid the anti-Bolsheviks in the civil war of 1919. Nor had certain of the Allied disputes over strategy during World War II relieved Soviet fears. Britain's counsels for delay in opening a Second Front in Europe and support for secondary operations in the traditional British sphere of influence, the eastern Mediterranean, could easily be interpreted as a desire to win the war with Russian blood while extending the British imperium wherever possible.

Living in fear

This desire for security in the face of a possibly hostile western Europe was a key factor in Soviet policy in the immediate aftermath of World War II, and many elements in the early stages of the Cold War can be traced back to this Soviet fear that its security was being undermined. There was another factor at work, too. Ever since the first Five Year Plan had begun to run into difficulties, Soviet society had been gripped in fear as the purges literally decimated the ruling groups and led to wholesale deaths and resettlement at other levels. The climate of always fearing the worst, always looking for the hidden catch in an official formula – in short, the automatic, inevitable suspicions of people living in a totalitarian state run by a paranoid megalomaniac (even in the early 1950s, just before his death, Stalin had his doctors arrested, accusing them of plotting against him) – permeated all Russian life, and naturally affected relations with the Western powers.

In this climate, certain actions of the Western allies caused a disproportionate response. The decision of the Western governments to go back on wartime agreements about reparations and to discontinue them in the Western-occupied zones of Germany was felt as particularly annoying by a Soviet leadership that saw its country as having suffered horrendously at the

Above: Demonstrators with placards saying 'we are hungry' march through Poznań during the June 1956 rebellion. Below: Polish troops march through Warsaw in the course of a military parade in 1962.

hands of this same Germany, and felt no sympathy for German economic problems if there was any way that German resources could be used to help Soviet industry. And other Western policies that were intended as mere reactions to Soviet pressure easily provoked a further range of Russian suspicions: the formation of Nato in 1949, for example, and the rearming of West Germany in the 1950s.

Of course, underpinning all this suspicion was the ideological divide, and the problem of opposed views of the function of the state in society. But if the West felt that the Marxist theory of world revolution was directed at subverting their social system, so too the Russians felt that Western statesmen would be only too happy to destroy communism in the Soviet Union.

Right: Russian T34 tanks deploy in the streets of East Berlin after the June riots of 1953, effectively closing off the Russian sector.

Above: A Soviet cartoon attempts to portray Nato leaders as a collection of latter-day Nazis.

up to a view of the Cold War that was very different from the perspectives in Washington, London or Paris. This is not to say that the Soviet Union did not have plans for what it would like to do to further world revolution; just that a constricted, fearful, ruling class felt under threat and were as much on the defensive as on the offensive.

The dilemma of Stalinism

Finally, on top of these general, strategic and ideological factors, was the question posed by old-fashioned nationalism. Josef Stalin was as cynical and calculating an expansionist as any previous Russian ruler; and he saw this as a natural way for states to behave. He expected Great Britain and the United States to expand their spheres of influence, just as he was determined to do in eastern Europe and also in the Far East.

Once the Stalinist system had been established over the satellites, however, the Soviet leadership found itself in a dilemma that added to its anxieties. Russian-imposed (or Russian-backed) communism rapidly became extremely unpopular, and the competitive nationalism of central and eastern Europe soon re-asserted itself. Yugoslavia, with geographical advantages, rapidly moved away from the Soviet orbit, but this was not possible elsewhere – except in Albania which itself withdrew from military participation in the Warsaw Pact in 1961. Any attempts at reform, or at introducing more flexible and efficient policies within the satellites, ran the risk of encouraging spontaneous outbursts that threatened to destroy the whole system; and this no Soviet government could permit. East Germany in 1953, or Poland and Hungary in 1956, were reminders to the men in the Kremlin that their defensive buffer, their security zone, regarded them with loathing.

So the very area that was designed to strengthen Russia's defences proved to be one of the major twists in the spiral of Soviet worries. The world's second greatest power felt that its position was threatened on many sides; and not least from within. Added to the problems of managing the Georgians, Ukrainians, Kazakhs and all the other nationalities of the USSR itself was the difficulty of coping with fiercely patriotic eastern Europeans, who found their Russian-sponsored regimes a hated imposition.

Ashley Brown

Again, from this point of view of armed confrontation, the Soviet Union did have important weaknesses that make its attitudes and policies seem, in retrospect, less aggressive than they appeared to the West at the time. The Red Army was an enormous presence; but the Russians had no atomic weapons until their successful test of 1949, and their first delivery system was the Tu-4 Bull; a medium-range bomber that could not reach the United States. By 1956, when the Tu-16 Badger, Tu-20 Bear and Myasishchev M-4 Bison were coming into service and giving the Russians this intercontinental capability, their atomic/nuclear stockpile was of about 2000 weapons, whereas the Americans at this time had between 7000 and 10,000 bombs and warheads.

A sense of strategic inferiority; a natural fear of invasion from the West; the automatic suspicions of the inhabitants of a totalitarian state. These all added

Poland 1956

The gradual relaxation of Stalinism after 1953 was accompanied by growing demands for reform in Poland, and on 28 June 1956 the workers of Poznań took to the streets in protest, requesting 'bread, freedom and the end of Soviet domination'. Marshal Rokossovsky, Polish Minister of Defence although a Soviet officer, ordered troops to break up the crowds. This resulted in 53 dead and over 300 injured. The atmosphere now became truly revolutionary. Wladyslaw Gomulka, who as deputy

premier had attempted to introduce reforms in the late 1940s but had been imprisoned in 1951, was re-admitted to the politburo in October in an attempt to calm the situation; but Rokossovsky began to deploy Soviet troops toward Warsaw. In return, troops loyal to Gomulka moved into the city and blocked all approaches.

In this tense and explosive atmosphere Gomulka persuaded Soviet leaders that domestic concessions must be instituted. Troops were withdrawn and Gomulka set about developing the 'Polish road to socialism'.

Hungary 1956

When the people of Budapest rose up against Soviet military might

For a short time the Hungarian rebels held the might of Russian forces at bay. The rebellion happened in two stages: street protests (top) followed by more violent armed insurrection (above).

At the time of Stalin's death in March 1953, Hungary gave every appearance of being a docile Soviet satellite. Yet three and half years later, that country, alone among the Soviet satellites, erupted in bloody revolution against Stalinism and Russian domination.

Stalinism in Hungary was particularly brutal and bloodthirsty. The exact figures are unknown, but at least 150,000 people out of a population of less than 10 million found themselves in prison or in detention camps, while several thousand were executed, or died after torture. All opposition, real or imaginary, inside or outside the Communist Party, was eliminated without mercy.

Presiding over the Stalinist terror was Mátyás Rákosi, the First Secretary of the Hungarian Communist Party and, since 1952, prime minister. A brilliant tactician, Rákosi excelled at eliminating opponents or potential rivals through a mixture of cunning, duplicity and utter ruthlessness. Generally feared, he seemed unchallengeable. In the spring of 1953, however, after Stalin's death, he ignored clear signals from Moscow that collective leadership and a less harsh regime were now required. It was a passing fashion, he assumed, and policies did not change.

In June 1953 Rákosi and three other prominent communists were summoned to the Kremlin. There the Soviet leaders, Nikita Khrushchev, Georgi Malenkov and Lavrenti Beria told them bluntly that Rákosi's methods and policies were leading Hungary to ruin and the party to perdition. He was ordered to hand over the premiership to Imre Nagy but was still allowed to continue in the all-important post of first secretary of the party.

Imre Nagy seemed a sensible choice for prime minister. A life-long communist, like Rákosi, he had spent many years in the Soviet Union and was trusted by the Russians. Since the end of World War II he had held various high ministerial and party offices but had never been associated with the Stalinist terror. Now, in charge of the government, he launched Hungary on a new and very popular course. He announced the end of over-ambitious industrialisation, gave priority to consumer goods, halted compulsory collectivisation of agriculture, promised greater freedom of speech and the restoration of the rule of law. This last signalled the end of terror by the political police, the hated Államvédelmi Osztaly (or AVO). If implemented, Nagy's programme would have transformed life in Hungary.

Rákosi, however, had a different idea on how the country should be run. While making some grudging concessions by allowing, for instance, the rehabilitation of many victims of the purges, he set out to sabotage and discredit Nagy's reforms. Helped by the party apparatus under his control, he both aggravated and exploited the difficulties of a quick transition from a Stalinist to a more consumer-orientated economy, and never stopped plotting against Nagy both at home and in Moscow. By April 1955 his case was ready. The Central Committee of the Hungarian Communist Party, meeting in the presence of Mikhail Suslov, the Kremlin theoretician, condemned Nagy's policies as 'right-wing opportunism, inimical to the interests of the working class'. Nagy was dismissed from the government and expelled from the party.

The triumphant Rákosi set about steering Hungary onto a more authoritarian course but the relatively liberal interlude under Nagy had awakened Hungarian intellectuals from the torpor induced by years of terror.

Angry voices

In 1954 a number of writers, academics and journalists, most of them party members, had formed the Petöfi Circle, a debating society named after Sandor Petöfi, the romantic poet, hero of the revolution of 1848. Their meetings were held behind closed doors until, emboldened by Khrushchev's denunciation of Stalin in February 1956, they decided to admit the public. Thousands flocked to hear their debates, which dealt with increasingly controversial subjects, and listened to speakers demanding greater freedom of expression and the punishment of those responsible for the terror.

Rákosi eventually prohibited further meetings of the Petöfi Circle and, in July 1956, submitted to the politbureau a list of some 400 names, mostly intellectuals (including Imre Nagy), whom he wanted arrested for allegedly plotting against the party. The politbureau meeting was interrupted by the sudden arrival of two envoys from the Kremlin, Anastas Mikoyan and Mikhail Suslov, who carried orders for Rákosi to be removed from the party leadership. After telephoning Khrushchev, who offered no comfort, Rákosi resigned and left Hungary for ever.

Having at last got rid of Rákosi, the Kremlin chose Ernö Gerö as his successor; but Gerö too was a thoroughly discredited and generally hated Stalinist. The appointment of János Kádár, who had spent several years in prison, as Gerö's deputy was not enough to give respectability to the new party leadership. Admittedly Gerö tried to pacify public opin-

Above: Hungarians await the next attack by Soviet forces. Although able to obtain quantities of smallarms, the rebels had few heavy support weapons.
Right: Ernö Gerö's last-minute concessions failed to forestall the 1956 uprising. Below left: A dead AVO man bedecked with the Hungarian emblem lies in the street.

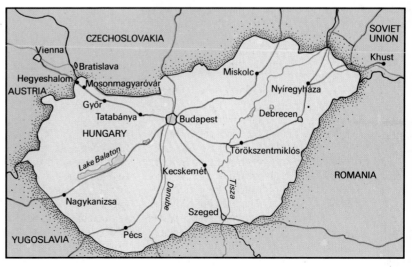

scene of mass demonstrations of solidarity with Poland. University students and the Petöfi Circle, who had called the people out into the streets, presented demands for internal reforms, a more equal relationship with Russia, and the return of Nagy to the councils of the party. Gerö, who had just returned to the capital, responded with a short, harsh broadcast which yielded nothing and merely inflamed tempers. Shortly afterwards, the first shots were fired by the AVO guard at the radio headquarters, which was besieged by demonstrators clamouring that their demands be broadcast. Ordinary police and army units, called in to help the AVO, sided with the crowds, often handing over their weapons.

A panic meeting of the party's central committee at midnight decided to recall Nagy to the premiership and, at the same time, asked for Soviet military help to restore order. In the early hours of Wednesday morning, Soviet tanks entered Budapest and sporadic fighting developed; a peaceful movement for reform turned into a bloody revolt against Stalinism and Soviet domination.

On Wednesday, 24 October, the revolution spread to the provinces. Nagy broadcast an appeal for calm and order. Martial law was proclaimed (though it is not certain by whom). The much travelled Mikoyan and Suslov arrived in Budapest once more.

On the Thursday there was a massacre of peaceful demonstrators outside Parliament, probably an AVO provocation, which led to Soviet tanks firing at the crowd. The Kremlin envoys told Gerö to resign, and put János Kádár at the head of the party. Kádár in turn broadcast an appeal for order, promised no reprisals and undertook to review Hungarian-Soviet relations. But party authority had collapsed and nobody was listening any more. The apparatus of the state was dissolving too. A general strike, which had started in Budapest, spread nationwide. Workers' committees were taking over factories, revolutionary councils were replacing local administration. The police and many units of the army, notably a tank regiment under Colonel Pál Maléter, openly joined the revolution. Only the AVO remained loyal to the party, and they were under siege everywhere, their members lynched

ion by making a number of concessions: he allowed the Petöfi Circle to resume public debates, permitted easier travel abroad and allowed the body of Lásló Rajk, a former government minister who had been executed for alleged treason, to be moved to a place of honour in the national cemetery.

The reburial of Rajk on 6 October turned into a massive demonstration against Stalinism; 300,000 people, led by Rajk's widow and Imre Nagy, filed silently past the new grave. Even the chief party newspaper was forced to note the following day that 'people were numbed not only by a deep sense of grief but also by burning hatred'.

At the time of the funeral, Gerö and Kádár were in the Soviet Union, and were soon to travel to Yugoslavia. In their absence – they did not return until 23 October – the drama of the 'Polish October' fired the imagination of the Hungarians.

There were, however, important differences between the situation in the two countries. In Poland, a section of the politbureau had been working with Wladyslaw Gomulka, the former deputy premier who had been disgraced and arrested, to get rid of the Stalinists and return him to power. In Hungary, Imre Nagy had no such powerful allies in the party, and he himself had shown few signs of wishing to lead the popular movement for reform. All he did was to apply for re-admission to the party and, when this was granted, left for a holiday on Lake Balaton. Thus Hungary approached its hour of crisis with the party completely out of touch with the popular mood, the unorganised opposition without a leader.

On Tuesday, 23 October 1956, Budapest was the

Above: Domesticity and militarism side by side in the streets of Budapest. Note the hole in the flag where the communist emblem has been cut out.

Right: Scenes of devastation in the Hungarian capital. The young men in the foreground are armed with pre-World War II rifles.

whenever they fell into the hands of the mob.

If anyone could restore order and control the temper of the nation, it was Imre Nagy. But during the first few days Nagy was either unwilling or unable to put himself at the head of the revolution. The new government announced on the Saturday was still full of Stalinists and included only two token members of the suppressed democratic parties. This was not enough to gain public confidence, especially since Nagy was blamed, unjustly, for calling in the Russians.

Support for the rebels

On Sunday, however, a transformed Nagy spoke on the radio. For the first time he sided openly with the revolutionaries and announced that there would be negotiations about Hungary's relations with the USSR, including the question of withdrawal of Soviet troops. The following day some Red Army units did leave Budapest. Nagy also told the nation that a unified democratic police force would be formed. On the following Tuesday he announced that the new government would be a coalition of the communists and the three old democratic parties. That day Mikoyan and Suslov were back in Budapest, apparently to give Nagy the Kremlin's seal of approval. When they left on Wednesday they told reporters that agreement had been reached. It looked as if the revolution had succeeded. But on Thursday morning, 1 November, it became clear that, instead of leaving Hungary, the Red Army was moving in fresh units. Furious, Nagy summoned the Soviet ambassador, Yuri Andropov (future leader of the USSR), and warned him that if Russian troops were not withdrawn, Hungary would declare neutrality and leave the Warsaw Pact. Later that day reports were received of further Red Army units entering Hungary. With the backing of Kádár, and the entire government, Nagy crossed his Rubicon by proclaiming to the world his country's neutrality.

A few hours later, Budapest radio broadcast a speech by Kádár announcing that the Communist Party would be dissolved and a new one formed to follow a national road to socialism. But Kádár himself was no longer in the capital; he was on his way in

Above: Soviet T55 tanks swing into action while Hungarian civilians stand watching.

Below: Imre Nagy, dismissed as prime minister and expelled from the Communist Party in 1953 for 'right-wing opportunism', was recalled as premier by a desperate party at the height of the crisis in 1956. Bottom: Pál Maléter, the colonel who became minister of defence in the revolutionary government. He, like Nagy, was subsequently executed by the Russians.

secret to the Soviet Union. From that moment on, the fate of the revolution was sealed, though the Hungarians themselves did not realise it. On Saturday, 3 November, the country was delighted by the announcement of a genuine four-party government in which Pál Màléter, promoted to General, was Minister of Defence, and János Kádár a Minister without portfolio. A Soviet military delegation arrived for talks with Maléter and his colleagues to discuss details of Red Army evacuation. Some progress was reported when the talks adjourned, to be resumed in the evening at the Soviet Army HQ. But Maléter and his fellow delegates never came back: they were arrested by the head of the NKVD, General Serov.

At dawn on Sunday, 4 November, the Red Army attacked Budapest in overwhelming strength. Nagy broadcast a fighting message of defiance. Kádár, using a Soviet transmitter on a Hungarian wavelength, announced the formation of a Hungarian Revolutionary Workers' and Peasants' Government, calling at the same time for Soviet armed help in restoring order. By the evening Budapest was in the grip of the Red Army. Imre Nagy escaped to the Yugoslav embassy where he was given political asylum. The revolution had been crushed, though desperate fighting in isolated centres went on for another 10 days, and strikes continued for weeks.

Kádár returned to Budapest on 7 November to face a grimly hostile nation. Relying almost entirely on Soviet help, he set about rebuilding the party, restoring its rule, and destroying every vestige of opposition. All traces of the revolution, now officially labelled a 'counter-revolution', were obliterated and former revolutionaries persecuted. Imre Nagy and his friends, enticed by promises of safe conduct to leave the shelter of the Yugoslav embassy, were arrested by the Russians and taken to Romania. In 1958 it was announced that following a trial for treason, Nagy, Maléter and two others had been executed.

The revolution cost Hungary dearly: 25,000 died in the fighting, about 200,000 fled the country, countless unknown thousands found themselves in jail. Was it all in vain? Not entirely, for Kádár was not a Rákosi. After a period of ruthless repression he gradually relaxed his regime, proclaimed amnesties, introduced economic reforms, and turned Hungary into one of the more 'liberal' and also relatively prosperous countries of the Soviet bloc.

Konrad Syrop

Battle for the streets

At the time the Hungarian uprising reached its climax in October 1956, Gordon Brook-Shepherd of the Daily Telegraph *was one of the few Western journalists able to see events at first hand. Throughout this period he kept a detailed diary, which provided the material for the following account.*

❝ Wednesday, 24 October

Hegyeshalom on the Austro-Hungarian border, 11.40am. Though the revolution had erupted like a volcano yesterday afternoon, here, either the old regime – or perhaps it was just the indestructible bureaucracy – was still in charge. The Hungarian lieutenant commanding the post could do nothing about my visa. It was undeniably 'kosher', having been stamped in weeks before when, out of curiosity rather than prescience, I thought it would be a good idea to see how the volatile Magyars might one day react to the summer riots in Poznań and the reinstatement of Wladyslaw Gomulka to power in Poland. 'One day' was now here; but though the besieged neo-Stalinist regime of Ernö Gerö in Budapest had ordered a clamp-down on all Western journalists, his minions were powerless to stop the entry of this particular one. (Were that visa transferrable, and I willing to transfer, I could have sold it for a thousand dollars to anyone in that phalanx of my frustrated colleagues fretting and champing behind the red-white-red Austrian frontier pole of Nickelsdorf, 1500 yards behind me.)

That dead border zone was about the only thing still in Gerö's grip. The moment the car left it, we entered the furnace. Even at the little village of Hegyeshalom itself – only 5km (3 miles) inland and the local security police (AVO) headquarters – there were shouts and waves for a Western car (in my case a staid 1953 Rover saloon). And Mosonmagyaróvár, the first big town 16km (10 miles) further in, showed all the scars of a place that was now being torn violently apart. A brown official car lay burnt out on its side; shattered windows everywhere; a fresh spray of bullet holes on the yellow walls to cover the dirty pock-marks of the 1944-45 fighting; and civilians with arm-bands patrolling the streets with a piratical assortment of pistols and knives stuck in their belts.

At Györ, the western county capital, two Hungarian Army tanks were stationed on the bridge, the hatches open and the crews leaning out, smoking, as though it were a peaceful break on manoeuvres. Whose side were they on? At any rate it was not they who stopped my car but a group of youths headed by an older man in blue beret and sheepskin jacket. One of the boys carried something that I soon came to know as the symbol of the uprising: the red-white-green flag of Hungary with a hole in the middle where the wheat-sheaf, hammer and sickle, emblem of communism, had been ripped out. Kossuth purified of Marx. The man saw my own flag, a paper Union Jack, stuck hastily on the windscreen in Vienna.

'Do you have any arms for us? Is it true the Americans are coming?' he asked in a mixture of English and German.

I shook my head, told him of the sealed border, and

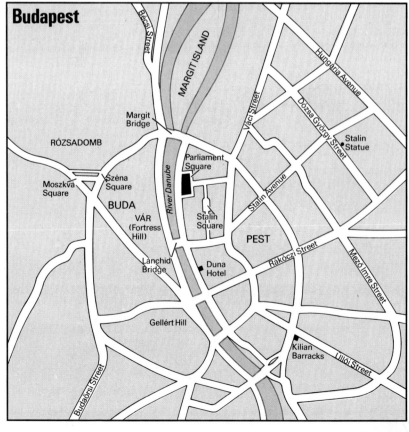

Budapest

Bécsi Street · MARGIT ISLAND · Hungária Avenue · Margit Bridge · RÓZSADOMB · Váci Street · Dózsa György Street · Stalin Statue · Parliament Square · Moszkva Square · Széna Square · River Danube · Stalin Avenue · BUDA · VÁR (Fortress Hill) · Stalin Square · PEST · Lánchíd Bridge · Duna Hotel · Rákóczi Street · Mező Imre Street · Gellért Hill · Kilian Barracks · Üllői Street · Budaörsi Street

who I was.

'Well drive on then, and good luck in Budapest. Make sure they hear all about us outside.'

It was Almasfuszitö, only 80km (50 miles) from Budapest, which brought the proof that this was a truly national uprising. To the west it had been all solid Catholic peasant country. But this ugly town, dominated by its great aluminium plant still belching out dark silver smoke, was proletarian Hungary. Yet here too, Kossuth flags, not red flags, waved from every building and a crowd of workmen at the factory gates cheered the Rover with its paper Union Jack as I drove by. Where on earth was the Red Army?

I met it for the first time on the outskirts of the capital, which had been ringed with Soviet light tanks and lorry-borne infantry. The Russian officer who was halting traffic clearly had no instructions, except to search all Hungarian cars for arms. But though he didn't know what the lion and unicorn on my passport meant, he didn't seem to like the look of them.

'Journalist – Izvestia,' I lied hopefully as he waved me back.

'Diplomat,' I tried next, but at that dirty word he only swung his machine pistol round. Then I had an inspiration.

'Delegate! Delegate!' I cried, remembering this vaguest but most respectable of communist credentials. The scowl faded and I was through. An hour later, just as a misty dusk was spreading up from the Danube, I was picking my way through the northern suburbs of Budapest.

The isolated capital seemed at first sight to be in the same trance-like limbo as the countryside. There were plenty of signs of fighting. Near the Margit Island Bridge, for example, a trolley bus lay on its side, its overhead wires coiled up on the pavement like a Medusa's head of steel. But instead of driving in through pools of warm blood and hail-storms of bullets, everything seemed hushed and frozen in the night. The only sound was an occasional chatter of smallarms fire from the hills of the Vár and the Gellért above me. They were black, not a house or street light showing.

Before long I had booked in at the crowded reception desk of the Duna Hotel, whose foyer was like a bright and noisy circus after the eerie emptiness outside. At 6 pm, a few minutes earlier, the revolutionaries had triumphed in one of their main demands: Imre Nagy had been reinstated as prime minister and was issuing his first emergency decrees.

Below: Hungarians destroy the statue of Stalin.

Left: Crowds surround Soviet tanks. Above: A dead soldier and burnt-out tanks.

Thursday, 25 October – Saturday, 27 October

No pattern to these days, just as there was no pattern to the uprising itself. Happenings just seemed to pull you towards them.

Soon after dawn on the first day I set out, first for the radio building where, in the first hours of the uprising, the AVO had poured fire into an unarmed and passive crowd. The blood patches were still there, so was that acrid smell of debris and corpses I had not felt in my nostrils since the war. Then slowly up broad Rákóczi Street to Stalin Square to look at what remained of the memorial to the dictator whose dead hand had still ruled Hungary until 36 hours ago. All that was left were two jagged bronze feet, each the size of a man, on the plinth.

As we were gazing at this historic piece of desecration, the cry went up: 'They are burning the Russian books.' Slowly back down Rákóczi Street again. As we drove, a white-haired old man – who looked old enough to have fought against Genghis Khan, let alone Stalin – thrust a rusty curved cavalry sabre through the open window and waggled the blade under my nose. (He could just as easily have slit my throat.) 'This is what we are fighting with,' he roared. 'When are you going to help us?'

At the Soviet Information Centre there, sure enough, was the bonfire – a pile of Soviet propaganda 1.8m (6 feet) high and 3.5m (12 feet) across, blazing on the pavement. Whenever it threatened to die down, fresh supplies of Marx and Lenin were brought out from the looted shop and tossed on to the simmering heap. And this, until that Tuesday, had been one of the communist Holy of Holies.

It was, I think, the next morning that a Hungarian friend dashed into the Duna and pulled me from the dining-room. A party of school-children, he said, were 'taking on' a squad of Russian heavy tanks across the river with nothing more than stones and petrol bombs. The 'battle area', which we approached from the flanks, turned out to be the Moszkva Square and the Széna Square, twin squares below the fortress hill which normally formed a double-loop for Budapest's tram-car system. Now they presented a very different sight. The steep road was blocked by a line of five Soviet tanks, gun barrels tilted down to command the area below. Quite unde-terred, a group of boys darted out from behind an upturned tram not 45m (50 yards) away, lobbing their home-made petrol bottles. Suddenly another boy was seen, creeping slowly down the hill behind the tanks. He had evidently been told that the only safe way to deal with these metal monsters was to come close up where the gun barrels couldn't harm you. As though he were climbing an apple tree, he clambered up the back to one battened-down tank and carefully emptied a can of precious petrol on its tracks. Alas, he had forgotten the matches, and disappeared again – furious with himself, but to loud applause.

The hatch of the commander's tank opened and the fur-lined helmet of an officer popped cautiously up. Immediately, a woman with a shopping basket darted forward from the shelter of the wall and shouted something at him in Hungarian, but with some Rus-sian words to ram home the point.

'She asked, ''Do we look like fascists?'' ' said my guide.

I wondered what the young Soviet lieutenant made of that. Like all of his comrades, he had been ordered into action because, as his political commissar had assured him, 'Budapest was in the hands of fascist counter-revolutionaries, backed by American troops.' Soon after that, the lieutenant saved his red face by pulling out his tanks altogether.

I went behind the tram barricade to ask about the boy with the petrol can.

Above: Politically embarrassed by events in Hungary, occupying forces attempted to discourage Western journalists from highlighting the situation. Here Soviet officers show their displeasure at the photographer.
Right: Wrecked Soviet tanks smoulder as a rebel, armed with a Hungarian Model 48 7.62mm sub-machine gun, keeps a lookout for Russians.

Men against tanks

Despite the overwhelming presence of the Soviet tanks, they were often at a distinct disadvantage during the street-fighting that occurred as a spontaneous reaction to the Russian intervention in Hungary. The lack of supporting infantry to patrol the streets with the tanks, combined with the elusive nature of the street-fighters, made the tanks in an urban situation virtually useless.

The street-fighters, usually armed with smallarms and grenades, were extremely efficient at both disabling tanks and eliminating their crews. Such were their successes that tank crews were loathe to leave their vehi-cles. Consequently, the tanks them-selves became terribly vulnerable to the assortment of methods used by the Hungarians.

The basic anti-tank weapon em-ployed by the street-fighters was the Molotov cocktail. T34 tanks, which carried their fuel to the rear, could be easily taken out by a well-placed Molotov on their rear deck. Indeed, the Russians soon discovered that tanks were least vulnerable when on the move.

Liquid soap, oil, or oil-soaked silk spread across the road could all dis-able a tank, causing it to slide uncon-trollably. The freedom-fighters also preyed on the reluctance of tank crews to leave their vehicles by plac-ing dummy mines, usually made from soup-bowls or saucepans, across the road. The tank crews would neither leave their tanks to check the objects nor run the risk of them being genuine.

Another method was to drop over-head tram cables onto the tanks, elec-trocuting the crews inside. To all this the Russians simply responded with the use of maximum firepower, though later on they did begin to de-ploy infantry along with tanks, artillery and rocket launchers.

'He had to run off home,' came the reply. 'He said there would be a row if he was late for supper.'

It was nice to reflect that a child who could defy five tanks was still afraid of a box over the ears from mother . . . .

Tuesday-Wednesday, 30-31 October

There was no doubt about it, the Russians were withdrawing, at least from Budapest. I toured the two areas where a really sustained battle had been going on for the past week: the Kilian barracks in the middle of the city and the great industrial complex on Csepel Island, where the workers had shown what they really thought about the 'workers' paradise'. Hitherto I had edged towards these places very gingerly (my Rover once getting a bullet ricochet); but now I could drive about freely – so far as the mounds of rubble permitted. And that was not the only change.

'The cardinal is free!' The news rang round the city like a carillon. After eight years of communist captivity, József Mindszenty was at liberty again. We piled in our cars and drove up to the old castle area where, back in his town palace at Uri Street. the cardinal was waiting to face the world again. He was surrounded by black-frocked priests, nearly all in tears.

There were to be no political statements, so I just

asked him how he was. The large burning eyes swivelled round.

'Thank you, I'm quite fit. Prison conditions were tolerable – for the last year or two at least.'

Was this, as Radio Budapest claimed, 'the only man who can save the country'?

On the drive back I noticed something of which the austere cardinal would have been proud. A notice in an empty food shop window read: 'Contents NOT stolen but removed inside for safety.'

Thursday, 1 November – Saturday, 3 November

Ominous days, with the end really always in sight, if one could have brought oneself to look at it. '304 Soviet tanks counted coming across the Soviet-Hungarian border at Záhony'; 'another 300 reported entering from Romania. Twenty stayed at Debrecen, the rest continuing to Budapest.' These were among many gloomy reports. Worst of all, perhaps, Russian troops had ringed the main Budapest airport at Ferihegy again. István Dudas, who had emerged as the leader of the civilian resistance – a burly thick-set man wearing leggings – was not reassuring when three of us went to see him. After some desultory talk about forming a new multi-party government he suddenly exploded: 'Plans! Plans! What's the point of them? The Russians will never let us carry any of them out. We're all deluding ourselves, in true Hungarian style!' The words, coming from him, carried a steely conviction.

For me, the prophecy came true in a yellow-washed building (formerly an archducal shooting lodge) at Mosonmagyaróvár in the early hours of Sunday morning, 4 November. I had joined a convoy of other Western cars for a weekend trip to Vienna, and the patriots had quartered us there after reports that Soviet troops had suddenly appeared and sealed off the border. At 5 am, brandishing machine pistols, they stormed into our bedrooms, beginning what was to turn into 48 hours of temporary captivity. At dawn, over my car radio in the courtyard (exit now blocked by a Soviet tank), I heard Vienna reporting the all-out Russian attack on Budapest and other key cities. It was all over. **"**

Above: A female insurgent in the streets of Budapest.

Right: Communist flags and literature provide the material for a bonfire.

Combined manoeuvres

The reasons behind the creation of the Warsaw Pact

The foundation of the Warsaw Pact in 1955 marked a major change in the relationship between the Soviet Union and its east European allies, although it did not alter the underlying reality that the Soviet position depended on military strength. The essence of the change was a shift from Stalin's system of totally subservient communist regimes, all modelled on Soviet lines, to a system which recognised some elements of national autonomy, as long as the Communist Party retained political power.

During the 1930s, Josef Stalin had built the Soviet Union on the basis of a one-party state in which all power derived from the centre, and ultimately from Stalin himself. Often unpopular policies were enforced by a police state using terror on the widest scale. The secret police guaranteed the Stalinist state

Above: Polish tankmen discuss their deployment during Warsaw Pact manoeuvres.

Below: The Soviet premier, Nikolai Bulganin, signs the Warsaw Treaty – the East's answer to Nato.

from internal enemies but threats from outside remained, particularly from Nazi Germany. Stalin tried to insure against these threats by building up the armed forces and pushing his own frontiers further to the west. In 1939 and 1940 Stalin made considerable gains at the expense of his neighbours but even so, in 1941, German troops penetrated to within sight of Moscow. Victory in 1945 did not remove this trauma from Stalin's memory. He established the Soviet border further west than ever before and determined to create a buffer zone between Russia and her potential enemies in the West.

At the end of the war the Red Army occupied most of eastern Europe and by 1948 East Germany, Poland, Czechoslovakia, Hungary, Romania, Bulgaria, Albania and Yugoslavia were communist one-party states. Stalin made it quite clear how this happened when he told the Yugoslav leadership why there was a communist government in Yugoslavia but not in France or Italy. It had nothing to do with the merits of the respective communist parties but was simply because 'the Soviet Army came to the aid of the Yugoslav people, crushed the German invader, liberated Belgrade and in this way created the conditions which were necessary for the Communist Party of Yugoslavia to achieve power. Unfortunately the Soviet Army did not and could not render such assistance to the French and Italian communists.'

It would not have been in Stalin's nature to have constructed these new eastern European regimes on any other model than his own Soviet system. The police state, one-party rule, centralised economic planning, concentration on heavy industry and collectivisation of agriculture were all imposed. Only the Yugoslavs under Marshal Tito managed to break the mould and try to create their own style of communism. Stalin's anger was immense, but Yugoslavia's geographical remoteness, the military difficulties of subduing the country and the possibility of Western intervention kept him from trying to force the Yugoslavs back into line. But he redoubled his efforts to ensure that the Yugoslav 'disease' did not spread.

Stalin's ruthless rule

It was not enough that eastern European leaders should be communists; they must also put the Soviet Union's interests, as interpreted by Stalin, above national interests, because the Soviet Union was the foundation of the entire communist bloc. Eastern Europe was to look to Moscow for leadership in every matter, whether political, economic, cultural or military. Communists with their own local power bases were purged from the party. In their place came the 'Muscovites' who had mostly spent the war in Russia and who depended absolutely on Stalin for their political position. Show trials were held to discredit people tainted with the crime of 'Titoism'.

A parallel process occurred in the eastern European armed forces. Many of them had fought against the Soviet Union during the war. Stalin was also eager to exclude those who had led the resistance to the Nazis. So during the late 1940s all the eastern European armies were thoroughly purged. New officer corps were created from suitable stock among the working class, peasants and 'creative intelligentsia'. Not only did such newcomers lack military expertise; but even they worried Stalin, who was still not convinced that they were politically reliable.

He therefore placed thousands of Soviet officers in the satellite armies. The most extreme example was Poland. Marshal of the Soviet Union Konstantin Rokossovsky, a Pole by birth but a Russian by upbringing and a Soviet Army officer by career, was made Polish minister of defence in November 1949. Some 17,000 Soviet officers served under him in the Polish armed forces, equivalent to about half the officer corps. Elsewhere Soviet officers were either appointed directly to posts in national armies or served as 'advisers' at every level of command. Under their guidance these armies were re-modelled on Soviet lines.

East Germany was a special case because, in theory, the defeated Germans were not allowed to have armed forces. In 1948, however, 7500 men were transferred from the normal police to special Alert Units, organised on military lines. By 1953 the force had been re-named the Barracked People's Police and numbered 100,000 men. Soviet officers were appointed as advisers and the chief of the Barracked People's Police had been trained in Moscow.

Stalin did not ask a great deal from the armies of his satellites. He wanted them to be a large as possible (at his death in 1953 they numbered 1.5 million men) and he expected them to be politically reliable; but they were trusted only with obsolete Soviet equipment and were capable only of internal security duties. The real basis of communist power in eastern Europe remained the Soviet Army, which was kept segregated in barracks, out of contact with the local population. There was no attempt at joint training among the different national armies.

Above: Emerging from a river in Czechoslovakia, a frogman leads an armoured car ashore on Warsaw Pact manoeuvres.

Above: Marshal Ivan Konev, the Soviet commander who was given control of the entire Warsaw Pact forces.

Above: Marshal Konstantin Rokossovsky, the Soviet officer who became the Polish Minister of Defence in 1949.

The strains in Stalin's system were becoming obvious by 1953 and, not long after his death, riots occurred in East Berlin and elsewhere in Germany and Czechoslovakia. They drew attention to a problem which Moscow could not ignore.

The basic problem was to give legitimacy to the regimes which the Soviet Union had established by force. The process of change began in 1955 with the so-called 'new course' which gave greater flexibility to individual governments to plan on the basis of their own economic circumstances. In the same year the Soviet leadership patched up the quarrel with Yugoslavia and in 1956 Nikita Khrushchev made his 'secret speech' to the 20th Party Congress, denouncing Stalinism. Thus although it was claimed that the Warsaw Pact was founded as a response to West German rearmament in 1955, it can be more realistically seen as part of the liberalisation process.

The Warsaw Treaty of Friendship, Cooperation and Mutual Assistance was signed on 14 May 1955. The signatories were the Soviet Union, Albania, Bulgaria, Czechoslovakia, East Germany, Hungary, Poland and Romania. East Germany did not formally contribute military forces to the pact until January 1956. The treaty established a political structure which was loosely similar to Nato's, but almost nothing was made public about its military organisation.

As more details of the working of the pact emerged it became apparent that it contained many bogus elements. The eastern European states were presented as sovereign allies of the Soviet Union, but real power was concentrated in Soviet hands. Thus a Political Consultative Committee (PCC) was established, which was nominally the supreme decision-making body. It was supposed to meet twice a year, but met only 10 times in its first 14 years. The secretary-general of the PCC was General Antonov, a Soviet officer who was also chief of staff of the pact's forces. The political and military headquarters of the pact were located in Moscow. The first commander-in-chief of the pact's forces was Marshal Ivan Konev, like all his successors a Soviet officer responsible to the Soviet minister of defence. The staff of the pact was a branch of the Soviet General Staff.

After the Hungarian Revolution of 1956, when the

significant contribution of the Warsaw Pact to Soviet nuclear strategy was in air defence. Eastern Europe became an extension of the Soviet air defence system, with all the national defences being controlled from Moscow. The Warsaw Pact allies had little part in Soviet plans for a nuclear war. They were allowed some battlefield weapons but the warheads remained in Soviet hands.

The other reason for the improvement in the standards of the Warsaw Pact was political. During the late 1950s several states pressed for greater autonomy and this was reflected in military matters. The most extreme examples, however, occurred in Albania and Romania. Albania exploited the rift between China and Russia to remove itself from Soviet hegemony by looking to China for leadership. Romania did not go as far as this but did begin to take embarrassing liberties in its foreign policy, associating with Yugoslavia and the West. In both countries these political moves were accompanied by the abandonment of Soviet military doctrine in favour of doctrines of total national defence. These entailed preparing the nation for a protracted guerrilla war against an invader and were based on Yugoslav ideas.

Such ideas were anathema to the Soviet Union, which was always aware that it might be necessary to use force to maintain the cohesion of its bloc, as in Hungary in 1956. The Russians had no desire, in such circumstances, to be met by a nation in arms. The reforms in organisation, doctrine and training which Grechko introduced were designed to limit the usefulness of the eastern European armies as a defence against Soviet police actions by fitting them only for offensive action on a nuclear battlefield.

By the time that Khrushchev was deposed in 1964 the Warsaw Pact could be regarded in most respects as a Soviet success. The satellite armies were better equipped, organised and trained than in 1955 but they mostly remained subordinate to Soviet military control. Their governments had gained a certain amount of room to manoeuvre and even some leverage against Moscow, but this did not threaten Soviet predominance. Only in the Balkans were there serious problems: Albania abandoned active military participation in the pact in 1961 and withdrew Soviet base facilities. And Romania was becoming increasingly skilful in pursuing its own policies, forcing the regime of Leonid Brezhnev to create new machinery to bypass Romanian obstruction.   **Michael Orr**

Nagy government tried to withdraw from the pact but was prevented by a Soviet invasion, the pact had little political life. In military terms it remained weak, with grave doubts about the reliability of its forces. In 1953 the East German armed forces had remained passive during the disturbances; afterwards they were completely re-organised. A new army was gradually created but, by the time that the Berlin Wall was built in 1961, over 25,000 East German servicemen had defected to the West. In Poland in 1956 the Soviet Union threatened to intervene militarily to prevent Wladyslaw Gomulka returning to power and Soviet troops actually began to move on Warsaw. But Marshal Rokossovsky discovered that he could not control the Polish Army, which was preparing to resist the intervention. In Hungary some members of the armed forces, including senior officers, did actually join the fight against the Soviet forces.

The Soviet Union seemed content to accept the Warsaw Pact as a largely paper organisation until the early 1960s. The changes that occurred then are associated with the appointment of Marshal Andrei Grechko as commander-in chief in July 1960. New equipment was introduced and, most significantly, in 1961 Grechko began a series of multi-national exercises.

There are two explanations for these improvements. The first is military. In the late 1950s nuclear weapons became the dominant element in Soviet strategy. Conventional forces were reduced in size and re-equipped with new tanks, armoured personnel carriers and rockets to fit them for the nuclear battlefield. The emphasis was on mobile, hard-hitting forces exploiting nuclear strikes, and the Warsaw Pact armies were obliged to conform. The most

Above: The Polish Army on parade. Top: In an effort to consolidate the Warsaw Pact, large scale military manoeuvres were instituted, along with rearmament, in order to create a solid military force throughout eastern Europe. High-ranking officers from Russia, Hungary, and Bulgaria are shown watching troops on exercise.

The SCORPION

During the late 1950s the British Army began to review its armoured reconnaissance vehicles then in service. All of the vehicles under review – the Saladin, Saracen and Ferret – were wheeled, and they were seen as coming towards the end of their service lives. The army decided upon a single, though tracked, replacement vehicle which would be able to fulfil all the essential requirements of battlefield reconnaissance.

The new vehicle had to have a fast top speed, be air-portable and be of a weight which would not exceed 8200kg (18,000 lb), thereby making it lighter by a third than the Saladin. But at the same time the new vehicle would have to maintain its independence from back-up units for fire support and communications. The most demanding specification was that, as a multi-role vehicle, it would be called on to perform three major duties: fire support, reconnaissance and anti-tank. Several experimental vehicles were put forward with main armaments ranging from 76mm to 105mm, but they were all far too heavy; and as the designers had drawn a blank in this field of research, it was decided to develop a basic vehicle from which a whole range could be developed by equipping them to meet the various role demanded of them.

By 1963, the first outline of the new project, known as TV15000 Test Vehicle, was in hand. The results of TV15000 matured into a mobile test rig, which

incorporated most of the main engine, transmission and suspension elements which were to become standard on the Combat Vehicle Reconnaissance (Tracked) or CVR(T). In September 1967, satisfied with the initial trials, the Ministry of Defence placed a contract order with Alvis of Coventry to supply 17 prototype vehicles. The new vehicle was to be called FV101 Scorpion.

The first Scorpion prototype rolled out of the Alvis plant in January 1969, and a year later all of them had been delivered. There now followed exhaustive field trials in all extremes of terrain and climate. Following the satisfactory conclusion of the field trials, Alvis were awarded a production contract for 2000 Scorpion vehicles in May 1970. This order was soon

Above left: Armed with Swingfire missiles, with a machine gun mounted on the hull, an FV102 Striker prepares to fire. Above right: A forward view of the FV107 Scimitar; four such Scorpion variants served in the Falklands. The highly accurate 30mm Rarden gun carried by the Scimitar makes it very effective against soft-skinned vehicles. Thus the Scimitar would be capable of taking on the latest Soviet MICVs with success.

increased when the Belgian Army placed its own order for 700 vehicles.

Two years later the first production model was completed. Over the next few years, Alvis were to produce no fewer than eight variants in the Scorpion range: the FV101 Scorpion (with a 76mm gun or a 90mm gun), FV102 Striker, FV103 Spartan, FV104 Samaritan, FV105 Sultan, FV106 Samson, FV107 Scimitar and finally Streaker (without FV prefix number). All of the Scorpion family of CVR(T)s share a number of common design features, such as the engine, tracks, suspension and running gear, which help in production and maintenance, and keep costs down.

All of the CVR(T)s are constructed mainly from a

Page 483: Two FV101 Scorpions advance across rough terrain in an armoured vehicle training area. Above left: This Scorpion is armed with the larger 90mm gun made by Cockerill in Belgium; the intention is to provide the Scorpion with greater battlefield punch.

Right: The FV103 Spartan, the armoured personnel carrier of the Scorpion range. The Spartan can also carry radar and night observation devices, and be fitted with Blowpipe missiles.

Left: An FV107 Scimitar (distinguishable by its long 30mm gun) and a Scorpion advance together on an armoured patrol.

welded aluminium alloy, which reduces weight while maintaining a reasonable degree of protection. The actual armour thickness is classified, but it is sufficient to afford protection from smallarms fire to 12.7mm calibre.

The layout of the Scorpion design is such that it places the engine, which can be either a de-rated Jaguar 4.2 litre J60 petrol engine developing 190bhp or a Perkins 5.80 litre T6-3544 diesel with 155bhp, to the front while the turret is positioned to the rear. In this configuration the Scorpion has a high power-to-weight ratio and has an agility and cross-country capability which is second to none. The turret of the Scorpion and Scimitar is occupied by two members of the three-man crew: the commander to the left and the gunner to the right; the gunner is responsible for both the main armament and the 7.62mm machine gun. The driver sits forward of the turret and to the left.

The vehicle made its first impact by successfully participating in Exercise 'Glory Hawk', with the 17th/21st Lancers and 14th/20th King's Hussars in 1976, and since then it has seen regular service with the British Army in which it equips four armoured reconnaissance regiments of 1 (Br) Corps in West Germany. However, there are now some doubts as to the effectiveness of the L23A1 76mm main armament of the Scorpion. While this gun is seen to be effective in the fire support role and against light armour, it is not capable of defeating heavier armoured vehicles. To overcome this problem a Cockerill 90mm gun can be installed in a modified turret. This new variant is proving effective, but whether the 90mm gun will become the standard main armament of the Scorpion in the future remains to be seen. The Scorpion was one of three types of CVR(T) to see action in the Falklands in 1982, serving as a fire support vehicle along with the Scimitar.

Role of the Scimitar

Although its FV number is 107 the Scimitar was, in fact, the second vehicle of the series to go into production, and apart from its main armament and some turret features it is the same vehicle as the Scorpion. Armed with a 30mm L21 Rarden cannon the Scimitar has been designed to act in a fire support role. The L21 is capable of firing up to 90 rounds per minute with great accuracy, and with a maximum range in excess of 4000m (4400yds) it is a highly effective weapon. Alongside the Scorpion, the Scimitar first saw action in the Falklands and during the fighting around San Carlos Bay a number were dug in to act as infantry support weapons.

The FV102 Striker entered service in 1978, and is currently deployed in West Germany with 1(Br) Corps. This is the true anti-tank version in the Scorpion family. Being armed with 10 Swingfire missiles it can take on main battle tanks up to a range of 4000m (4400yds). The missiles, produced by British Aerospace, are contained in five launcher bins which are raised to 35 degrees when firing. They can be reloaded from within the Striker. The Swingfire missiles can be fired either from the vehicle or from a remote unit outside. When the launcher bins are lowered, the Striker is almost indistinguishable from the less deadly Spartan.

The FV103 Spartan is the vehicle which most infantrymen are likely to come in contact with, because it is the APC (armoured personnel carrier) in the family and provides the necessary mobility required

Scorpion CVR(T) series

Vehicle	Crew	Length (overall)	Width	Height	Weight (loaded)	Ground pressure	Speed (road)	Range (road)	Armament
FV101(76) Scorpion	3	4.79m (15ft 8½in)	2.24m (7ft 4in)	2.10m (6ft 10½in)	7938kg (17,485lb)	0.36kg/cm² (5.1lb/in²)	80.5km/h (50mph)	644km (400 miles)	one 76mm gun one 7.62mm machine gun two ×4 smoke grenade launchers
FV101(90) Scorpion	3	5.29m (17ft 4in)	2.24m (7ft 4in)	2.10m (6ft 10½in)	8723kg (19,213lb)	0.38kg/cm² (5.4lb/in²)	72.5km/h (45mph)	644km (400 miles)	one 90mm gun one 7.62mm machine gun two ×4 smoke grenade launchers
FV102 Striker	3	4.83m (15ft 10in)	2.24m (7ft 4in)	1.73m (5ft 8in)	8346kg (18,383lb)	0.345kg/cm² (4.9lb/in²)	80.5km/h (50mph)	483km (300 miles)	ten Swingfire anti-tank missiles one 7.62mm machine gun two ×4 smoke grenade launchers
FV103 Spartan	3+4	4.93m (16ft 2in)	2.24m (7ft 4in)	2.26m (7ft 5in)	8172kg (18,000lb)	0.338kg/cm² (4.8lb/in²)	80.5km/h (50mph)	483km (300 miles)	one 7.62mm machine gun two ×4 smoke grenade launchers
FV104 Samaritan	3+4/5	5.07m (16ft 7½in)	2.24m (7ft 4in)	2.41m (7ft 11in)	8664kg (19,084lb)	0.358kg/cm² (5.1lb/in²)	72.5km/h (45mph)	483km (300 miles)	two ×4 smoke grenade launchers
FV105 Sultan	5/6	4.8m (15ft 9in)	2.13m (7ft)	2.56m (8ft 4in)	8664kg (19,084lb)	0.358kg/cm² (5.1lb/in²)	72.5km/h (45mph)	483km (300 miles)	one 7.62mm machine gun two ×4 smoke grenade launchers
FV106 Samson	3	5.0m (16ft 5in)	2.43m (7ft 11½in)	2.25m (7ft 4½in)	8738kg (19,247lb)	0.358kg/cm² (5.1lb/in²)	72.5km/h (45mph)	483km (300 miles)	one 7.62mm machine gun two ×4 smoke grenade launchers
FV107 Scimitar	3	4.99m (16ft 4½in)	2.24m (7ft 4in)	2.10m (6ft 10½in)	7750kg (17,070lb)	0.338kg/cm² (4.8lb/in²)	80.5km/h (50mph)	644km (400 miles)	one 30mm Rarden cannon one 7.62mm machine gun two ×4 smoke grenade launchers
Streaker	variable	4.88m (16ft)	2.21m (7ft 3in)	1.83m (6ft)	5354kg (11,793lb) unladen 9075kg (19,989lb) laden	0.221kg/cm² (3.14lb/in²) unladen 0.375kg/cm² (5.3lb/in²) laden	80.5km/h (50mph)	483km (300 miles)	none

on today's battlefield. But as the Spartan can only carry four fully equipped men, plus its three-man crew, its role as an APC is consequently limited, especially so when compared to the FV432 – the army's main APC – which has a capacity for 10 men plus crew. Thus the Spartan's role would seem to be that of a battlefield transport vehicle for units of sub-section size, such as pioneer assault teams and other specialised patrol groups. In addition, it can be employed as a carrier for Blowpipe anti-aircraft missiles or Milan anti-tank missiles. The latest development of the Spartan variant has been the introduction of the FV4333 Stormer, which is an enlarged Spartan (capable of carrying up to 10 men) whose prime use, however, would be to act in an anti-aircraft role.

Due to its non-combatant status, the FV104 Samaritan is not armed except for smoke grenade launchers which are for personal protection. As the ambulance vehicle, Samaritan has had to have slight modifications made. The roof, for example, is higher than its counterparts, in order to allow more stowage space for casualties and equipment. The Samaritan can carry a mixture of cases: four stretchers, five sitting wounded, or even two stretchers and three sitting. Another modification is the extra large door at the rear, which allows easy access for both the medical crew and the wounded.

The brains of the CVR(T) series are supplied by the armoured command vehicle, the FV105 Sultan. The Sultan can be fitted with any type of combination of radios, map-boards and accessory equipment. As it is most likely to be found in rear areas, away from the heavy fighting, it is armed with only a 7.62mm

machine gun and smoke grenade launchers for local defence. The crew complement is five or six men, though if additional personnel are needed a collapsable screen, called a 'penthouse', can be erected over the rear. The Sultan has extra air-conditioning fitted because of its vast array of electrical equipment.

The FV106 Samson acts as the workhorse; it is the vehicle recovery variant, a task for which it is adequately supplied. An internally mounted winch, with 229m (250 yds) of steel rope, is fitted. This particular

Opposite page: An FV104 Samaritan armoured ambulance (top); an FV105 Sultan command vehicle (centre); an FV106 Samson recovery vehicle with its bulkhead-mounted blades dug-in (bottom). Below: The Streaker high-mobility load carrier.

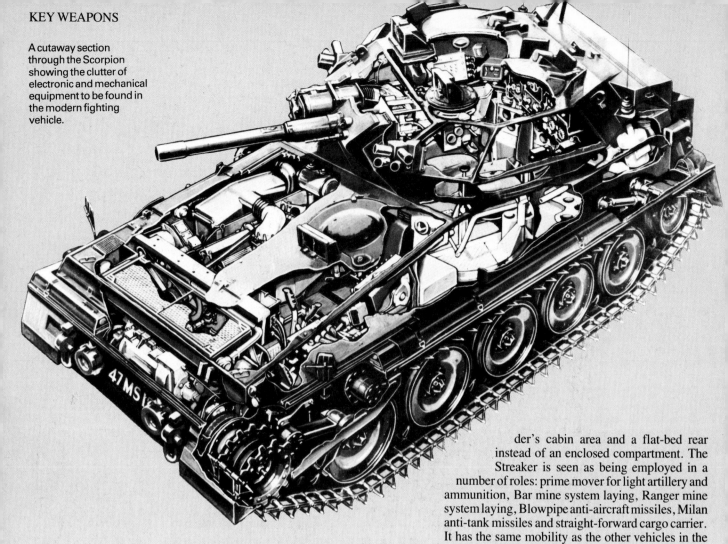

A cutaway section through the Scorpion showing the clutter of electronic and mechanical equipment to be found in the modern fighting vehicle.

Below: A Scorpion of the United Arab Emirates traverses deep sand during manoeuvres in the desert. Its light ground pressure is a considerable asset in conditions such as these. Below right: A British Army Scorpion churns across a ploughed field at high speed.

item of equipment has variable speeds, and with a 4:1 snatch block it can pull a 12-tonne load. For assistance in these matters the Samson is equipped with a pair of heavy blades fitted to the rear bulkhead. With these blades lowered into position the vehicle will not move backwards when pulling a load heavier than itself. A small jib crane, bench vice and other ancillary equipment make this mobile workshop a valuable vehicle on the battlefield. In fact one Samson was sent to the Falklands, where it serviced the Scorpions and Scimitars.

The final member of the CVR(T) family, and the very latest addition, is the Streaker. This vehicle is classed as a high mobility load carrier, without local armament. It is of the same design as the rest of the Scorpion family but has only a small driver/comman-

der's cabin area and a flat-bed rear instead of an enclosed compartment. The Streaker is seen as being employed in a number of roles: prime mover for light artillery and ammunition, Bar mine system laying, Ranger mine system laying, Blowpipe anti-aircraft missiles, Milan anti-tank missiles and straight-forward cargo carrier. It has the same mobility as the other vehicles in the range, and incorporates all of the other Scorpion features, notably reliability and durability.

Scorpion CVR(T)s are a successful range of vehicles. They have been sold in most variants to many countries, including Iran, Kuwait, Nigeria, Thailand, the Philippines and the United Arab Emirates. All of the eight variants in this range can be equipped with NBC (nuclear, biological and chemical) survival packs. Water-fording screens and propulsion units can be fitted, to enable the vehicles to cope with deep-water obstacles. In view of its success in the Falklands, during which only one Scorpion 76mm was lost, hit by a mine, the future of the Scorpion CVR(T) looks assured. And with its ability to be able to meet almost any requirement it will, no doubt, be in service for a long time to come.

The French Empire

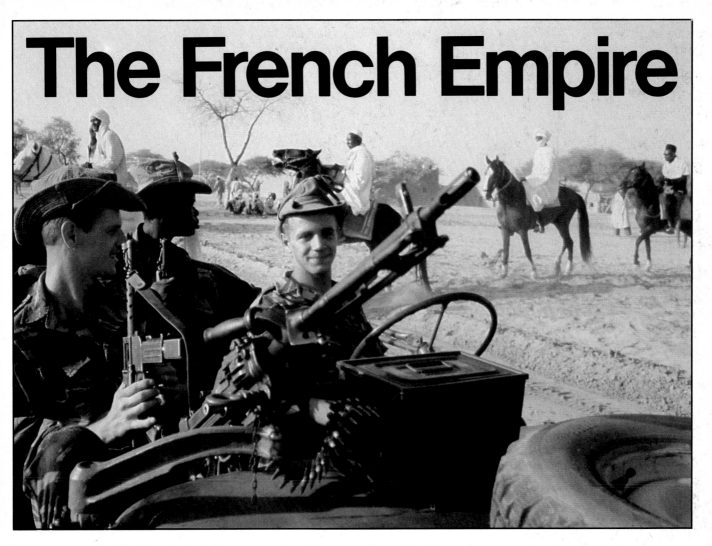

The painful withdrawal of a colonial power

For France, like Britain, the postwar years were a period of imperial withdrawal. Between 1945 and 1962, France granted independence to all her major imperial possessions, thus disintegrating an overseas empire which had been second in size only to Britain's; and for the French, the process of decolonisation was even more painful than it had been for the Anglo-Saxons. Decolonisation gave rise to considerable bitterness in France, particularly as the French Army fought two protracted and costly wars in order to preserve the empire. Indeed, until the late 1950s the French showed great reluctance to part with their imperial possessions.

This reluctance to disengage from empire cannot be explained wholly or even largely in terms of economics. Although parts of the French Empire were profitable for investors, most of it was not. The French generally did 'less well' from their empire in economic terms than did the British. Nor can this reluctance to withdraw be attributed primarily to strategic factors. True, the French Empire provided a reservoir of manpower for the French Army and a network of military bases, but unlike the British the French suffered from no overwhelming desire to protect the trade routes to the East. But the French needed their empire for political reasons. It was large enough to give France the prestige of a first-rank power; without the empire this status would be lost.

France's reluctance to decolonise also stemmed from sentiment. Traditionally, the very basis of French colonial policy had been 'assimilation'. According to this concept, the overseas possessions were extensions of France and the colonial natives, whether yellow, black or brown, were to be turned into Frenchmen by a process of Gallicisation. This policy was maintained, if not strengthened, by the Fourth Republic. Under the new constitution, introduced in 1946, the French Empire was replaced by the French Union, which comprised France, her overseas *départements* and territories, associated territories and states. The very basis of the *Union française,* according to the constitution, was full citizenship rights for all, regardless of race. Despite some successes, however, the policy of assimilation proved to be no prophylactic against colonial nationalism. Either because the policy was not applied properly, or because it was unacceptable to native peoples, resistance to French rule was widespread. As a result, the French were compelled to use force in order to maintain the Union in a long series of wars in Asia and Africa.

An early manifestation of colonial resistance came in Madagascar. In March 1947, in an attempt to oust the French, members of the Hova tribe launched an armed insurrection. France responded by sending reinforcements to the island and launching a ferocious

Local people seem oblivious to the French military presence as a patrol, armed with 9mm sub-machine guns, drive their jeep (mounting a 7.5mm machine gun) through the dry countryside of Chad. The French gave Chad independence in 1960 but their armed forces intervened on behalf of the Chad government several times in the next two decades during the civil wars that seemed endemic in the country.

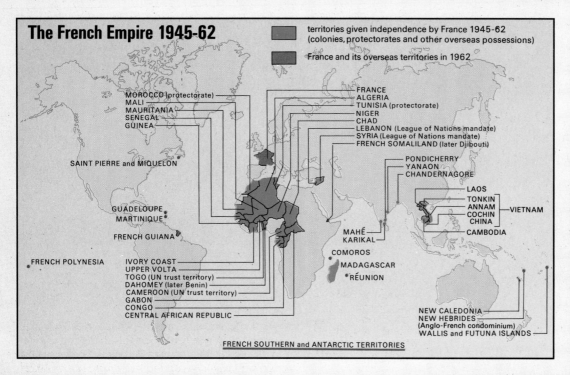

The French Empire 1945-62

territories given independence by France 1945-62
(colonies, protectorates and other overseas possessions)

France and its overseas territories in 1962

MOROCCO (protectorate)
MALI
MAURITANIA
SENEGAL
GUINEA
FRANCE
ALGERIA
TUNISIA (protectorate)
NIGER
CHAD
LEBANON (League of Nations mandate)
SYRIA (League of Nations mandate)
FRENCH SOMALILAND (later Djibouti)
SAINT PIERRE and MIQUELON
PONDICHERRY
YANAON
CHANDERNAGORE
GUADELOUPE
MARTINIQUE
FRENCH GUIANA
LAOS
TONKIN
ANNAM
COCHIN
CHINA
VIETNAM
CAMBODIA
MAHÉ
KARIKAL
COMOROS
MADAGASCAR
RÉUNION
FRENCH POLYNESIA
IVORY COAST
UPPER VOLTA
TOGO (UN trust territory)
DAHOMEY (later Benin)
CAMEROON (UN trust territory)
GABON
CONGO
CENTRAL AFRICAN REPUBLIC
NEW CALEDONIA
NEW HEBRIDES
(Anglo-French condominium)
WALLIS and FUTUNA ISLANDS
FRENCH SOUTHERN and ANTARCTIC TERRITORIES

Right: The retreat from Algeria was a traumatic experience for France. These Algerian women display the independent nation's flag next to a monument erected on the centenary of French conquest. Below: French troops at Dien Bien Phu. The final defeat in Indochina heralded the general decline of French colonial power.

counter-offensive. After considerable loss of life on the rebel side, the revolt was crushed by 1948.

Far more prolonged and successful was the revolt in Indochina. During World War II, the territory had been taken over by the Japanese. By the time the French were able to return in strength in 1946, Vietnamese nationalists led by the Viet Minh had proclaimed Vietnam independent. Initially France attempted to negotiate with the Viet Minh, who had gained local support, but by December 1946 discussions had broken down. Open warfare between the Viet Minh and French Union forces followed.

The war lasted for eight years. It was a heavy drain on French financial and military resources. Although the French Union forces included many local troops, the Viet Minh proved an elusive and formidable enemy. The psychological strain of an apparently unending war also took its toll in Paris. After the fall of Dien Bien Phu in May 1954, the balance of opinion tilted decisively against the war. By the Geneva Accords of July 1954, France agreed to evacuate the whole of Indochina, which was divided into four states: Cambodia (now known as Kampuchea), Laos, North Vietnam and South Vietnam. France retained some influence in the region, particularly Saigon, but each of the new states became fully independent outside the French Union.

France's other holdings on the Asiatic mainland, the five territories of French India, were given up without bloodshed. One, Chandernagore, was transferred to India in 1952. The other four – Pondicherry, Yanan, Karikal and Mahé – followed in 1954, their accession to India being formalised in May 1956. France also gave up Morocco and Tunisia with relatively little loss of life. In both cases, conflict could have been widespread, given the strength of nationalist sentiment by the mid-1950s, and when trouble began there, France responded by reinforcing her troops in both protectorates. By March 1956, however, the French had decided to cut their losses and recognise the independence of both.

By contrast, the independence of France's other North African territory, Algeria, took place only after prolonged, bloody and bitter conflict. Unlike Morocco and Tunisia, Algeria was administered

Above: The parachute drop into Kolwezi in 1978 was a reminder that France could still influence Third World affairs – in this case to bolster President Mobutu and to rescue European technicians.

Left: Moroccans celebrate independence from the French. Morocco had long been a protectorate of France and it had always been difficult to control. In the 1920s, 300,000 French troops had been tied down by the nationalist rebel Abd-el-Krim.

not as a protectorate but as an integral part of metropolitan France. Algeria's population of 9 million included some 900,000 European settlers, most of whom were second or third generation Algerians. Known as *colons* or *pieds noirs,* they were resolved upon keeping Algeria French. When the Algerian nationalists launched an open revolt against French rule in November 1954, thousands of French troops were poured into the territory.

The war in Algeria had profound repercussions. For one thing, it led directly to French involvement at Suez in October 1956. From the French standpoint, the Anglo-French operation against Egypt was partly in order to save Algeria. The aim was to topple Colonel Gamal Abdel Nasser of Egypt, who had been aiding and abetting the Front de Libération Nationale (National Liberation Front or FLN) since 1952.

Coups and terrorism

The war in Algeria also had an influence upon French colonial policy in black Africa. In order to prosecute the war in Algeria, peace had to be maintained in the other African territories and concessions were therefore made to African nationalism.

The Algerian conflict had even more profound consequences within metropolitan France. The French public, directly implicated in the war through a conscript army of some 500,000 men, were deeply divided. Many favoured a settlement, on the grounds that the war was too costly in financial, human and even moral terms. The *colons,* however, had powerful allies. They were supported not only by a segment of French public opinion, but also by many senior army officers. These men, having seen France defeated in 1940 and again in 1954, were in no mood to contemplate any further debacles. The settlers also managed to build up a powerful political lobby in Paris, a lobby adept at preventing the unstable coalition governments of the Fourth Republic from taking decisive steps towards Algerian independence.

By 1958, the elements favouring *Algérie française* had gained the upper hand. In May of that year, the *colons,* enraged by FLN atrocities and dismayed by

talk of a negotiated settlement between Paris and the nationalists, launched a coup in Algiers which gained the backing of local army commanders and brought down the French government. The outcome of this was the fall of the Fourth Republic and the return to power of the war hero, General Charles de Gaulle. While de Gaulle was regarded by the *colons* as the man who would save Algeria, he was seen by others as the man who would stave off a military takeover and restore stability.

The latter view proved correct. Under de Gaulle's leadership, stability was restored. The shaky parliamentary system of the Fourth Republic was replaced by an executive presidency and the Fifth Republic, and de Gaulle set about revamping French domestic and foreign policy. The Union as a concept was abandoned, but de Gaulle introduced a replacement in the form of the French Community, a much looser organisation that entailed not integration but association. One African territory, Guinea, refused to accept even this arrangement and was duly given independence in 1958. Two years later, with black African leaders pressing for greater autonomy, de Gaulle was forced to go further and so, in 1960, the whole of French West and Equatorial Africa, plus Madagascar, was granted full independence. Fourteen new states thereby came into being. The French Community, introduced to maintain the empire, was used instead to smooth the path to independence.

Algeria, on the other hand, remained a source of conflict and bitterness. Initially de Gaulle proposed that Algeria should become an internally self-governing territory within the French Community, but this compromise satisfied neither the nationalists nor the *colons.* Although the war was going reasonably well militarily, de Gaulle became convinced that it was not in France's political interests to continue the campaign. By September 1959, he was speaking in terms of Algerian self-determination, which alarmed the *colons* and their supporters. In April 1961, the proponents of *Algérie française* launched a further coup in Algiers – but this time the bulk of the army refused to respond. De Gaulle pressed ahead with his peace proposals. In March 1962 agreement was reached with the FLN on independence for Algeria. This outcome did not endear de Gaulle to the *colons,* who left Algeria in droves, but it was supported by the French people as a whole. France's last major colonial problem had been settled by negotiation. The army, for the first time since 1946, was no longer at war. **Francis Toase**

Slaughter in Madagascar

Tragic results of a nationalist revolt

In 1947, before most of the nations of mainland Africa had organised political independence movements, the people of the island of Madagascar staged a revolt which resulted in the death of more than 60,000 people and nearly brought French rule to an end. Although the rebellion was quickly defeated and order restored to the island, Madagascar was slow to recover from the violence of 1947. The Malagasy people obtained independence from France in 1960, but the country continued to be torn by political strife alternating with periods of authoritarian rule.

Madagascar became a French protectorate in 1895 after French troops, including the Foreign Legion, landed at Majunga and fought their way to Tananarive and occupied it. The French then subdued the dominant tribe on the island, the Merina, and established a colonial regime based on military force. Resistance to French rule continued until the outbreak of World

War II, inspired by primitive tribal disapproval of modernisation and later by the growth of nationalism among the educated elite amidst the Merina. In 1945 two Malagasy politicians, Raseta and Ravoahangy, were elected as deputies to the French Constituent Assembly and, along with Jacques Rabemananjara, a French-educated Catholic, they formed the Mouvement Démocratique de la Rénovation Malgache (MDRM). In 1946 MDRM claimed to have 300,000 members representing most of the tribes on the island. Other political movements, Catholic and Protestant, joined in the campaign for independence.

The initial success of the 1947 revolt was due mainly to the element of surprise. The authorities appear to have greatly underestimated the strength of political feeling among the native population and the people's ability to organise themselves. That the revolt was not entirely spontaneous was shown by the

Above: Many of the French colonies provided manpower in the strangely contradictory role of fighting to help France retain other colonial possessions. Senegalese troops (a term used to describe forces from all of French black Africa, not merely those from Senegal) were the main forces used to put down the Malagasy revolt.

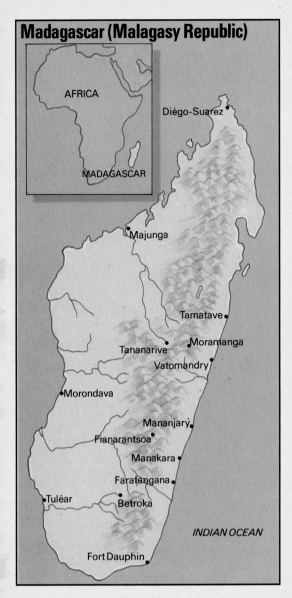

Madagascar (Malagasy Republic)

AFRICA

MADAGASCAR

Diégo-Suarez

Majunga

Tamatave

Moramanga

Tananarive

Vatomandry

Morondava

Mananjary

Fianarantsoa

Manakara

Farafangana

Tuléar

Betroka

Fort Dauphin

INDIAN OCEAN

coast region which provided most of the crops for export and where the Malagasy felt themselves to be most harshly exploited by the European settlers.

Brutal retaliation

Once the authorities had recovered from their initial surprise they reacted with great speed and much brutality. In the late summer, reinforcements of Senegalese troops from North Africa and parachutists of the Foreign Legion from France began to arrive in Madagascar. They quickly sealed off the main rebel area and set about clearing out the rebels, who lacked food and ammunition and were forced to surrender or to seek temporary refuge in the forests.

Operations were interrupted by the rainy season but resumed in April 1948. By the end of the year the last pockets of resistance in the forests had been wiped out. Some 558,000 rebels were registered as having surrendered to the authorities, but estimates of the number of casualties vary. Critics of the French put it at 90,000, but the administration gave several different figures, finally arriving at a total of 11,000. The actual figure, impossible to establish with any precision, is probably somewhere between these two extremes. Certainly tens of thousands of the islanders died, mostly villagers who played no part in the fighting but, fearing reprisals, fled into the forests where they died of hunger and exposure. In addition, several hundred Europeans died. French military casualties were given as a thousand killed.

Opinions differ regarding the success of the revolt as a military operation. One authority argues that it was 'so badly planned and so poorly executed that even the few troops stationed in the island were able to hold the rebels in check'. Another takes the contrary view that the revolt was well organised and 'militarily effective and enabled small groups with few arms and rudimentary supplies to hold out against greatly superior French forces'. A third ventures the opinion that, if the nationalists had had modern weapons and other supplies from abroad, the French would have been in serious difficulty.

In the event the French remained in possession of Madagascar, but not for long. The revolt revealed the strength of nationalist feeling and the great distance separating the French and the indigenous administration from the ordinary people of the island. The long-term effect of the revolt was seen in 1960, when Madagascar became independent of France.

David Floyd

fact that it broke out simultaneously in several parts of the island.

It was at midnight on 29/30 March that the rebels struck. Armed mostly with spears, axes and a few captured rifles and shotguns, they attacked the French army garrisons in the towns. In Moramanga, which lies between the capital of Tananarive and the east coast, the Senegalese garrison suffered heavy losses from an attack by 2000 rebels. But they succeeded in counter-attacking and subsequently massacred many of the local population.

In Tananarive itself the rebels were quickly dispersed, and in Fianarantsoa they were all arrested after they had cut some power lines. The larger towns, like Tamatave and Mananjary, remained in French hands, but the smaller and more isolated ones were occupied by the rebels. From March to August the revolt spread along the east coast and into the forest zone until the rebels controlled the whole of the coastal region from Tamatave to Farafangana. Road and rail communications were attacked and destroyed by the rebels, cutting the capital off from the coast. They killed white settlers and pro-French Malagasy and set fire to crops.

Even at the height of their success, however, the nationalists did not control more than a sixth of the island and that, significantly, was mainly the east

Below: Madagascan rebels armed with spears. Their pitiful armaments and lack of organisation doomed their movement to defeat.

Bourguiba's revolution

Tunisia's uneasy road to independence

In 1881 the kingdom of Tunisia became a protectorate of France under the terms of the Treaty of Bardo. In theory, the country still retained its sovereignty under the rule of its hereditary monarch, the Bey, but in practice power was exercised by a French Resident General who quickly established control over every aspect of the country's internal administration. French settlers, offered special privileges, soon began to arrive in large numbers.

Until 1945 the system worked reasonably well and, by and large, the relationship between the French and the indigenous population was a harmonious one. By then, however, a generation of educated Tunisians had emerged who felt that they were entitled to participate democratically in the management of their own affairs. Nationalist elements began to intensify their pressure and civil unrest grew. To this the French reacted with a barely disguised policy of repression. During a riot in Sfax in 1947, troops opened fire on the crowd, killing 29 and wounding 59. Tunisian attitudes hardened. Whereas adequate reform would once have sufficed, now complete independence was the goal.

The Tunisian nationalist movement began with the founding of the Destour (Constitutional Liberal) Party in 1920. The party recognised the benefits of French rule but insisted that Muslim interests and culture must be represented in government. The party was too fragmented by sectional interests to make any headway and in 1935 was replaced by the Neo-Destour Party, which was much more radical in its approach.

One of the most prominent figures in the new party was Habib Bourguiba, nowadays regarded as the father of his country. Bourguiba was looked upon as a trouble-maker. He was arrested several times and forced to leave the country, but returned in 1949 to become president of the Committee of National Liberation, which worked secretly through the agency of trade unions, student associations and sporting bodies. Despite this, Bourguiba remained a Francophile and in 1950 declared: 'The choice rests between gaining independence under French guidance with freedom and cooperation, and winning independence by means of hate and bloodshed.'

In 1956 France bowed to the United Nations' principle of self-determination and on 17 March granted Tunisia full independence while retaining several military bases, of which Bizerte was the most important. Four months later the Bey Sidi Lamine, a figurehead, was peacefully deposed and Bourguiba became president of the new republic.

Relations with France continued to deteriorate, however. The Algerian War of Liberation was now raging, and the Front de Libération Nationale (National Liberation Front or FLN) was using Tunisian territory both as a refuge and as a base from which operations could be launched against the French. The latter reacted first by suspending technical and economic aid to Tunisia and then by mounting 'hot pursuit' forays across the frontier. In one such punitive raid the village of Sakiet Sidi Youssef was virtually flattened by an air strike, an event which provoked deep anger. To Bourguiba's protests that the French were flagrantly violating Tunisian sovereignty, Paris retorted that his country was offering sanctuary to the enemy, and indeed there was little doubt where Tunisian sympathies lay.

Above: Troops and medical staff in the streets of Bizerte after savage fighting. French action in 1961 caused more than 1900 casualties.

A lethal barrier

The French solved the problem for themselves by sealing the Algerian-Tunisian frontier with a barrier named the Morice Line, after the then minister of defence. Every subsequent attempt by the FLN to penetrate Algeria from their Tunisian bases ended in complete disaster and heavy loss, but substantial FLN forces remained inside Tunisia until the end of the conflict.

All this left a legacy of general bitterness. In 1961 French voters endorsed General Charles de Gaulle's proposals for Algerian self-determination and peace talks with the FLN began. Bourguiba decided that the moment had come for his country to be rid of its last French presence.

On 19 July a column of 'death volunteers' set off to plant the Tunisian flag in a disputed area of the Sahara; it clashed with local French troops and was dispersed after sustaining 100 casualties. On the same day the base at Bizerte was blockaded, with tragic consequences. The blockade was probably intended to be nothing more than a lever to be used in negotiations for a French withdrawal, and was mounted not only by troops but also by a large number of civilians, whose presence was designed to give the event a 'popular' look. Bourguiba was later to admit that this was a serious error of judgement. In the event, the situation quickly got out of hand, and the weight of evidence suggests that it was Tunisian hot-heads who opened fire first.

The base was hit by artillery, mortar and heavy machine-gun fire, and several unsuccessful attempts were made to storm its perimeter. The 4000-strong garrison reacted sharply. French jets hammered the Tunisian positions with rockets and cannon. Paratroop reinforcements were flown in and went into action as soon as they arrived, supported by Panhard armoured cars. Soon they were pursuing the Tunisians through Bizerte itself. Three cruisers, *Colbert, Chevalier Paul* and *Bouvet,* then penetrated the channel connecting the base with the open sea, effectively breaking the blockade.

After three days of fighting the United Nations imposed a ceasefire. Tunisian casualties amounted to approximately 700 killed, 1200 wounded and 650 captured; French losses were 25 men killed and about 100 wounded.

Despite being roundly beaten in a battle that should never have taken place, Bourguiba emerged the ultimate victor. Such was the spirit of the times that no former colonial power could expect any sympathy from the United Nations General Assembly. Moscow described the French reaction as 'a foul crime' and as 'a new bloody provocation against the peoples of Africa,' and a bloc of 36 Afro-Asian nations led a campaign of censure. France bowed to world opinion and in 1962 withdrew completely from Tunisia, retaining only the right to use certain air bases if required. It is some measure of Bourguiba's statesmanship that, after this troubled period, he was able to maintain amicable relations with the West that remain to the present day. **Bryan Perrett**

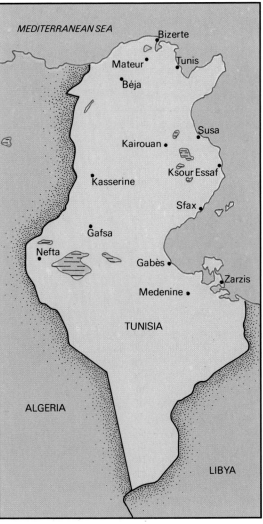

Right: Habib Bourguiba, the man who led Tunisia to independence and who guided the new republic through the difficulties of the late 1950s and early 1960s. Below: French paras inspect the streets after the fighting in Bizerte in July 1961.

Storms over the Sahara

Bloody conflict in French Algeria

The Algerian struggle for independence was so out-standingly cruel and bitter because it destroyed a genuinely colonial regime. History since World War II is littered with epics of national resistance that dismembered the empires of the European powers, but very few of the nations that emerged from these wars had been seriously colonised. Algeria was completely different in that, by 1945, 10 per cent of its population were European settlers, known as *colons*. By the time Algeria gained independence from France in 1962, her estimated population had been reduced by 1 million Muslims (believed to have been killed in the struggle) and the vast majority of European settlers who left or were expelled at its conclusion.

There was no inkling of tragedy and loss on such a scale as the war in Europe drew to a close in the spring of 1945, but by that time, the roots of the confrontation were very deep. Algeria had been a Muslim country since the 8th century and it was loosely governed by a Turkish dey when the French trumped up an excuse to invade in 1830. At first the French looked only for a glorious distraction for the fading regime of King Charles X, but they soon found themselves involved in a 19th century preview of the 20th century's savage war. Algiers quickly fell, but a young man named Abd-el-Kader led a fierce guerrilla resistance in the interior. French patrols were

ambushed and isolated garrisons overwhelmed in a pattern that was to become disturbingly familiar. Abd-el-Kader was unable, however, to unite Algeria's clannish, tribal people behind him, and a ruthless campaign under the French Marshal 'Père' Bugeaud forced him to surrender in 1847. By this time the seeds of future dispute had already been sown: in 1841 there were 37,374 *colons* cementing France's rule over an estimated 3 million *indigènes*. As a final, fateful step towards the eventual conflict, Algeria was declared an integral part of France in 1848 and divided into three French *départements*.

Being regarded as a part of France made Algeria unique in North Africa and displayed France's intentions towards her newly acquired land. Four times the size of metropolitan France, with the distance from Algiers in the north to Tamanrasset in the south roughly equivalent to the distance from Newcastle to Algiers, there was a vast new territory for the expan-

Above: After the massacre of French civilians in Philippeville on 20 August 1955, French troops killed hundreds of Muslims in a day of vengeance. Muslim corpses are shown laid out in a stadium. Below: As early as 1945, disaffection with French colonial rule was expressed by the Algerian people when, during peace celebrations, Europeans were attacked in the Muslim town of Sétif. French reaction was harsh, leading to the capture and detainment of many tribesmen – such as these, who are surrendering to French troops.

sion of the French nation, even though most of Algeria consisted of the bleak vastness of the Sahara desert.

Any dreams of expansion by France across the Mediterranean were tempered, however, by reality. France herself had a declining population so that the *colons* who poured into Algeria came chiefly from Spain, Italy and Malta; it was estimated in 1917 that only one in five settlers was of French origin. Even these willing subjects were more than counterbalanced by the native population.

To the French the Muslims were a resource and a difficulty. In no case were the Muslims treated as French citizens under French law, but rather as French subjects under their own Islamic law. Besides this, they were deprived of any effective role in government because the *colons* would never accept an official, mayor or deputy who was a Muslim. French democracy was for the *colons* only, which set a cauldron of resentment simmering. The situation was exacerbated by the benefits of French rule. Better education enabled the indigenous population to recognise discrimination; European draining and farming techniques made the land more productive but enriched the *colons* and drove the Muslims back to the poorer land; most ironic of all, improved medical techniques brought a population explosion that resulted in grinding poverty.

The 1914-18 war provided a last opportunity to deflect the wrath to come. Some 173,000 Muslims rallied to France's colours and 25,000 of them died in her cause. There is little doubt that many of these soldiers hoped that their loyalty would be rewarded by reforms and a greater measure of equality. Instead, the French remained complacent and both they and the *colons* were aware that the swelling Muslim population would swamp them in a true democracy. Injustice continued, poverty grew and frustration reigned supreme. Resistance to French rule was established long before the debacle of 1940.

There were three main strands to this dissent. The Association des Ulema founded by Sheikh Abdulhamid Ben Badis in 1931 was an Islamic fundamentalist

Above: French paras, one armed with a sniper's rifle, during a massive cordon and search operation in the casbah in Algiers. Below left: Abd-el-Kader who led a fierce guerrilla resistance to the French forces in Algeria in the mid-19th century. Below: French gendarmes pour scorn on a captured FLN flag.

movement that stressed the incompatability of a devout Muslim life and an infidel rule. The liberals led by the French-educated Ferhat Abbas strove, at first, merely for the full equality of Algerian and Frenchman. The most important party, however, was the most radical: the Parti Progressiste Algérien (PPA), under the ex-communist Messali Hadj, believed in the confiscation of the *colons'* land for redistribution.

During the years of World War II there was little overt resistance, but frustration continued to grow until it became apparent to both sides that the ending of the European war would see some kind of demonstration in Algeria. Never dreaming the extent of popular resentment, the French authorities arrested Messali Hadj in advance of the victory celebrations,

about which they were uneasy. The set date for triumphal parades was 8 May 1945. Incidents of stone throwing broke out before it and threatening graffiti appeared on walls, though this was little warning of the horror yet to come.

It was in the small, largely Muslim town of Sétif that the peace celebrations first turned into massacre. The parade assumed a threatening character and shots were fired. The Muslims responded with a five-day orgy of murder, mutilation and rape. The 20 gendarmes at Sétif were overwhelmed and 103 Europeans killed. Many of the dead men had their genitals cut off and sewn in their mouths, and the women (one as old as 84) were raped and their breasts hacked off. It was, in fact, a spontaneous outburst of savagery.

Reign of terror

The reaction of the French military was blunt. Army units made an indiscriminate sweep of villages and carried out summary executions; Muslim settlements were bombed from the air and, off the coast, a warship shelled Muslim suburbs. At least 500 Algerians perished this way but a more full-blooded vengeance was exacted by the *colons*. A wave of lynchings gave terror a full rein and anything between 4000 and 35,000 Algerians (according to whose version can be believed) were killed in return for the horror of Sétif.

Both sides had had a glimpse of the cruel excesses that lay in store, and this gave pause for thought. It was, in fact, nine and a half years before violence broke out again on any scale, but they were years which saw a hardening of attitudes on both sides.

Shortly after the Sétif bloodbath, the 7th Regiment of Algerian Tirailleurs disembarked, home from the war in Europe. They were horrified by what they learnt of the reprisals and a good number of future leaders of the resistance were to be men who had soldiered for France. Theirs was to be a harder determination than that behind the established parties of dissent. Ferhat Abbas's liberals and Messali Hadj's radicals became irrelevant in the face of the most adamantly revolutionary party which arose from splinter groups in Messali's faction and, by October 1954, became known as the Front de Libération Nationale (National Liberation Front or FLN).

Years of conspiracy between Algerian hardliners went into the formation of the FLN and by 1954 it was established that they wanted full independence and that this could only be achieved by war. In order to guarantee its success, the FLN needed both strong leadership and support. The appeal of total independence combined with an absence of strong political reaction from the French, meant that plenty of support existed for the FLN. By mid-1956 there were some 20,000 active members, though most Muslims offered passive support.

As the membership of the FLN increased, it changed its style from that of loosely based guerrilla units and adopted a formal military structure. The movement was led by a committee because the Algerian population was a mixture of Arabs and Berbers with the Berber population strongest in the mountain areas of the Aurès and Kabylia. Mistrust between the Muslims made unity dependent on a shared leadership and responsibility. By the autumn of 1954 the shadowy leaders of the FLN had agreed that a general rising against the French should take place at 0001 hours on 1 November, All Saints Day.

The FLN divided Algeria into six independent

commands or Wilayas: Wilaya 1 in the Aurès; Wilaya 2 around Constantine; Wilaya 3 was Kabylia; Wilaya 4 was the Algérois around Algiers; Wilaya 5 the Oranie around Oran and Wilaya 6 the hinterland behind the Algérois. The only significant FLN armed force in existence was the Kabylia maquis under the ex-soldier Belkacem Krim, so the main task of the other groups was to raid armouries. Killing French soldiers and Muslim collaborators was an important secondary aim.

The French had some knowledge of the revolt to come. The security police even knew the location of the main bomb-making factory in Algiers, but they knew little of the organisation of the FLN and persisted in believing that its real leader was the Cairo-based Ahmed Ben Bella. Because they knew something was afoot they were not much shocked by the rising on All Saints Day – especially since most of the FLN's raids were ineptly executed causing few

Top: A Moroccan goumier armed with a French 7.5mm rifle, guards the approaches to a pass in the Aurès mountains. Above: The rebel leader Ben Bella outside a police station after his arrest in 1956. Right: Motor-borne French troops keep guard over loyal Algerian farmers as they bring in the harvest. Reprisals carried out by the FLN against pro-French Algerians led to increasing military protection for loyal civilians.

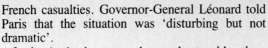

French casualties. Governor-General Léonard told Paris that the situation was 'disturbing but not dramatic'.

In the Aurès, however, the revolt smouldered on and the French Army's clumsy sweeps had little impact in the wild country. The liberal Paris government of Pierre Mendès-France felt that it was time for change and replaced Léonard with the more intellectual and progressive Jacques Soustelle. Soustelle was greatly mistrusted at first by the reactionary *colons* and his attempts at reform were frustrated, but his views soon underwent a sea-change. The sheer cruelty of the FLN's excesses quickly destroyed the new governor-general's sympathy.

The resistance only just survived into the spring of 1955. A regiment of paratroops, under their legendary Colonel Ducournau, gave them a hammering in the Aurès and captured their leader Ben Boulaid. Only terror stood between the FLN and extinction and they applied it with a will. Any Muslim who smoked or drank – thereby supporting the *colon* tobacco barons and wine growers – was liable to wear the 'Kabyle smile' when his lips and nose had been cut off. Murders were always made as gruesome as possible: 'loyal' Muslims would be found with their throats cut but staked to stand upright with their right arm fixed in a mockery of salute, and the corpses of French soldiers were often found with their genitals misplaced in the cruel 'Algerian cocktail'. By these ferocious means, opposition from supporters of Messali or Abbas was stamped out and recalcitrant leaders

of the FLN itself liquidated: Bachir Chihani, who took over command in the Aurés, was executed for paederasty in the summer of 1955.

In April that year the first of the Algerian *tirailleurs* began to desert to the FLN, but the resistance was at such a low ebb throughout the summer that desperate measures were needed. On 20 August a general uprising was staged in Philippeville (now known as Skikda) by Wilaya 2. French civilians were lynched and women and babies mutilated in the most disgusting scenes of carnage. The result was predictable. The first French soldiers on the scene started a day-long execution of Muslims. Jacques Soustelle himself called for 'vengeance for the dead'.

Soustelle's generous nature had not been totally destroyed by the horror of Philippeville, but his instinct for reform was crippled, and in January 1956 he was recalled by the new French government. As he tried to reach Algiers dock on 2 February the *colons* showed how their opinion of him had changed: a huge, frenzied crowd tried to stop him leaving and delayed him several hours as they begged him to stay. He would indeed return in the future, but for the meantime French rule in Algeria awaited the changes ordered by the new socialist prime minister, Guy Mollet, who arrived to look over the troubled scene on 6 February. None of this mattered to the FLN, which was preparing for a conference of its leaders at Soummam in Kabylia. It was there that the fateful seeds of the Battle of Algiers were planted.

P. J. Banyard

Turmoil in Morocco
How a French protectorate was destroyed

The bloodshed that gained independence for Morocco in 1956 was savage but shortlived. Only 30 years later it seems incredible that a nominally self-governed people had to fight to throw off the shackles of a Western protecting power in order to establish a constitutional monarchy. The trouble stemmed from the fact that the imperial powers of Europe consistently underestimated the aspirations of developing countries and overestimated their own strength after victory in World War II.

It was not as if the protectorates originally established over Morocco had much constitutional validity. Britain had protected Moroccan independence during the second half of the 19th century; but eventually Morocco's internal situation became so chaotic, and the threat of German intervention so strong, that the British acquiesced in the establishment of French and Spanish protectorates in the south and north of the country respectively. The Treaty of Fez, signed in 1912, was the instrument by which the French forced their 'services' upon the sultan of Morocco. Its provisions gave them a great deal of power but not actual sovereignty.

Although a Spanish protected zone was established in the north and the 'special characteristics' of the city of Tangier effectively made it an internationally administered city, the main part of the country came within the French protectorate. In this zone, the French had powers to make whatever reforms they wished. Yet they were bound to support the sultan and his heirs, protect his religious status, respect and prestige, and undertook not to interfere with the exercise of the Muslim religion. The one real power left to the sultan was slight enough but was eventually to be used effectively: he had to sign draft decrees

before they could become legal.

It was soon abundantly clear that the French did not expect their protectorate to be temporary or provisional, and equally clear that there would be Moroccan resistance. Indeed, the Treaty of Fez had a fairly gory reception within the city itself. Almost as the ink on the treaty was drying, 73 French people, mostly military men, were lynched and their bodies grotesquely treated as a prelude to a full-scale attack on the city by dissident tribesmen. The French Army

Above: French military action against rebels in the field often involved long hours of reconnaissance and observation. These soldiers man a 7.5mm 1924 M29 light machine gun. Below: French troops move at speed in pursuit of rebels.

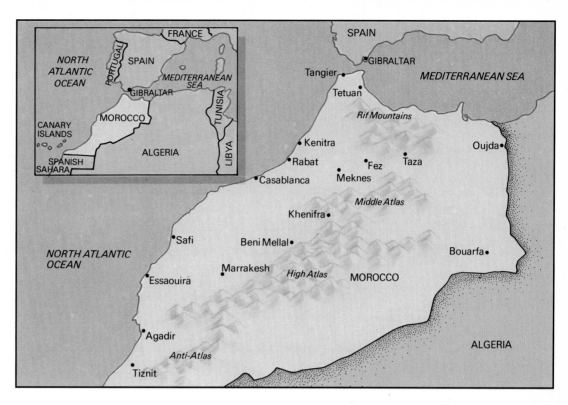

proved quite capable of dealing with such problems and, indeed, of suppressing the more long-standing threats to the sultanate which existed in the south of the country and around Taza. They showed themselves well able to provide the military security that the sultan had bargained for when he had agreed to ask for their assistance.

Many Moroccans admit that there was much that was good about the French protectorate. Education, the construction of roads, the improvement of public services, the establishment of phosphate mining and some industry, were all benefits brought by the French. The darker side of the achievement, however, was the emphasis on French culture and language at the expense of Moroccan and Arabic, together with the introduction of French settlers. The numbers of these new colonists were always tiny in proportion to the indigenous population, but they made Moroccan nationalists fear that their country was destined to become a province of France and, in the final struggle, increased French willingness to fight.

Many of the 44 years of the protectorate were calm enough, but there was never complete freedom from war or the rumbling of revolt. Probably the largest operation undertaken was against the Berber resistance leader Mohammed Abd-el-Krim, who established a 'Republic of the Rif' in 1921. Abd-el-Krim had the distinction of inflicting major defeats on both Spanish and French armies, so no chances were taken in the 1926 campaign: the French deployed 325,000 men commanded by 80 generals and one marshal, while the Spanish put 100,000 men in the field. Abd-el-Krim was captured and exiled but resistance smouldered on in the Anti-Atlas mountains until 1934. Despite this, Morocco was never a drain on French military resources; the contribution of Moroccan troops to the French Army in two world wars far outweighed the difficulties of policing their country.

It was evident that old-fashioned types of tribal resistance would never loosen the French grip and, in any case, a new type of nationalist was born in the

Below: Moroccan police and soldiers try to keep an angry crowd in order in 1955 as a convoy of French dignitaries passes through.

1930s. Intellectual university graduates such as Ahmed Balafrej in Rabat and Allal al-Fasi in Fez put forward demands for reform but, when these demands were contemptuously ignored, they began to adopt a harder line and espouse the use of violence. In 1937 a quarrel between French settlers and Moroccan farmers over water resulted in a major confrontation in which shots were fired. The police and military suffered casualties but killed 13 demonstrators and wounded 100 more. Allal al-Fasi was deported and detained for nine years.

The gathering storm was postponed by the outbreak of war in Europe in 1939 and the young Sultan Mohammed V – himself already suspected of complicity with the nationalists – called for total support for France. Moroccan forces served with distinction

in the French Army but the course of the war undermined the matchless prestige of the French military. The shattering collapse of the French in 1940, followed by the appearance of huge, magnificently equipped Anglo-American armies in Morocco, served to break the illusion of invincibility which had hitherto surrounded the French military and had convinced the people of Morocco that resistance was hopeless. By January 1944 the various opponents of French rule showed that they had digested the lessons of the war and were prepared for action.

The first move in this new situation was significant enough. The nationalist movements reorganised themselves to form a new party calling itself Istiqlal (Independence). The French responded by arresting the leaders of the new party, including Balafrej. However, signs of the troubles to come were immediately apparent when widespread disorder and rioting broke out in protest at the arrest of the Istiqlal leaders. In Fez alone, at least 30 Muslims were killed before order was restored.

With the Istiqlal leaders in prison, the standard of revolt was taken up by the sultan himself. In 1947 he visited the international city of Tangier, passing

through the Spanish zone to reach it. Everywhere he went he was received with open and tumultuous acclaim, much to the embarrassment of the protecting powers. Fear that the situation was becoming unmanageable led to the recall of the French resident general and his replacement by a strongman in the person of General Alphonse Juin – himself of French colonial stock from Algeria. As the sultan's revolt increased to the extent of refusing to sign draft decrees, Juin began to work with dissident tribal chiefs who saw rich pickings for themselves in opposition to the sultan.

Chief among Juin's new allies was Thami al-Glaoui, whose family fief had been greatly enlarged through cooperation with the French in the High Atlas and who was sometimes known as the Pasha of Marrakesh. He and others were able to make some pretence at a tribal revolt against the Istiqlal, which gave Juin a chance to surround the sultan with troops 'for his protection' and coerce him into disavowing

Above: As the riots in Marrakesh became more violent, the widespread deployment of troops on the streets became commonplace. Here angry crowds protest at the shooting of civilians by French forces.

the nationalists. After this success, General Juin was transferred to high command in Europe and succeeded by General Guillaume who took an even harder line and promised, soon after his arrival, that he would 'make the nationalists eat straw'.

A nation in revolt

In January 1952, hundreds of Istiqlal activists were arrested and detained by the French, who were planning to move against the sultan himself. In August 1953 al-Glaoui called for more firmness from the French, who responded by deporting the sultan and his family and replacing him on the throne with an elderly, more malleable member of the royal family. For a few days the French authorities were able to congratulate themselves on their move, but then the country rose in revolt.

The elderly sultan only just escaped assassination when he attended Friday prayer and was soon virtually confined to his palace. All over the rest of the country, nationalists resorted to tactics of terrorism. Because their leaders were in prison, these attacks were sporadic and dislocated but, where they could, the nationalists killed Frenchmen and 'loyal' Moroccans. The French colonists were not to be outshone when it came to murder and they struck back by killing nationalist leaders and liberal Frenchmen.

It was a battle that could only be won by the Muslims. The mounting disorders meant there was an increasing need for troops, something France found difficult to supply due to the fact that she was heavily committed to the war in Indochina which was not going well and was soon to end in the humiliation of Dien Bien Phu (May 1954). Further problems were caused by the rising in Algeria on 1 November 1954 and demands from the governor general there for more troops. In the long run, Algeria was much more important to France as it was not a protectorate like Morocco, but designated a part of France itself and one tenth of its population consisted of European colonists (*colons*). The resources to fight the Moroccan nationalists did not exist, so Guillaume was replaced by a more liberal resident general who had the task of placating the dissidents with reforms. His efforts were sabotaged by the colonists and the violence dragged on until 18 August 1955, when an horrific massacre of Frenchmen at Wadi Zem illustrated the point that the country had become ungovernable.

The French now made concessions with great haste and tried to persuade the puppet sultan to relinquish his throne, but all the while they negotiated and legislated, the security situation deteriorated. Isolated killings and bombings continued, reinforced by the fact that a Moroccan guerrilla army had been formed and took the field against French garrisons on the Rif. By the end of October, the Pasha of Marrakesh had declared his support for the exiled sultan. The French now had little choice but to agree to independence and the return of Mohammed V, and negotiated to that effect. On 18 November 1955, the sultan returned and the violence petered out almost instantly. In March 1956 the Treaty of Fez was annulled and Morocco was granted independence. There is no doubt that embarrassing commitments elsewhere had undermined French confidence, but equally little argument that the Moroccans would not have won independence if they had not fought for it.

P. J. Banyard

Key Weapons

SOVIET FIGHTERS

Part 1

At the end of World War II the Soviet Air Force's front-line fighter strength consisted of some 8000 aircraft, and these were backed by substantial reserves. All of these aircraft were piston-engined fighters and for the remainder of the 1940s they formed the mainstay of the Soviet fighter regiments. The most important types were the Lavochkin La-9, La-11, Yakovlev Yak-9U and Yak-9P. As they had been developed late in the war, they differed from the majority of previous Soviet fighters in being of all-metal rather than wooden construction. Nonetheless, at a time when the air forces of the major Western powers were rapidly converting to jet fighters, the Soviet machines were outdated if not entirely anachronistic.

The Soviet Union was well aware of the urgent need to develop a jet fighter aircraft. Amongst its war booty had been German jet engines and jet-powered aircraft, together with large numbers of captured engineers and technicians. A Messerschmitt Me-262 twin-jet fighter was evaluated in 1945 and consideration was given to putting the type into production for the Soviet Air Force. However, it was felt that the design was too complex for Soviet needs, lacking the simplicity and ruggedness that Soviet pilots and groundcrew had come to expect from their aircraft. Consequently it was decided to give priority to a home-designed jet fighter.

The German BMW 003A and Junkers Jumo 004B jet engines had been put into production in the Soviet Union as the RD-20 and RD-10 respectively and so were available to power the first Soviet jet fighters. They were the Mikoyan-Gurevich MiG-9 and Yakovlev Yak-15, both of which made their first flights on 24 April 1946. The MiG-9 fighter was powered by two RD-20s mounted side-by-side and fed by a nose intake. Each engine developed 1760lb of thrust, giving the MiG-9 a maximum speed of 900km/h (560mph) at 5000m (16,400ft). This straight-wing, all metal fighter carried an armament of two 23mm and one 37mm cannon mounted in the nose. Some 550 MiG-9s were built during 1948-49.

Unlike the MiG-9, which was an entirely original design, the Yak-15 jet fighter was simply an adaptation of the piston-engined Yak-3 airframe. A new fuselage was designed to house a single RD-10 jet engine, while the wing, undercarriage and tail surfaces of the original design were retained. After 280 Yak-15s had been built, production switched to the

improved Yak-17 (Nato code-name Feather) with a nosewheel undercarriage in place of the original, unsatisfactory tailwheel-type and a more powerful RD-10A powerplant. Maximum speed of the Yak-17 was 830km/h (515mph) at 3000m (9840ft) and armament for both Yak fighters was two 23mm cannon. The Yak-17UTI was a two-seat conversion trainer built in parallel with the fighter and total production of the two versions was 430 aircraft.

The first-generation of Soviet fighters only served

Previous page: Soviet pilots and MiG-21s in eastern Europe. Above: A MiG-15bis of the Czechoslovak Air Force. Below: A MiG-15 in North Korean markings. Bottom: The Junkers Jumo 004B engine powered the Yak-15.

MiG-15 (Fagot)

Type Single-seat fighter
Dimensions Span 10.08m (33ft 1in); length 10.86m (35ft 8in); height 3.4m (11ft 2in)
Weight Empty 3400kg (7500lb); maximum take-off 5112kg (11,270lb)
Powerplant One RD-45 turbojet

Performance Maximum speed 1055km/h (656mph) at 3050m (10,000ft)
Range Combat range 900km (560 miles); maximum ferry range 2000km (1250 miles)
Ceiling 15,500m (51,000ft)

Armament Two 23mm NS-23 cannon, one 37mm N-37 cannon; underwing hardpoints for a maximum of 500kg (1100lb) stores

Above: A two-seat conversion trainer MiG-15UTI of the East German Air Force is prepared for flight. Armament consisted of a single 12.7mm machine gun or a 23mm cannon.

Two Soviet-built MiG-17s of the Czechoslovak Air Force: the MiG-17PF Fresco-D (below) was a late variant with more advanced electronics while the MiG-17 Fresco-A (bottom) was the initial production version shown here with a 400 litre (88 gallon) drop tank.

in small numbers alongside the far more numerous piston-engined types. They were essentially interim equipment, intended to give Soviet pilots early experience of jet operations pending the availability of more capable jet fighters. The powerplants for the new breed of Soviet fighters were made available by the British government, which supplied the Soviet Union with Rolls-Royce Nene 2 and Derwent 5 engines in 1947. These were immediately placed in (unlicensed) production as the RD-45 and RD-500. The latter engine was used to power the Yak-23 (Nato code-name Flora), a manoeuvrable and fast climbing straight-wing fighter, which saw little service with the Soviet Air Force but was exported to the east European satellite countries.

Speeding Fagot

The RD-45 engine, together with German-derived research into swept-back wings, made possible the design of the MiG-15 (Nato code-name Fagot). This was one of the most effective fighter aircraft of its era, and at the time of its combat debut in Korea was matched only by the North American F-86 Sabre. The first pre-production examples of the MiG-15 were tested by the Soviet Air Force in the autumn of 1948 and deliveries to the fighter regiments began shortly afterwards. A relatively light fighter with a maximum take-off weight of 5112kg (11,270lb), the MiG-15 had a service ceiling of 15,500m (51,000ft), an initial rate-of-climb of 2760 metres per minute (9050fpm) and reached a top speed of 1055km/h (656mph) at 3050m (10,000ft).

Its excellent rate of climb and service ceiling were, however, offset by various shortcomings in the design: control became difficult at high air speeds and a 'snaking' movement, which developed at speeds above Mach 0.86, made gun aiming difficult. The MiG-15's rate of turn was good, but if turned too tightly the fighter would flick into a spin. Conversely its rate of roll was poor. In comparison with its principal antagonist over Korea, the F-86 Sabre, the MiG-15's acceleration and altitude performance were superior. The Soviet fighter's poor showing in the Korean air battles – 78 Sabres shot down for the loss of 792 MiG-15s – was due more to the inexperience of the pilots than to the shortcomings of the aircraft.

In 1950 the improved MiG-15bis was put into production. This differed from the original fighter in having a 2700kg (5952lb) thrust Klimov VK-1 powerplant (an improved version of the Nene) and a better radio and instrumentation. Armament of both versions comprised a 37mm cannon with 40 rounds of ammunition and two 23mm cannon each with 80 rounds. Up to 500kg (1100lb) of ordnance could be carried on underwing hardpoints, but auxiliary fuel tanks were more usually carried. Production of the MiG-15 totalled more than 15,000 aircraft.

The MiG-17 (Nato code-name Fresco) was an aerodynamically refined version of the MiG-15, which it began to replace from 1952 onwards. The wing was entirely redesigned, having more sweep-back and a thinner section, the rear fuselage was lengthened and the tailplane's span and sweepback was increased. Early versions of the MiG-17 retained the VK-1 powerplant, but the MiG-17F introduced the VK-1F fitted with a simple afterburner. The MiG-17F was the most widely used variant, this model having a maximum speed with reheat of

1145km/h (711mph) at 3000m (9800ft) and a service ceiling of 16,460m (54,000ft). Armament remained the three-cannon installation used on the MiG-15.

When the MiG-21 became available in quantity during the early 1960s, the MiG-17 was retained in service as a ground attack aircraft and continued in this role until the end of the 1970s with the Soviet Air Force. Some 8800 were built before production ended in 1957. It was widely exported, seeing combat service in many parts of the world, most notably in the Middle East and Southeast Asia. During the air battles over North Vietnam from 1965 to 1972 the then-obsolescent MiG-17s performed creditably against US fighters. They were generally used to defend North Vietnamese airfields and to attack heavily-laden strike aircraft at low altitudes. Their successes came when they were able to lure the high-performance US fighters into turning dogfights. In the Middle East wars of 1967 and 1973 the MiG-17 was employed as a fighter-bomber by the Arab air forces.

One serious shortcoming of the Soviet fighter forces in the late 1940s was the lack of all-weather capability. This deficiency was made good to some extent in the early 1950s by the development of all-weather versions of the MiG-15 and MiG-17, fitted with Izumrud radar. One of these all-weather fighter conversions, the MiG-17PFU, was armed with four AA-1 Alkali air-to-air missiles (AAMs) to become the Soviet Air Force's first missile-armed interceptor. However, these fighters were essentially stop-gap measures, and the first true all-weather fighter in Soviet service was the Yak-25 (Nato code-name Flashlight) of 1953. Powered by two 2500kg (5500lb) RD-9 turbojets, the Yak-25 reached a maximum speed of Mach 0.9 and a service ceiling of 15,240m (50,000ft). Radar was carried in the fighter's nose with two 37mm cannon mounted beneath the forward fuselage. A pilot and radar operator

Right: A MiG-19, the first Soviet production fighter capable of supersonic performance at level flight. This MiG-19PM was manufactured to act in an interceptor role and was armed with four AA-1 Alkali air-to-air missiles, visible under the leading edge of the plane's wings.

Left: A MiG-17PF Fresco-D. Below: A flight of MiG-17 Fresco-As on patrol. The MiG-17 has had a long service record and gave a good account of itself in the wars in the Middle East and in Vietnam although by the mid-1960s it was clearly obsolete.

MiG-17F (Fresco)

Type Single-seat fighter
Dimensions Span 9.63m (31ft 7in); length 11.09m (36ft 4½in); height 3.35m (11ft)
Weight Empty 4100kg (9040lb); maximum take-off 6700kg (14,770lb)
Powerplant One 3400kg (7500lb) Klimov VK-1F afterburning turbojet

Performance Maximum speed 1145km/h (711mph) at 3000m (9800ft)
Range Maximum ferry range 2250km (1400 miles)
Ceiling 16,460m (54,000ft)

Armament Two 23mm NS-23 cannon, one 37mm N-37 cannon; underwing hardpoints for a maximum of 500kg (1100lb) stores

MiG-19 (Farmer)

Type Single-seat fighter, limited all-weather interceptor

Dimensions Span 9m (29ft 6in); length 12.6m (41ft 4in); height 3.9m (12ft 9½in)

Weight Empty 5172kg (11,402lb); maximum take-off 8900kg (19,620lb)

Powerplant Two 3250kg (7165lb) Tumansky RD-9B afterburning turbojets

Performance Maximum speed Mach 1.4 or 1450km/h (900mph) at 10,000m (33,000ft)

Range Maximum ferry range 2200km (1370 miles)

Ceiling 17,370m (57,000ft)

Armament Three 30mm NR-30 cannon; rocket pods on underwing pylons

Above: A MiG-19P, an uprated variant provided with an Izumrud radar.
Left: A Soviet MiG-19 flies skyward; particular features of this model were its good rate of climb and overall manoeuvrability.

Below: The MiG-19S was a redesign of the initial MiG-19 and had improved flying controls and an all-moving tailplane.

were seated in tandem and additional armament was provided by 55mm unguided air-to-air rockets, carried in a belly pack and in underwing pods.

The Soviet Air Force's first supersonic fighter, the MiG-19 (Nato code-name Farmer) began its service trials in 1953. However, the early production MiG-19F and all-weather MiG-19PF were found to suffer from serious powerplant and structural failures. This necessitated a major redesign of the fighter, and it was not until 1955 that the definitive MiG-19S entered service with the Soviet Air Force's Frontal Aviation and the Air Defence Forces (under the Soviet military system an entirely separate armed service from the air force).

The MiG-19S was powered by two Tumansky RD-9B turbojets and attained a maximum speed of Mach 1.4. Its initial climb rate was 6890 metres per minute (22,640fpm), with a service ceiling of 17,370m (57,000ft). Armament comprised three 30mm cannon, one mounted on the underside of the nose, offset to starboard, and the other two in the wing roots. Because of its high thrust-to-weight ratio and low wing loading the MiG-19S was a very manoeuvrable aircraft with a good initial rate of climb. By comparison with its US Air Force contemporary, the

507

F-100 Super Sabre, the MiG-19 was considered to have a better all-round performance and a harder hitting armament than the former's quartet of 20mm cannon. In 1957 production of the MiG-19 ended in the Soviet Union after some 2500 had been built. A further 850 were manufactured under licence in Czechoslovakia, while an unlicensed version continues to be built by the People's Republic of China as the Shenyang F-6.

Undoubtedly the most famous Soviet postwar fighter, the MiG-21 (Nato code-name Fishbed) first entered service in 1959. It was designed in the aftermath of the Korean War as a high-performance point-defence and air-superiority fighter, with the accent on combat performance at the expense of payload and range. The MiG-21F was a Mach 2 fighter of tailed-delta configuration, powered by a 5770kg (12,670lb) thrust afterburning Tumansky R-11 turbojet. It was armed with one 30mm cannon (with provision for a second) and two AA-2 Atoll infra-red homing AAMs. It was a highly-maneouvrable aircraft, was pleasant to fly and easy to maintain, but did not have an all-weather capability.

During the 1960s and 1970s successive improvements to the basic MiG-21 design sought to overcome some of the type's shortcomings. The MiG-21PF replaced the MiG-21F's simple ranging radar with a more capable search-and-track radar, carried additional fuel in a saddle tank atop the fuselage and introduced the rapid-fire, twin-barrel GSh-23 23mm cannon. The MiG-21PFMA had two additional wing pylons (making four in all, plus one on the fuselage centreline) thus improving the fighter's ground-attack potential by increasing its ordnance load, or allowing four AAMs to be carried. This weight increase required additional power, which was provided by the MiG-21MF's 6620kg (14,550lb) Tumansky R-13 turbojet. The latest MiG-21 variant, the MiG-21bis, has the even more powerful 7500kg (16,500lb) Tumansky R-25 powerplant. Over 500 MiG-21s remain in Soviet Air Force Service.

Top: An experimental variant of the MiG-21 – the Ye-166 – in 1962 set a new world speed record of 2680km/h (1666mph). Above: One of the MiG-21s in service with the Soviet Air Force in 1977. Below: The underside of a MiG-21.

MiG-21bis (Fishbed)

Type Single-seat fighter, ground-attack aircraft
Dimensions Span 7.16m (23ft 6in); length 15.75m (51ft 8in); height 4.49m (14ft 9in)
Weight Empty 6200kg (13,668lb), maximum take-off 10,000kg (22,045lb)
Powerplant One 7500kg (16,500lb) Tumansky R-25 afterburning turbojet

Performance Maximum speed Mach 2 or 2125km/h (1320mph) at 11,000m (36,000ft)
Range Combat radius 500km (310 miles)
Ceiling 15,000m (50,000ft)

Armament One twin-barrel 23mm GSh-23 cannon; four underwing hardpoints for K-13AA-2 Atoll or AA-8 Aphis air-to-air missiles, AS-7 Kerry air-to-surface missiles or unguided rockets

The Suez affair

Why Great Britain and France invaded Egypt

The Suez crisis was one of the major turning points in modern history. It saw the humiliation of two powers that had hitherto been predominant in the Middle East, and President Nasser's escape from complete military disaster firmly established him as the representative of a new order in Arab affairs.

The Suez Canal in 1956 presented all interested parties with problems, for it was a foreign commercial enterprise of immense importance to world trade within the territory of a state wracked by nationalist upheaval and revolution. The failure of the Arab world to prevent the emergence of Israel, the Israeli success in the 1948-49 War, and general dissatisfaction with a corrupt and inefficient monarchy all contributed to a rising tide of revolutionary nationalism in Egypt, a tide that ran particularly strongly in the army.

In 1952 a military coup toppled the unpopular and corrupt King Farouk. General Mohammed Neguib assumed the presidency but was little more than a figurehead – the real power lay in the hands of his prime minister, Colonel Gamal Abdel Nasser. The Revolutionary Command Council demanded a formal end to monarchy, expulsion of the British and reform of the social and economic structure of Egypt along vaguely socialist lines. These policies proved too extreme for the more conservatively-minded Neguib but he was easily outmanoeuvred by Nasser who, within a couple of years, emerged as the virtual head of state.

Nasser was determined that his country should play a full part in international affairs. First, however, it was necessary to rid Egypt of the British military presence, which had its origins in Britain's occupation of Egypt in the 1880s. The British Middle East Headquarters had already been moved to Cyprus, which reflected the declining importance of the Suez Canal as a strategic line of communication after India had become independent. Washington pressed London to be 'reasonable', for US Secretary of State John Foster Dulles was anxious to recruit Nasser into the Western camp.

Terms over Britain's withdrawal were agreed by July 1954. The British were allowed to retain a base maintained by locally contracted labour on a seven-year lease, but the existing garrison was to start the evacuation of its facilities immediately. Agreement was also reached over the Sudan, which was jointly ruled by Britain and Egypt; in the event, the Sudanese chose independence rather than union with Egypt. And so on 31 March 1956, the 2nd Battalion, The Grenadier Guards and D Squadron, The Life Guards embarked at Port Said. Their departure brought 74 years of military presence to a close.

In April 1955, Nasser had attended the Bandung Conference, embraced the ideologies of the non-aligned world, and returned to Cairo determined to create a neutral Arab bloc under Egyptian leadership. In the process he succeeded in alienating the major Western powers one by one. Radio Cairo kept up a constant tirade of propaganda against the Baghdad

Below: The Suez Canal had long been crucial to British interests in the Middle East and Asia. Britain was the largest single shareholder in the Suez Canal Company and used the waterway more than any other nation. By taking over the canal in 1956 President Nasser of Egypt openly challenged Britain's position in the Middle East.

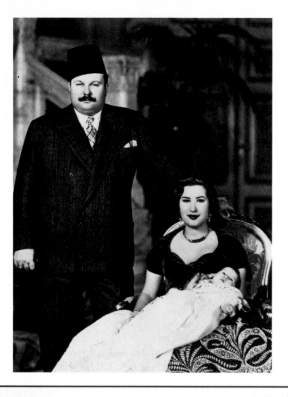

Left: King Farouk of Egypt poses for an official photograph with Queen Narriman and their newly born son. Farouk, profoundly unpopular, was deposed in the military coup of July 1952. Below: Anti-British feeling in Cairo. The banner reads: 'Gallows await the necks of the British.'

Pact, which angered the United States, and Nasser's support for the Mau Mau rebels in Kenya and the nationalists in Algeria made him deeply unpopular in Britain and France. Because of this, the West refused to grant military aid to Egypt, but Nasser still hoped that financial assistance would be forthcoming for the building of the Aswan High Dam. Although the Western powers initially agreed to fund it, the offer was rescinded on 19 July 1956, in part because of doubts that the Egyptian economy could bear the burden of debt on the $1400 million project. A week later, on 26 July, Nasser nationalised the Anglo-French Suez Canal Company as a means of financing the dam. By this act he set in train the events that were to lead to war.

Britain was bound to contest Nasser's actions for she was both the largest shareholder in the company, the profits from which exceeded £35 million annually, and the biggest single user of the canal. France, too, had a large investment in the canal. Furthermore, the Suez Canal was the subject of an international treaty signed in 1888 whereby freedom of navigation was guaranteed by the signatories for all states, irrespective of flag, in time of war and peace, and one of the first acts of the Nasser regime had been to refuse passage to Israeli shipping, a blatant contravention of the treaty.

This direct challenge to Britain's interests caused many to argue that Nasser should be 'taught a lesson'. Prime Minister Sir Anthony Eden's firm stand against 'giving in to fascism' enjoyed a large measure of international support, too, for maritime powers had a vested interest in free passage through the canal. There were also a number of Arab states that were not

Right: Prime Minister Sir Anthony Eden bids farewell to US Secretary of State John Foster Dulles after the Suez Canal conference, which was held in London in August 1956. Below: Egypt's President Gamal Abdel Nasser (seated third from right) with other military personnel in 1955. By this time Nasser had shown himself to be a forceful head of state eager to promote Arab unity under Egyptian leadership.

in the least averse to the radical Nasser being humiliated or even toppled.

American attitudes were, from the outset, more ambivalent and were not helped by the strained relations between Secretary of State John Foster Dulles and Eden. In part the United States favoured a strong reaction because of their own interests in the Panama Canal, and Dulles had no sympathy for Nasser's non-aligned stance. But Dulles did not want to see an over-reaction, which might drive Nasser and indignant Arabs into the Soviet fold.

A diplomatic solution?

The late summer of 1956 saw a flurry of diplomatic activity. Britain convened a conference in London, attended by the major maritime powers and the signatories of the 1888 treaty, in which it was proposed that the canal should be nationalised. Robert Menzies, Australia's prime minister and Commonwealth elder statesman, led a delegation to Cairo to place the proposals before Nasser, who turned them down.

In some desperation the United States proposed a Suez Canal User's Association (SCUA) whose members would convoy their ships through the canal and collect their own tolls. Dulles then had second thoughts, fearing that the British and the French might use SCUA to create an international incident. On 5 October Britain and France took the issue to the United Nations Security Council. They proposed that control of the canal should rest with an international body. Initial private discussions seemed promising, but neither Britain nor France was prepared to guarantee publicly that force would not be used to protect their interests. The Soviet Union vetoed the Anglo-French scheme.

Convinced that all the diplomatic channels had been exhausted, and believing that the United States would remain at least benevolently neutral, the Brit-

ish and French determined upon a military solution – and shed all their international support in the process. Britain had hoped to solve the crisis in a week, but neither the armed force nor the military expertise was available to enable this objective to be attained. Instead reservists were recalled to the colours and joint Anglo-French command structures were established in order to prepare an expeditionary force.

In October Israel entered the picture. A number of secret meetings were held in France in an attempt to reach agreement with the Israelis, who were becoming increasingly concerned about guerrilla outrages perpetrated by the Palestinian fedayeen (freedom fighters) from sanctuaries in Sinai. The Israelis wanted Britain to bomb Egypt's air bases, where the Soviet-supplied air force was deployed, so that she could attack into Sinai.

The official position was that war between Israel and Egypt would present the Anglo-French forces with the opportunity to intervene. A contingency plan was agreed whereby, on the outbreak of hostilities, the belligerents would be presented with an ultimatum to accept a ceasefire and withdraw from the canal. This would allow the Anglo-French to occupy, as a temporary measure, Port Said, Ismailiya and Suez, key points along the canal. The Israelis would accept but the Egyptians would certainly reject such a ceasefire. The way would then be clear for the Royal Air Force to bomb Egypt's air bases as a prelude to an armed intervention.

By late October, in the full glare of international publicity, an armada of transports and warships gathered in the eastern Mediterranean while airborne and air force units were deployed to British and French bases. On 29 October 1956 the Israeli Defence Forces launched Operation Kadesh and crossed into Sinai on four fronts. The Suez War had begun.

Eric Morris

Above: Guy Mollet, the French Prime Minister, collaborated with the British in the Suez venture. His hope was that Nasser would be toppled, so ending Egyptian support for the FLN revolutionaries fighting French rule in Algeria.

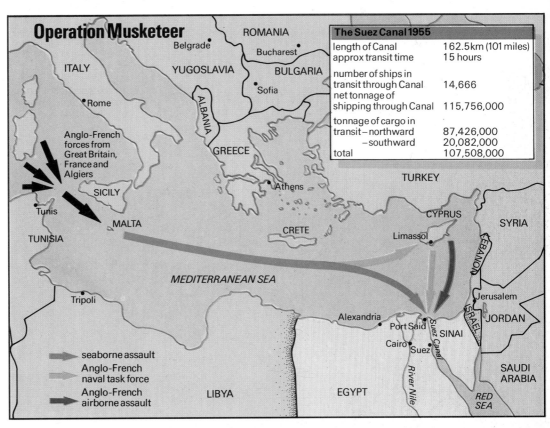

Operation Musketeer

The Suez Canal 1955	
length of Canal	162.5km (101 miles)
approx transit time	15 hours
number of ships in transit through Canal	14,666
net tonnage of shipping through Canal	115,756,000
tonnage of cargo in transit – northward	87,426,000
– southward	20,082,000
total	107,508,000

Anglo-French forces from Great Britain, France and Algiers

ROMANIA
Belgrade
Bucharest
ITALY
YUGOSLAVIA
BULGARIA
Rome
Sofia
ALBANIA
GREECE
TURKEY
Athens
SICILY
Tunis
CYPRUS
MALTA
CRETE
Limassol
SYRIA
TUNISIA
LEBANON
MEDITERRANEAN SEA
Tripoli
Jerusalem
ISRAEL
JORDAN
Alexandria
Port Said
SINAI
Cairo
Suez
Suez Canal
River Nile
SAUDI ARABIA
LIBYA
EGYPT
RED SEA

seaborne assault
Anglo-French naval task force
Anglo-French airborne assault

In with the paras

The air assault on Port Said

The original plan to restore the status of the Suez Canal, code-named Hamilcar and later Musketeer, envisaged the capture of Alexandria followed by an attack on Cairo. This would be achieved by an airborne assault on a ridge southwest of Alexandria, backed up by a seaborne landing. However, mainly for political reasons, in that a local operation merely to seize the Suez Canal itself would be more acceptable internationally, the objective was changed to Port Said. The operation was to be in three phases. Initially, air attacks would destroy the Egyptian Air Force on the ground, there would then be an airborne/seaborne assault, and finally an armoured column would advance to secure the length of the canal while remaining resistance was suppressed by air attack.

British troops available for the operation included

3 Royal Marine Commando Brigade and the 16th Independent Parachute Brigade. France allocated the 10th Colonial Parachute Division and the 7th Light Mechanised Division. The airborne assault would be launched from Cyprus, while the amphibious forces would sail from Britain, France and Algeria, link up at Malta and then move to Egypt. Originally it had been hoped to launch the operation in mid-September, but planning changes, problems of coordination, as well as complications on the political front, delayed the offensive until early November.

As far as the airborne forces were concerned, the British 1st and 3rd Battalions, The Parachute Regiment were already in Cyprus when the crisis blew up, engaged in counter-insurgency operations against EOKA. During August, therefore, the remainder of

Above: Brigadier M.A.H. Butler, commander of the 16th Independent Parachute Brigade, is shown in Cyprus immediately prior to embarking for Egypt. Below: Canopies fill the air as British paras land at Gamil. Above right: Safely down, paras swop helmets for berets.

The 'Maroon machine' goes into action

'Nicosia, Nov 5. About half an hour after dawn today British and French parachute troops began landings from the air in the Port Said area. Throughout the early hours of the night, lorries in a steady stream brought men wearing the maroon beret to the lines of transport aircraft parked along the edges of the runways of an airfield in Cyprus. At another airfield in the island similar movements of French troops were taking place. In the glare of orange floodlights the men made adjustments to their packs and parachute harness, standing in little groups alongside the aircraft...

'Precisely at 0445 hours the engines of the first aircraft broke silence, and the roar was taken up in succession along the tarmac. The night was turned into a booming, glaring, orange fog as engine exhaust blew dust across the airfield and into the path of the floodlights.... Then at 15-second intervals, with longer pauses between the larger transports, the British pilots gave their engines full power and took off in an evenly spaced stream.

'As each aircraft took off, its particular cluster of red and green navigation lights seemed among all the noise on the ground to be coloured stars floating silently away. It was 0515 hours. The airfield was silent.... The airborne spearhead of the landings was on its way. It was, as their commander phrased it earlier, "the Maroon machine going into action".'

Report in The Times, *6 November 1956.*

the 16th Independent Parachute Brigade, including reservists, was concentrated there. One immediate problem was that both 1 and 3 Para, employed as they were in an infantry role, lacked current parachute training and so, once the rest of the brigade had arrived in Cyprus, they were flown back to England for a quick refresher course. By contrast, the French airborne regiments had seen much active service in their proper role in Indochina and Algeria.

Going in at dawn

The seaborne assault, preceded by an hour's naval bombardment of coastal defences, would go in 35 minutes after sunrise, and then, 30 minutes later, the parachute drops would be made. Apart from the fact that these would be in the Port Said area, and were designed to get a grip on the town before the Egyptians could attack, the precise objectives remained in doubt almost until the last moment. A major limiting factor was the restricted capacity of the airfields in Cyprus. This meant that only two battalions' worth of troops could be used in the initial assault. There were also severe logistical problems to be faced by the British which, in the main, did not affect the French.

Suez caught the British airborne forces at an unfortunate time. Apart from the lack of recent airborne experience, there were severe inadequacies in air transport. Most airborne forces, including the French, had gone over to aircraft with rear boom doors, which meant that heavy equipment could be carried (and dropped from) within the aircraft. The British had such an aircraft, the Beverley, on order, but there had been technical delays in bringing it into service. They were consequently forced to rely on obsolete Hastings and Valettas with side doors. However they had already adapted their ancillary equipment (harness, dropping gear and indeed transport) as well as training, to the Beverley. They therefore had to re-train in the old methods, scrounge obsolete equipment and readapt to underslung loads, as well as obtain wartime jeeps to replace their newly issued Austin Champs (which would not fit in either transport).

The French, with their Nordatlas aircraft, had no such problems, and their recent operational experience meant that they could drop a stick of 17 men in 10 seconds. The Hastings, by contrast, could cope with only 15 men spread over 20 seconds. This meant that, provided the conditions were right, the French stick would not be dispersed by more than 0.8km (½ mile)

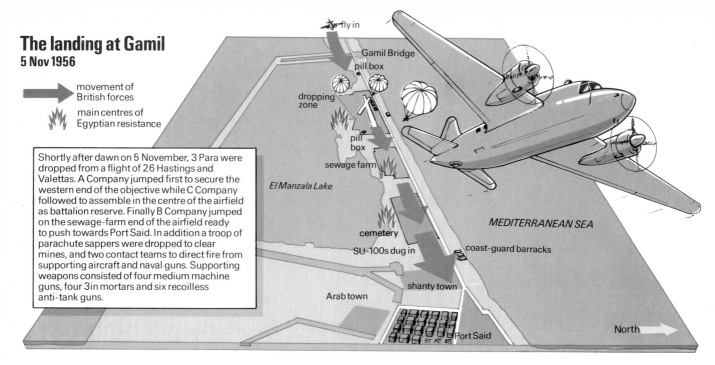

The landing at Gamil
5 Nov 1956

→ movement of British forces

main centres of Egyptian resistance

Shortly after dawn on 5 November, 3 Para were dropped from a flight of 26 Hastings and Valettas. A Company jumped first to secure the western end of the objective while C Company followed to assemble in the centre of the airfield as battalion reserve. Finally B Company jumped on the sewage-farm end of the airfield ready to push towards Port Said. In addition a troop of parachute sappers were dropped to clear mines, and two contact teams to direct fire from supporting aircraft and naval guns. Supporting weapons consisted of four medium machine guns, four 3in mortars and six recoilless anti-tank guns.

fly in

Gamil Bridge
pill box

dropping zone

pill box

sewage farm

El Manzala Lake

MEDITERRANEAN SEA

cemetery

SU-100s dug in

coast-guard barracks

shanty town

Arab town

Port Said

North →

on the ground, but for the British it could be as much as 1.6km (1 mile). Also, the French paras had folding butts on their weapons which enabled them to be carried across the chest, so permitting them to give suppressive fire during the descent – unlike the British, who had their weapons strapped to weapons-containers dangling beneath them.

On the evening of 31 October 1956, with the Israelis three days into Operation Kadesh, the first phase of Musketeer was launched, when Valiants and Canberras from Malta and Cyprus bombed Egyptian airfields. These attacks continued for the next four days and succeeded in virtually destroying the Egyptian Air Force, isolating Port Said and preventing any reinforcement. Meanwhile, the 16th Parachute Brigade, who apart from their commander knew nothing of their part in the operation, had been sent into the Troodos mountains of Cyprus in an anti-EOKA drive for six days as a cover operation. They did not return until 29 October, when they were confined to barracks.

On 31 October the French proposed that, in view of the success of Phase I and the Israeli advance, Port Said could be seized by air assault alone, with the British dropping on Gamil airfield, the Royal Marine Commandos making a helicopter assault on the bridges south of the town, and the French seizing Port Fuad. All three would then turn inwards to take Port Said. The British were less optimistic, however. They thought that the Egyptians had been reinforcing Port Said, and that the air defences would make the use of helicopters very dangerous. The French, impatient for action, then agreed to take over the Royal Marines' task.

On 1 November Brigadier Butler of 16 Para briefed Lieutenant-Colonel Paul Crook, commanding 3 Para which had been selected for the initial assault. There followed a period of frantic last-minute preparations for the attack, which was to go in on 5 November – 24 hours before the amphibious landings. 3 Para's objective, Gamil airfield, was a long narrow strip 2400m long and 800m wide (1½ miles by ½ mile) with water on both sides. Preceded by fighter ground attack, the Valettas would take the lead with the Hastings, carrying the heavy equipment, following behind. The

troops were to drop from heights of between 183 and 245m (600 and 800 feet); the heavy equipment would be dropped from 300m (1000 feet) and over in order to minimise the risk of accidents. The aircraft would fly in in pairs, and it was hoped to have the entire force on the ground within eight minutes.

Colonel Pierre Château-Jobert's 2nd Colonial Parachute Regiment (RCP) had the task of seizing the bridges. Their first objectives were the twin Raswa bridges, which crossed the Interior Basin waterway and formed a vital link in the Port Said – Suez route. It was a very tight dropping zone (DZ), 460 by 185m (500 by 200 yards) and bounded by water, roads and buildings. Château-Jobert elected to jump from 90m (300 feet), virtually the minimum safe height for a descent, with aircraft also in pairs, but more closely bunched than the British. He estimated he would have his men down in four minutes.

In the early hours of Monday 5 November both units were driven to their respective airfields, 3 Para to Nicosia and 2 RCP to Tymbou. Take off began at dawn. Once in the air, the British struck another problem. The Hastings Mark 2s were carrying heavy equipment only and had taken off before the Mark 1s, laden with troops and light equipment. It had been thought that the latter would overtake the former, but the drag produced by the underslung loads meant that this did not occur. Although some of the heavy equipment did arrive on the DZ before the troops, there ultimately was no cause for alarm.

Surprisingly little was known about the Egyptian

Below: French paras from 2 RCP take cover behind earthworks after landing in the Raswan area, which was stiffly defended by Egyptian infantry.

defences apart from the fact that, of the three battalions in the Port Said zone, one was responsible for protecting the area around Gamil from both air and sea assault and there were a number of supporting weapons capable of bringing down fire onto the airfield. Accordingly, 3 Para only had a vague idea of what opposition they might expect. Nevertheless, they managed to get down in 10 minutes – though one or two of the Hastings Mark 2s had to make a second run in order to ensure a safe landing for the heavier equipment.

Falling casualties

The air defences were not as strong as feared, but even so nine aircraft were damaged. As for the paras themselves, two were blown out across the sea and took some time to get ashore, one was killed when he landed on a minefield, and a fourth was injured when he landed on top of the control tower; a number also suffered minor injuries from smallarms fire during the descent. A Company secured the northwest end of the airfield with little difficulty, but B Company, which landed literally on the heads of the Egyptian defence forces, had a slightly more difficult time in seizing the Port Said end. Nevertheless, the employment of a continuous 'cab rank' of support aircraft helped to secure the airfield within 30 minutes, at which point 3 Para set off towards Port Said, with reinforcements in Cyprus standing by for the second lift.

2 RCP actually managed to get down in their bogey time of four minutes, but they received a very hot welcome from units of Egyptian infantry, machine guns and Bofors anti-aircraft guns. They, too, used the 'cab rank' system but, unlike the British, exercised control from an aerial command post run by General Gilles, commanding French airborne operations. Although his aircraft was rocked from time to time by anti-aircraft fire, Gilles remained overhead for most of the day, directing operations on the ground. After some tough fighting, 2 RCP managed to capture the western Raswan bridge intact, although the other had been demolished. The route south from Suez was now ready to exploit at a cost of just 10 French casualties.

While 3 Para pressed on slowly along the coast towards Port Said, encountering stiff opposition en route, stores plus 3 Para's fourth company, for which there had not been room on the first lift, were dropped into Gamil. At the same time a helicopter shuttle from HMS *Bulwark* and HMS *Albion*, 240km (150 miles)

Above: After a successful military operation, ended only as a result of international diplomacy, French troops look out over the western breakwater at Port Said.

off the coast, evacuated the wounded, both British and Egyptian.

During the afternoon, the French dropped a further battalion from 2 RCP (under Lieutenant-Colonel Fossey-François) south of Port Fuad. Although fired on as soon as they landed they quickly seized the salt pans to the south and moved north into the town, capturing the police station, while the majority of the defenders fled across the ferry stage to the east bank of the canal. At this point Colonel Château-Jobert received a telephone call at his headquarters at the waterworks. Apparently, the Egyptian commander was willing to negotiate a ceasefire. Chateau-Jobert then contacted Brigadier Butler.

While the two worked out terms, a signal was sent to General Stockwell, the Land Task Force Commander, in HMS *Tyne*, requesting a cessation of all air attacks in the area. After negotiations, during which Butler and Château-Jobert demanded that the garrison troops should lay down their arms and march out of the town, the ceasefire eventually came to nothing. Nasser had taken encouragement from a note from Soviet Premier Nikolai Bulganin to the British and French prime ministers that Russia was prepared to assist the Egyptians, and ordered the fight to continue. Crates of Russian weapons were opened and the contents issued to the local populace. Nevertheless, the night passed comparatively peacefully, with only the occasional outburst of smallarms fire, and, as dawn broke, the airborne forces eagerly awaited the imminent amphibious assault. **Charles Messenger**

Forward observer

It was into this inferno that we were headed as the buffaloes waddled forwards. First to swim off, we were on the ramp before it was fully lowered, but we plopped safely off the end into calm water. Just as we did so, an ear-splitting crash and a vicious blast of air knocked me sideways from where I was standing in the bows of the amphibian. I ducked below the gunwale, thinking that a shell had landed on *Suvla's* bows. Everybody else in the buffalo was already sitting down, unable to see what was going on, so my precipitate dive closely following the crash could not have re-assured them; and it was some seconds before I'd recovered myself sufficiently to realize that the blast and noise had been caused by the forward turret of HMS *Decoy*, which had crept level with *Suvla* and then stopped only twenty yards to starboard to fire her

Douglas M.J. Clark had been on the army reserve for just six weeks when he was recalled for service in August 1956 as the Suez crisis developed. A highly experienced Forward Observation Officer, Clark went ashore at Port Said with the first assault waves of Royal Marine Commandos in order to direct offshore naval gunfire. In this extract from his book Suez Touchdown *he describes the initial landing.*

66 'The men of Forty-two Commando are about to go,' he said. 'We all wish them the best of luck and God speed. Three cheers for the Commando! Hip, hip...' Wherever they were, about the ship, the sailors cheered, led by the stentorian voice of their captain. It was a touching moment. Even Colonel Peter's voice betrayed a certain amount of emotion as he in his turn spoke into the microphone. 'Forty-two Commando, I know you'd like to thank the captain and crew of *Suvla* for looking after us so well this last week, and for their good wishes. Three cheers for *Suvla*!'

We cheered with all our might. The shouting gave us an opportunity to blow off steam, thereby loosening taut nerves. By the time it was over, the bow doors had creaked open and the ramp was going down. Above the ramp I could see a strip of blue sky. It was the beginning of a glorious day.

But as the ramp lowered and I could see more, the impression suddenly altered. We were close to land – far too close for an invading convoy. Barely half a mile away was the water's edge and the beach, blotted out by rolling clouds of smoke; grey smoke from shell bursts and brown smoke from fires. As shells landed the smoke was pin-pricked with flashes, while here and there fierce red flames showed where the lines of wooden beach huts were on fire. The thud of the guns added to the confusion, and screaming aircraft plummeted earthwards, their guns and rockets blasting.

Above: Port Said, 1956. The coastal landing zones of the British force are to the right of the white bathing huts. In the distance is Gamil airstrip where the British paras made their drop. Left: The White Ensign is raised after the Navy House in Port Said had been captured.

main armament. An unexpected multi-gun salvo from naval 4.5s just sixty feet from one's right ear is liable to be a little stupefying; but even this didn't prevent me from feeling extremely foolish.

I stood up again. My job was to control gunfire, and in order to control I had to see, and in order to see I had to stand up. Small wonder that being the only one doing so, I should feel conspicuous. Perhaps something of my feeling must have conveyed itself to the Marine training major who was in command of this first wave of the assault; when I looked behind me I saw he had hoisted himself up in the stern of the buffalo and was sitting there, unconcernedly smoking a cigarette. As he saw me look at him, he gave a huge grin and a thumbs-up sign. His action in putting himself in the same position as me was a gesture of comradeship which can only be imperfectly understood by those who have never been in the same position. Certainly it did me good to see him there.

'Message from *Decoy*, sir,' said Symons, handing me a signal form.

'From *Decoy* to FOB 5. What do you think of the Casino? I got it with my first round. Everytime a cokernut. Good luck.'

I looked at the Casino. It was blazing merrily at the end of its stubby pier.

'Please reply,' I said, searching my mind for something to say. 'Excellent *rouge et noir* effect. From that range you could have knocked it over with a croupier's rake.' My poor joke took Symons a long time to get down on paper. While he was busy, I looked about me. Every ship was flying a battle ensign, but *Suvla* was flying the biggest of all. From somewhere she had unearthed a piece of bunting the size of a tennis-court. So big was it, that it trailed in the water astern, and could only have been made, initially, for decorating the entire front of Admiralty Arch at the Coronation.

There was very little enemy fire coming back at us. It was a comfort to realize this. Certainly it made my job much easier, for I hadn't to be constantly on guard against flying splinters and shell bursts. Out in front of us a motor-cutter, manned by Marines, swept in towards the coast, looking for sea mines and underwater obstacles. Satisfied that there was nothing to impede us, she turned and darted out again to take up her station between the leading waves.

Striving to hold my binoculars steady, I found I had to adopt a nautical sway in rhythm with the buffalo, which unaccountably tended to plunge fore and aft in the almost indiscernible wavelets. It was as much as I could do to keep the beach in view. The four hundred yards allotted to us were being plastered with shells, and I felt, rather than observed, that the area would be free of the enemy. But to our right, the sand was golden and untouched, as though forgotten by everybody. To rest my eyes, more than anything else, I turned the binoculars to sweep along this untouched area. It was as well I did so. Just two hundred yards from the holocaust of Green Beach, I saw movement – the impudent movement of men who reckoned they were safe, setting up a machine gun to enfilade our touchdown area. They were dug into the sand, not ten yards from the water's edge. Had they lain low, I might have missed them, but seeing movement, I asked *Decoy* to switch one turret on to them. It was the only correction I had to give during the run-in: and within a minute, shells were falling all about the spot I had indicated.

Satisfied that the machine gun must have been – as Gunners have it – neutralized, and because we were now nearing the beach, I turned my attention to our immediate front.

Suddenly, at 0413, the shelling stopped as if cut off by a guillotine. In the comparative peace which followed, I could hear the sound of planes far out to sea. These planes were to strafe the beach from left to right during the last two minutes of our approach. This is the most dangerous time in any landing. The friendly guns have to stop firing so that they do not endanger the assaulting troops. It is now that a determined enemy can pop his head up in comparative safety and fire at the craft which, because they are so close, present easy targets. To lessen the risk of enemy reaction during these last, vital seconds, aircraft are required to strafe along the beaches, across the front of the assault craft, right up to the moment of touchdown. Our guns had stopped, but our aircraft were perhaps 15 seconds late. We seemed to be similarly ahead of our schedule, for we were merely a hundred yards from the beach by the time the aircraft appeared in front of us . . . .

If the planes had been frightening, at least I'd had the comfort of knowing that they were friendly. But now, another danger presented itself. The wooden beach huts were burning fiercely in a broad curtain of fire across our path. The enemy had dug weapon pits underneath the huts, and though these positions were now vacated, stocks of ammunition had been left in the huts themselves. This ammunition was exploding in the flames, and was spurting and whizzing about as we approached.

The drivers of the buffaloes made their best speed over the sand towards the gaps in the two rows of huts. But our progress through the gaps seemed pitifully slow as I stood there with flames on either side, and smoke billowing about me. At last, however, we were through and out into the sunlight once again. We bumped over the low kerb of the coast road, and the tracks ground on the tarmac as we slewed left to pull up in front of a school building.

We had made our first objective with nothing more than one short burst of three or four bullets hitting the side of the buffalo . . . .

Phase One had begun. **"**

Far left: The combination of heliborne and seaborne landing techniques was made in the British assault on Port Said.

Right: Troops from 45 Royal Marine Commando undergo a final inspection on board HMS *Theseus* prior to going in.

As the British and French prepared for military action against Egypt in 1956, they faced two major problems: agreement as to the ultimate aim of the proposed invasion, and the actual gathering together of an effective invasion force. If the aim was to topple President Nasser, then the initial landing ought to be made at Alexandria, whence the force could readily move on Cairo. If, however, the political decision was simply to seize the Suez Canal zone, then the landing should be somewhere on the canal, presumably Port Said, at its northern end.

Eventually, after all the factors had been considered, the decision was taken: the landing would be at Port Said on 6 November, following a paratroop drop the day before. The first date mooted for the landing was 15 September, but political and logistic factors intervened to cause D-day to be postponed again and again from 15 September to 25 September, then to 1 October and finally to 6 November.

Setting aside political considerations, preparations for the invasion rapidly became a nightmare for the joint Anglo-French planning teams. Firstly the men had to be found and trained, then the ships and aircraft earmarked and, last but not least, came the task of locating a base from which to launch the invasion. The choice was between Cyprus and Malta. The former was ideal geographically but had no deep-water ports; the latter had the necessary facilities but was too far away from Egypt to allow reasonable

surprise when the fleets sailed. In the event both islands were to be used, though Malta was the main support base.

The size of the force assembled was roughly equivalent to that which landed at Anzio in Italy during World War II. The British contributed 45,000 men, 12,000 vehicles, 300 aircraft and 100 warships. The French contributed 34,000 men, 900 vehicles, 200 aircraft and 30 warships. The British forces comprised 3 Royal Marine Commando Brigade with the 6th Royal Tank Regiment in support plus the 16th Parachute Brigade. As a back-up force, the 3rd Division was embarked from Britain to reinforce the landing and carry out occupation duties in the canal zone at a later stage. Both countries provided paratroops which landed prior to, and in preparation for, the sea landings.

After much confusion, and not a few mistakes, the various allied forces got under way from a variety of ports in Britain, France, North Africa, Malta and Cyprus. By 5 September all had linked up off the coast of Cyprus to form one great convoy bound for Port Said.

For a week before the landing Egyptian airfields, military installations and the immediate vicinity of the proposed amphibious landing areas around Port Said and Port Fuad were subjected to almost continuous air attack. By D −1, when the parachute landings were scheduled to be made, air superiority

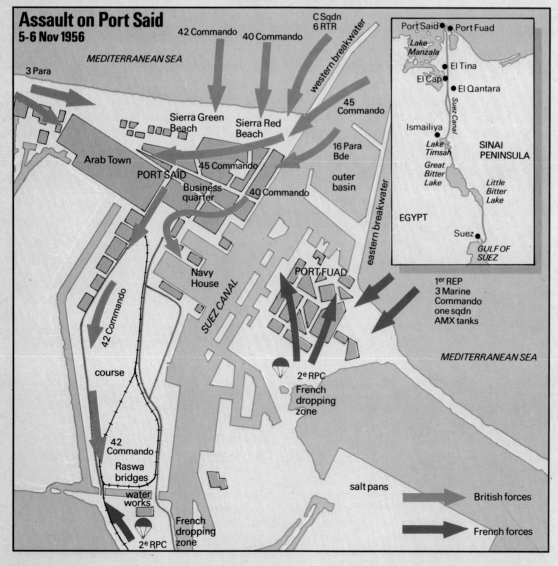

Assault on Port Said
5-6 Nov 1956

MEDITERRANEAN SEA

3 Para

42 Commando   40 Commando

C Sqdn
6 RTR

western breakwater

45 Commando

Sierra Green Beach   Sierra Red Beach

16 Para Bde

Arab Town

45 Commando

PORT SAID

Business quarter

40 Commando

outer basin

eastern breakwater

42 Commando

course

Navy House

SUEZ CANAL

PORT FUAD

1er REP
3 Marine Commando
one sqdn
AMX tanks

MEDITERRANEAN SEA

42 Commando

Raswa bridges

water works

2e RPC
French dropping zone

2e RPC
French dropping zone

salt pans

British forces

French forces

Port Said   Port Fuad
Lake Manzala
El Tina
El Cap
El Qantara
Ismailiya
Suez Canal
Lake Timsah
SINAI PENINSULA
Great Bitter Lake
Little Bitter Lake
EGYPT
Suez
GULF OF SUEZ

Said falls
ngs and

Top: French troops leap from landing craft as they go ashore at Port Fuad. Above left: The French take up positions and mount their 7.5mm M29 light machine gun on a pile of lumber. Above: A British soldier boards a ship in Britain bound for Suez. Left: The scene at the Abbas Hilmi Basin near the entrance to the canal soon after the landings. Landing craft and the British naval task force are visible in the background.

had been achieved by the allied air forces and, as was to be proved, the Egyptian capacity to resist the main assault had been drastically reduced.

When the airborne forces dropped on 5 November they had the task of securing the immediate areas forward of the assault beaches prior to the arrival of the combined fleet. The general picture by nightfall was that all objectives had been secured with the loss of very few allied lives. As twilight descended, the paratroopers settled down to await the arrival of the seaborne forces in the early hours of the following day.

Bombarding the beaches

At 0400 hours on 6 November, aircraft from the carriers flew the final attacking sorties against Egyptian strong points along the landing beaches themselves. There then followed an intense, but carefully controlled, naval gunfire bombardment, and a few minutes after 0430 hours the first assault troops hit the beaches.

The British landed at Port Said with 40 Royal Marine Commando on the left (Sierra Red Beach) and 42 Royal Marine Commando on the right (Sierra Green Beach). In reserve, 45 Royal Marine Commando waited patiently on board the carriers HMS *Ocean* and *Theseus* for their turn to go ashore. They were to be transported by helicopter, the first time such a method of landing had been attempted. The French assault forces made their landing at Port Fuad on the east bank of the canal. After consolidating their initial landings, the allies' first objective was to link up at Raswa on the canal to the south of Port Said.

The first troops ashore met with little resistance initially, but as they advanced towards the towns they came under persistent and frequently accurate sniper fire. The advance into and through the built-up areas of Port Said was made easier when, by 0530 hours, the first tanks of C Squadron of the 6th Royal Tank Regiment were ashore and able to support the commandos. By 0630 hours the first helicopters of 45 Royal Marine Commando had landed, and throughout the rest of the day the Commando Brigade advanced with armoured support until dusk called a partial halt to further action.

Throughout the daylight hours, frantic efforts had been made to clear mines and other obstacles from Port Said harbour in order to facilitate the landing of reinforcements there rather than on the comparatively difficult assault beaches. The HQ of 16th Parachute Brigade together with the 1st and 2nd Battalions, The Parachute Regiment, disembarked there as did A and B Squadrons of the 6th Royal Tank Regiment. No less than 14 Tank Landing Ships had unloaded before night fell on the day of the landing.

Even before dusk, British and French troops, having linked up at Raswa, were heading southwards along the bank of the canal with the aim of reaching El Qantara and Ismailiya. Preparations were also in hand for a parachute assault on both, but the news that the British and French governments had proposed a ceasefire (to be effective from midnight) halted further planning.

After weeks and weeks of order and counter-order, the assault had finally gone in successfully, but with the allied forces poised to exploit their initial success, they were suddenly called on to desist from further military action unless under attack from Egyptian forces.   **Major F.A. Godfrey**

Twilight of Empire

The consequences of British involvement in Suez

The Suez affair of 1956 had far-reaching effects. In the Middle East it marked the end of an era of European domination, as British and France were forced to withdraw their troops from Egyptian territory without having achieved their political objectives. Such public humiliation boosted the reputation of President Gamal Abdel Nasser, reviving his hopes of leading a movement based upon pan-Arab nationalism, but this proved to be only temporary. Of far more lasting significance was the fact that the Anglo-French withdrawal had taken place as a result of superpower pressure. This served to indicate that both America and the Soviet Union were determined to project their influence and rivalry into the Middle East, vying for control of its vital sea-lane, trade routes and natural resources. The region therefore became a centre of Cold War confrontation, a development which elevated its conflicts from local to global concern. The pattern was established in 1956, with Soviet-armed Egyptians fighting Israelis who, through their close cooperation with the British and French, were associated with the West. This alignment was one that would persist.

But the most traumatic effects of Suez were felt by the humiliated Europeans and, most especially, by Britain. At the beginning of the crisis she had all the attributes of a great power: a leading role in the United Nations, contact with Europe through the Nato alliance, a 'special relationship' with the United States, the remains of an apparently viable imperial trading system, large armed forces and nuclear weapons. Yet the events of 1956 suggested that these were little more than a facade. The ease with which the United States was able to exert economic pressure to ensure a ceasefire in early November and the failure of Sir Anthony Eden's Conservative government to cope with the run on sterling which accompanied the crisis, highlighted the parlous state of Britain's finances and exposed her Achilles' heel.

If Suez proved anything, it was that Britain could no longer afford to maintain the global commitments of a great power. When this was coupled to a realisation that, even if she could, she would be unable to act freely without at least the tacit backing of a superpower, it was obvious that her role in international affairs would have to be reassessed. If Britain was to exert any influence in the future, she would have to cut her commitments to match her capabilities.

Such a reassessment did not take place. In retrospect, given the problems of Suez, the logical move would have been to withdraw from the global responsibility of empire into the relative security of a unified western Europe, while at the same time nurturing the 'special relationship' with America to ensure superpower support. But this was impossible. No British politician of the 1950s, born and bred in the late-Victorian heyday of empire, was likely to accelerate the process of decolonisation just because of Suez. At the same time, the prospect of European integration was, as yet, unattractive. Moreover, after the humiliation of Suez, no French government was going to welcome the 'perfidious' British into a future alliance be it political, economic or military.

In the end, the only element of reassessment that did occur was the improvement of relations with the United States. Despite American actions in 1956, the Atlantic bond was swiftly re-established. But this did nothing to reduce Britain's global commitments – indeed, the Americans seem to have expected Britain to maintain them for as long as possible as part of the 'containment' of communism – and merely succeeded in driving a deeper wedge between Britain and a western Europe suspicious of American motives. The result was confusion over the direction of British foreign policy in the late 1950s and 1960s as successive governments sought to solve the central dilemma of their post-Suez world: how to maintain global commitments when the money to pay for them was not available.

Nor was this the full extent of the problem, for

The sun sets over the Suez Canal, blocked to shipping by sunken vessels. The Suez affair was deeply humiliating for Britain and drastically reduced her influence and standing in the Middle East.

Above: Duncan Sandys, Minister of Defence, presented the 1957 Defence White Paper to Parliament which contained provision for the ending of National Service without reducing Britain's military commitments abroad.

confusion in foreign relations inevitably caused confusion in defence policy. Contrary to expectations, the Suez crisis did not produce a particularly clear or radical defence reassessment. In purely military terms, the lessons of the crisis seemed crystal clear. Nasser's nationalisation of the Suez Canal Company in July had caught Britain with inadequate forces to mount an immediate punitive expedition. In order to mount even the delayed assault of early November, it had been necessary to take warships out of reserve, to charter merchant ships and commercial aircraft and to call up ex-conscript reservists. If, in the future, the politicians should demand a similar expedition, Britain would have to maintain a strong central reserve, backed by adequate air and naval resources.

But this would cost money which was not available in the late 1950s. Pressure to reduce defence spending had been growing for some time, particularly in light of the announcement made in July 1955 by the Minister of Defence, Selwyn Lloyd, that his department was absorbing nearly 10 per cent of the gross national product every year and that this was likely to rise as urgently needed re-equipment programmes were initiated. National Service, the 1940s answer to Britain's enormous defence commitments, was becoming increasingly unpopular and the Conservatives quickly recognised that its abolition would be a guaranteed vote-catcher and money-saver. So when the new prime minister, Harold Macmillan, appointed Duncan Sandys to the Ministry of Defence in January 1957, he directed him to alter the emphasis of British defence policy with a view, not to cutting down commitments, but to saving money and getting rid of conscription. It was an unrealistic approach and one that was to produce as many problems as it solved.

Sandys presented his recommendations to Parliament on 4 April 1957 in a White Paper entitled *Defence: Outline of Future Policy*. The central pro-

Above: French troops lead away captured Egyptian prisoners. Below: Protesters in Manchester demonstrate against Britain's invasion of Suez. The international outcry that the affair provoked effectively ended Eden's career. He resigned as prime minister two months later.

posal was that National Service would be gradually phased out, ceasing altogether in 1962. This was widely welcomed, not just by the youth of Britain, who saw an end to what, for many, had been a wasted experience, but also by industry (which stood to gain a substantial workforce) and even by the armed services themselves, who had grown tired of spending time and resources on an endless treadmill of recruit-training. But the effects were to be dramatic, reducing the future size of the armed forces from 690,000 men to an all-volunteer establishment of 375,000. As Britain had already been hard pressed to satisfy the demands of her defence commitments, this reduction would clearly affect capabilities for the future.

The suggested solution was contained in two further proposals, both of which were designed to substitute technology for manpower, with no attempt to cut down the scale of Britain's continued commitments world-wide. On the one hand, the need for large conventional forces in Europe (and, by implication, elsewhere) would be reduced by a new emphasis upon nuclear weapons both for deterrence and, if that failed, for war-fighting at a tactical (battlefield) level; on the

other, the maintenance of large garrisons overseas, outside Europe, would be ended by creating a strategic reserve, stationed in Britain, which could be flown out to trouble-spots as and when crises occurred. It seemed a neat and logical plan, apparently taking account of the military lessons of the Suez affair while at the same time offering substantial financial savings. Parliament accepted the White Paper with few reservations, particularly when Sandys presented a defence bill for 1957-58 which was £180 million less than that for the previous year.

Unfortunately the proposals were unworkable. Nuclear weapons on their own, without the backing of large conventional forces, were unlikely to prevent war in Europe – as the Americans were beginning to realise, dependence upon a massive retaliatory nuclear response to minor levels of aggression was less than credible – and they were inapplicable to crises elsewhere. Similarly, the use of a strategic reserve pre-supposed the existence not only of long-range transport aircraft (which were not available in sufficient numbers) but also of refuelling bases and undisputed overflying rights on the routes between Britain and potential trouble-spots, particularly east of Suez. But the Suez crisis had led to a distinct cooling of relations between Britain and many of the Arab states of the Middle East. Flights over such countries as Egypt, Syria, Jordan and Iraq were restricted and bases closed, requiring the maintenance of elements of the strategic reserve east of Suez – a return to the expensive, static garrisons which the 1957 White Paper had sought to avoid.

In the end, Britain gained little advantage and the problems of finance and overstretch remained. They were to be a feature of British defence policy until the mid-1970s, mute testimony to the missed opportunity for rationalisation and reassessment which the aftermath of Suez undoubtedly presented. **John Pimlott**

Pressures for a ceasefire

Within a few hours of the Anglo-French landings at Suez, the commanders were informed that a ceasefire agreement was to come into action forthwith – thus denying the assault force any opportunity to exploit their victory. The reasons behind this decision had been under discussion some time before the actual operation.

Prior to the invasion Sir Anthony Eden, the British prime minister, had been under pressure from the American administration not to exaggerate the situation in the Middle East and to tread carefully. After talks on 28 October 1956, and a further discussion at a meeting of the UN Security Council (after the Israeli invasion on 29 October) it became clear to both Britain and France that American support, or at least benevolent neutrality, would not be forthcoming.

The revelation of American disapproval of the Anglo-French ultimatum gave rise to severe criticism at home. The difficulties involved in reopening the canal, the lack of oil from the Middle East, and American disapproval all put pressure upon the British government to accept UN deliberations over Egypt. Yet the crucial factor that forced the British government to accept a ceasefire was economic. After a good start to the financial year, dollars began to flow out of the country during the period of crisis and soon some 15 per cent of the country's gold reserves had left London. An emergency loan of £1.5 billion from the International Monetary Fund was urgently needed. This could only be gained with US assistance and the price of that assistance was clear.

Above: A Soviet cartoon comments on the Suez affair, showing a French cockerel and British lion having been battered by an Egyptian Sphinx. Left: French troops prepare to depart from Suez. Despite an overwhelming Anglo-French victory against the Egyptians, the intervention of the United Nations compelled Britain and France to accept a ceasefire after just a few hours of fighting.

Key Weapons

SOVIET FIGHTERS

part 2

In 1959 the Soviet Air Force introduced a specialised ground-attack fighter, the Sukhoi Su-7 (Nato code-name Fitter). It was a large swept-wing aircraft with a span of 8.93m (29ft 3in), a length of 17.37m (57ft) and an all-up weight of 13,600kg (30,000lb). Power was provided by an afterburning Lyulka AL-7F-1 turbojet which produced 10,000kg (22,000lb) of thrust. This gave the Su-7 a maximum speed of Mach 1.6 at high altitude and a low-level performance of Mach 1.1 in clean condition (that is, when not carrying external ordnance). Built-in armament comprised two 30mm NR-30 cannon in the wing roots, each with 70 rounds of ammunition, and up to 1813kg (4000lb) of ordnance could be carried over a combat radius of 480km (300 miles), but this was a disappointing performance for a fighter-bomber of the Su-7's size. Indeed, its poor payload/range was considered to be one of the Su-7's major shortcomings. On the credit side, the aircraft performed well at low altitude, being fast, manoeuvrable and stable. Over 1000 Su-7s were built for the air forces of the Warsaw Pact and for export. The Su-7 saw combat service with the Indian Air Force during the 1971 war with Pakistan and with the Egyptian Air Force in the Yom Kippur War of 1973, and in both conflicts it was considered to have performed well in a low-level attack role.

The problem of improving the Su-7s payload/range was dealt with in an interesting and unusual way. In 1966 an experimental version of the design was produced to test a variable-geometry wing. The pivot points were positioned at mid-span, with the outer wing panels' sweepback being variable between 16 and 62 degrees. It is believed that this aircraft, designated the S-221, was intended purely for experimental purposes, as it was the first Soviet aircraft to be fitted with a variable geometry wing. However, so great were the improvements over the basic Su-7, that the type was put into production as the Su-17. Fitted with a more powerful Lyulka A1-21F turbojet, the new fighter could operate from much

shorter airstrips than the Su-7 and was able to carry twice the payload over a radius greater by 25 per cent. The Su-17 entered service in 1971 and some 800 are employed by the Soviet Air Force, being assigned to Frontal Aviation and to Naval Aviation as shore-based attack aircraft. Two export versions, the Su-20 and Su-22, have been produced, and in a much publicised incident over the Gulf of Sirte on 19 August 1981, two Libyan Air Force Su-22s were destroyed in combat by US Navy F-14A Tomcats flying from the USS *Nimitz*.

The Sukhoi Su-9 (Nato code-name Fishpot) was a parallel design to the Su-7 which was intended to carry out the all-weather interception mission with the Air Defence Forces. Entering service in 1959, the Su-9 was a tailed delta aircraft like its contemporary the MiG-21, although it was a much larger and heavier aircraft and lacked the MiG's multi-role development potential. A small radar was carried in the Su-9's intake centre body and armament com-

Previous page: Airbase groundcrew service a Soviet MiG-25. Designed for high altitude Mach 3 supersonic-dash interception missions, the MiG-25 has no role in normal air-to-air combat. Top: An Su-7, the standard Soviet strike fighter of the 1960s until the subsequent introduction of the improved Su-17 and the MiG-27. Above: An experimental variable-geometry model of the Su-7, Nato code-named Fitter-B, which first appeared in 1967 and, with further improvements to the weapon-aiming system and take-off capabilities, was redesignated Su-17.

prised four AA-1 Alkali air-to-air missiles (AAMs) carried beneath the wings. The Su-9's radar, codenamed Spin Scan by Nato, was a short range sensor, though this was not necessarily a great disadvantage in a Soviet interceptor, as these aircraft operate under rigid ground control throughout their missions. However, with the availability of the more powerful Skip Spin radar (which necessitated the modification of the forward fuselage), and with a more powerful engine and AA-3 Anab missile armament, the fighter was redesignated Su-11. In its improved form, powered by a 10,000kg (22,000lb) thrust Lyulka AL-7F turbojet, the interceptor reached a maximum speed of Mach 2.1, although when fitted with external fuel tanks and AAMs this was reduced to Mach 1.5.

The Su-9 and Su-11 were the mainstay of the Air Defence Forces' interceptor regiments throughout the 1960s and their successor, the Su-15 (Nato codename Flagon) which entered service at the end of the decade, was a further development of the basic design. In its initial form the Su-15 combined the wing, tail surfaces and undercarriage of the Su-11 with an entirely new fuselage, which housed twin turbojets fed by intakes mounted on the fuselage sides. However, the Su-15's wing design was soon changed to increase its span and introduce a compound leading-edge sweepback. The early Su-15's retained the Skip

Right: The basic production model of the Su-15 high-altitude interceptor, Nato code-named Flagon A. In keeping with the Soviet practice of improving and updating a basic design, the Su-15 is a development of the Su-9/11 family. An initial pre-series batch of Su-15s appeared at the Domodedovo air display in 1967 and a number of variants from the subsequently abandoned reduced-take-off-and-landing Flagon B to the latest production version, Nato code-named Flagon F, have been produced.

Su-15 (Flagon)

Type Interceptor
Dimensions 10.5m (34ft 6in); length 21.5m (70ft 6in); height 5m (16ft 6in)
Weight Empty 12,500kg (27,500lb); maximum take-off 20,430kg (45,000lb)
Powerplant Two 10,200kg (22,485lb) Tumansky R-27 turbofans or two 7260kg (16,000lb) Tumansky R-13 afterburning turbojets

Performance Maximum speed Mach 2.2 or 2120km/h (1320mph) at 11,000m (36,000ft); maximum speed at sea level Mach 0.9 or 1100km/h (680mph)
Range Combat radius 640km (400 miles)
Ceiling 20,000m (65,000ft)

Armament Two AA-3-2 Advanced Anab air-to-air missiles

Su-11 (Fishpot)

Type All-weather interceptor
Dimensions Span 8.43m (27ft 8in); length 18.28m (60ft); height 4.58m (15ft)
Weight Empty 9000kg (20,000lb); maximum take-off 13,620kg (30,000lb)
Powerplant One 10,000kg (22,000lb) Lyulka AL-7F afterburning turbojet

Performance Maximum speed 'clean' Mach 2.1 or 2250km/h (1400mph); maximum speed (combat loaded) Mach 1.5 or 1600km/h (1000mph)
Range Approx 1125km (700 miles)
Ceiling 20,000m (65,000ft)

Armament Two AA-3 Anab air-to-air missiles

Below: An Su-9 photographed at the 1967 Soviet Aviation Day display. Like most Soviet interceptors, the Su-9 is operated solely by the USSR. It was replaced by the Su-11 in the early 1960s although relatively few improvements were incorporated under the new designation. These included, however, a more powerful radar and the introduction of two AA-3 Anab air-to-air missiles in place of the four AA-1 Alkali missiles carried by the Su-9.

Spin radar (though later aircraft are believed to have a more powerful radar) and twin-Anab missile armament of the Su-11. The Su-15's engines are believed to be 10,200kg (22,485lb) thrust Tumansky R-27 turbofans and performance includes a maximum speed (carrying missile armament) of Mach 2.2 and a service ceiling of 20,000m (65,000ft). The Su-15 remains one of the most important interceptors in the Soviet armoury and more than 700 are in service.

Because of the vast land areas to be defended, especially over the inhospitable Arctic frontier, the Soviet Union's Air Defence Forces maintain a force of long-range interceptors. Since its service introduction in the early 1960s, the Yak-28P (Nato code-name Firebar) has carried out this role and more than 200 remain in service. A derivative of the

Yak-25, which it resembles in general layout, the Yak-28P is a twin-engined, swept-wing fighter which carries a crew of two. It is powered by the 6000kg (13,000lb) thrust Tumansky R-11 turbojet and has a maximum speed of more than Mach 1 and a service ceiling of 17,000m (55,000ft). Capable of operating in all weathers, the Yak-28P is fitted with a Skip Spin radar. Its armament comprises a pair of AA-3 Anab AAMs, one of which is infra-red guided and the other semi-active radar homing. Soviet tactics may require that these missiles are launched together at an enemy bomber, to make it more difficult to employ effective countermeasures. Some Yak-28Ps have an additional armament of a pair of short-range AA-2 Atol AAMs.

The Air Defence Forces' other long range interceptor – and incidentally the largest fighter aircraft in service anywhere in the world – is the Tupolev Tu-28P (Nato code-name Fiddler). A swept-wing, two-seat fighter, it has a length of 26m (85ft), a span of 20m (65ft) and maximum take-off weight is 38,500kg (85,000lb). Power is provided by two Lyulka AL-21F afterburning turbojets, each developing 11,000kg (24,500lb) of thrust. Maximum speed when carrying

Above: A fully armed export MiG-23 of the Libyan Arab Republic Air Force out on patrol. While MiG-23s operated by the Soviet Union carry both AA-7 Apex and AA-8 Aphid air-to-air missiles, the downgraded export models are armed with the older AA-2 Atoll or AA-2-2 Advanced Atoll.

Tu-28P (Fiddler)

Type Two-seat long-range interceptor
Dimensions Span 20m (65ft); length 26m (85ft); height 7m (23ft)
Weight Empty 18,160kg (40,000lb); maximum take-off 38,500kg (85,000lb)
Powerplant Two 11,000kg (24,500lb) Lyulka AL-21F afterburning turbojets

Performance Maximum speed (combat loaded) Mach 1.5 or 1600km/h (1000mph)
Range Combat radius 1300km (810 miles); ferry range 3200km (2000 miles)
Ceiling 18,000m (60,000ft)

Armament Four AA-5 Ash air-to-air missiles

---

missile armament is Mach 1.5, service ceiling is 18,000m (60,000ft) and range is 3200km (2000 miles). A powerful radar, code-named Big Nose by Nato, is fitted and armament comprises four AA-5 Ash AAMs, two of them guided by infra-red and the other two by semi-active radar homing.

One of the most significant Soviet warplanes of the early 1970s was the MiG-23/27 (Nato code-name

Left: A Soviet MiG-23S in the standard air-superiority light grey finish being readied for flight. Although the MiG-23 has no direct Western equivalent it is designed to fulfil similar combat roles to the F-4 Phantom. Clearly visible on the wing root is the missile-launching shoe for the formidable AA-7 Apex air-to-air missile.

Flogger). This was a variable-geometry Mach 2 fighter which for the first time gave the Soviet Air Force a true multi-role capability, broadly similar to that of the United States' F-4 Phantom. The Flogger has been built in three main versions: the MiG-23 air-superiority fighter and interceptor, the MiG-27 ground-attack fighter and a hybrid version (the MiG-23BM) which combines features of the two. The MiG-23MF which currently serves with both the Soviet Air Force and Air Defence Forces is powered by an 11,500kg (25,350lb) thrust Tumansky R-29B afterburning turbofan. Its maximum speed at altitude is Mach 2.2, reducing to Mach 1.1 at sea level. It is fitted with a pulse-Doppler radar capable of 'looking down' to pick up low flying targets. Standard armament comprises a twin-barrel GSh-23 23mm cannon, mounted beneath the fuselage, with two medium-range AA-7 Apex AAMs carried beneath the fixed inboard portions of the wing and two short-range AA-8 Aphid infra-red homing missiles beneath the fuselage.

The MiG-27 ground-attack/strike fighter differs from the MiG-23 in having fixed rather than variable engine inlets, thus reducing maximum speed at altitude to Mach 1.6, although the sea level speed remains the same. It has an entirely redesigned nose, giving the pilot a greatly improved view forwards and downwards from his cockpit. The bulky air-interception radar is replaced by a laser rangefinder, a simple ranging radar and a Doppler navigation radar. Other equipment necessitated by the ground-attack role includes armour plate fitted to the cockpit sides, larger wheels with low-pressure tyres for operation from rough airstrips and a new 23mm multi-barrel, rapid-fire cannon mounted under the fuselage. Maximum ordnance load is 3000kg (6600lb) and this can be made up of air-to-surface missiles or laser or

Above: Two photographs showing the main and front landing gear of MiG-23 number 30 from the Kublinka airbase. This MiG-23, Nato code-named Flogger G, is the current standard air defence version and was photographed in August 1981 during a four day visit by a Soviet squadron to the Swedish base at Ronneby.

MiG-23 (Flogger)

Type Single-seat air-superiority fighter/interceptor
Dimensions Span minimum sweep 14.26m (46ft 9in); maximum sweep 8.3m (27ft 2in); length 18.24m (59ft 10in); height 4.36m (14ft 4in)
Weight Empty 11,350kg (25,000lb); maximum take-off 18,614kg (41,000lb)
Powerplant One 11,500kg (25,350lb) Tumansky R-29B afterburning turbofan
Performance Maximum speed Mach 2.2 or 2330km/h (1450mph) at 11,000m (36,000ft)
Range Combat radius 925km (575 miles)
Ceiling 17,000m (55,000ft)
Armament One twin-barrel GSh-23 23mm cannon; two underwing hardpoints for AA-7 Apex air-to-air missiles; two under-fuselage hardpoints for AA-8 Aphid air-to-air missiles

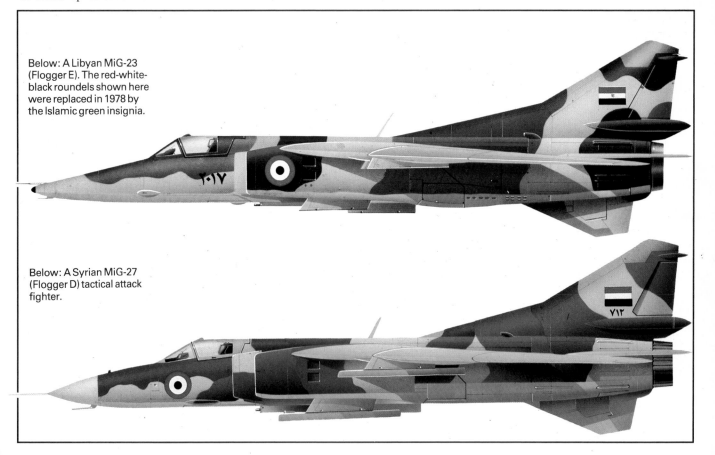

Below: A Libyan MiG-23 (Flogger E). The red-white-black roundels shown here were replaced in 1978 by the Islamic green insignia.

Below: A Syrian MiG-27 (Flogger D) tactical attack fighter.

Below: An underside view which clearly shows the massive inlet ducts and aft-set wing of the Mach 3 Mig-25.

Yak-36 (Forger)

Type VTOL carrier-based strike aircraft
Dimensions Span 7m (23ft); length 15m (49ft 2in); height 3.2m (10ft 6in)
Weight Combat loaded 7484kg (16,500lb)
Powerplant One 7500kg (16,500lb) class lift/cruise engine; two 2500kg (5500lb) Kolesov lift engines

Performance Maximum speed Mach 1.2 or 1290km/h (800mph) at 11,000m (36,000ft); maximum speed at sea level Mach 0.85 or 1050km/h (650mph)
Range Combat radius 250km (155 miles)
Ceiling 14,000m (46,000ft)

Armament Four underwing pylons for up to 1000kg (2200lb) stores including gun pods and AA-8 Aphid air-to-air missiles

Above: A Yak-36 VTOL strike fighter lifts from the flight deck of the Soviet carrier *Kiev*. To take off, the Yak-36's three engines have to be used together and failure of one of the lift engines usually results in loss of the aircraft. The Yak-36 compares unfavourably with the British Sea Harrier in that it has no STOL capability and combat manoeuvrability is limited by its inability to vector in forward flight ('viff'). It is expected that the Yak-36 will be replaced by a more sophisticated aircraft which can utilise the angled-deck of the Soviet carriers for rolling take-offs and thus increase its range and payload capabilities.

MiG-25 (Foxbat)

Type Interceptor
Dimensions Span 14m (46ft); length 22.3m (73ft 2in); height 5.64m (18ft 6in)
Weight Empty 19,976kg (44,000lb); maximum take-off 37,455kg (82,500lb)
Powerplant Two 12,250kg (27,000lb) Tumansky R-31 afterburning turbojets

Performance Maximum speed 'clean' Mach 3 or 3200km/h (2000mph) at medium and high altitude; maximum speed with stores Mach 2.8
Range Intercept radius 740km (460 miles); at Mach 3 1448km (900 miles)
Ceiling 23,000m (75,000ft)

Armament Up to four AA-6 Acrid air-to-air missiles

electro-optically guided 'smart' bombs, as well as the more usual free-fall bombs and unguided rockets. At present there are more than 2000 MiG-23s and MiG-27s in Soviet service, and this fighter is like to rival its predecessor, the MiG-21, in both longevity and importance.

Capable of a maximum speed of Mach 3 in a 'clean' condition and possessing a service ceiling of 23,000m (75,000ft), the MiG-25 interceptor (Nato code-name Foxbat) was one of the most impressive warplanes of its age. Introduced into service in 1970, the MiG-25 had been intended to counter the high-flying USAF B-70 Valkyrie bomber. The American warplane never entered service, but nonetheless the MiG-25 was produced in both interceptor and reconnaissance versions. The former, powered by two 12,250kg (27,000lb) thrust Tumansky R-31 afterburning turbojets, is armed with up to four AA-6 Acrid long range AAMs. in September 1976 a defecting Soviet pilot, Lieutenant Viktor Belenko, flew his MiG-25 into Japan, giving Western defence experts an opportunity to examine this advanced interceptor. Rather naively the MiG-25 was then criticised for its primitive construction and outdated electronics. The fact remains that the aircraft was capable of carrying out the highly demanding mission for which it was intended. A developed two-seat version (Nato code-name Foxhound) was introduced into service in 1982 and is capable of detecting and shooting down low-flying bombers (and possibly cruise missiles).

The capabilities of the Soviet Air Force were greatly expanded during the 1970s and two new fighters in particular gave the service hitherto unattainable operational capabilities. The Su-24 (Nato code-name Fencer) is an interdiction/strike fighter capable of penetrating deep into Nato air space. A March 2 variable-geometry wing aircraft, the Su-24 carries a crew of two. It can lift an ordnance load of 2000kg (4400lb) over a tactical radius of 900 miles, with the high-risk phase of the mission carried out at low level to avoid radar detection. The other innovatory Soviet fighter is the Yak-36 (Nato code-name Forger) vertical take-off naval warplane, which operates from *Kiev* class carriers. Although comparisons with the Royal Navy's Sea Harrier are inevitable, the Yak-36 is a much less capable aircraft. Its lift jet and lift/cruise powerplant arrangement is less efficient than the Sea Harrier's vectored thrust system and warload and performance are markedly inferior.

Three new fighter aircraft are known to be under development in the Soviet Union. One of these, the Su-25 (Nato code-name Frogfoot) is a specialized ground-attack aircraft, which has been operationally tested in Afghanistan. It is armed with a 30mm cannon and can carry 4000kg (8800lb) of ordnance. The Su-27 (Nato code-name Flanker) is a twin-engined air superiority fighter, while the MiG-29 (Nato code-name Fulcrum) is a dual role fighter with air-to-air and ground-attack capability similar to that of the US Navy's F-18 Hornet. Such aircraft are evidence of the narrowing technological gap between the Soviet Union and Nato.

Invasion of Sinai

Israel's stunning strike against Egypt

On 21 October 1956 David Ben-Gurion, Prime Minister of Israel, flew to Sèvres in France accompanied by Shimon Peres, Director-General of Israel's Ministry of Defence, and General Moshe Dayan, his Chief of Staff. The purpose of their visit was to confer with the French Prime Minister, Guy Mollet, and the British Foreign Minister, Selwyn Lloyd, on how best their three countries could coordinate their intended attack on Egypt.

The plan which emerged from the conference was to be implemented in two stages. First, Israel was to invade the Sinai peninsula and advance towards the Suez Canal; then Great Britain and France would 'intervene' to put an end to the fighting, effecting an assault landing which would result in an apparently defensive occupation of the canal zone. Initially, the Israeli advance was to resemble nothing more than the hot pursuit of fedayeen terrorist groups, escalating as the Egyptians reacted to this incursion into their sovereign territory. But, distrusting his allies, Ben-Gurion retained the right to withdraw his troops in the event of the British and French not fulfilling their part of the bargain.

For Israel, repeatedly threatened with destruction by the neighbouring Arab states, fear was a prime motive. Egypt had already established a joint military command with Syria and Jordan, the purpose of which was obvious, and the previous year she had, through the agency of Czechoslovakia, secured a large quantity of Soviet military equipment. Nasser was also actively encouraging fedayeen raids on Israeli settlements; 260 Israelis had been killed or wounded by these in 1955 and the tempo of attacks was steadily increasing. On the economic front Nasser not only denied Israeli shipping passage of the Suez Canal, but also blockaded the Straits of Tiran, the only entrance to the Gulf of Aqaba and the Israeli port of Elat. It was, in fact, this latter act which had prompted Ben-Gurion to instruct his General Staff to prepare an offensive in Sinai.

The Sinai peninsula is triangular in shape and is

Above: An Israeli commander briefs his troops prior to an assault in the Sinai. Below: Israeli French-built AMX13 tanks move across desert in the Sinai peninsula. The Israeli Defence Force had approximately 200 tanks by 1956.

separated from Egypt proper by the Suez Canal. In the north it has a maximum width of 210km (130 miles) and is 385km (240 miles) long from the Mediterranean to Sharm el Sheikh. From the northern coast the ground rises steadily across a rock, gravel and sand plateau to the 2640m (8664 foot) Mount Sinai massif, then falls sharply towards the Red Sea. The landscape is hot and arid, receiving less than 250mm (10 inches) of seasonal rainfall per year.

From Israel three routes cross Sinai to the Suez Canal. The best and most northerly follows the coast from Gaza through Khan Yunis, Rafah, El Arish and Mazar to reach El Qantara. In the centre the route lies from El Quseima through Abu Aweigila to Ismailiya. Further south a track from El Kuntilla passes through El Thamad and Nakhl to the Mitla Pass, from which the town of Suez can be reached. The principal north-south connection between these routes is a track running from El Arish through Bir Lahfan to Abu Aweigila and on past Gebel Libni to Nakhl, with a branch joining Abu Aweigila with Bir Gifgafa and the Mitla Pass. It will thus be apparent that Abu Aweigila is the hub of the central Sinai road network.

Egyptian dispositions in Sinai during October 1956 were, despite Nasser's threats, defensive in character. The 8th (Palestinian) Infantry Division was con-

centrated in the Gaza-Rafah area and the 3rd Infantry Division in the area from El Arish to Abu Aweigila, both being supported by tank and tank destroyer battalions. Further west was the 1st Armoured Brigade, based at Bir Gifgafa and equipped with T34/85 tanks and SU100 tank destroyers. An independent infantry brigade was stationed west of the Mitla Pass, protecting the town of Suez. Elsewhere, the frontier with Israel was covered by light motorised units.

On the eve of the war the Egyptian Army could muster 40 Centurions, 150 Shermans, 40 AMX13s, 150 T34/85s, 50 ISIIIs, 200 Archer and 100 SU100 tank destroyers, and 200 BTR152 wheeled armoured personnel carriers (APCs). Much of this, however, was retained in Egypt to counter the Anglo-French threat, and the same was true of the MiG-15 and Vampire jets flown by the Egyptian Air Force.

Israel had mobilised in secret and was deploying 10 brigades in the Negev desert: the 7th Armoured, the 27th and 37th Mechanised, which contained a substantial tank element, the 202nd Parachute and the 1st, 4th, 9th, 10th, 11th and 12th Infantry Brigades. Once hard pressed for weapons of every kind, the Israeli Defence Force (IDF) as a whole had benefitted from a limited provision of French arms, supplied in retaliation for Nasser's support of the FLN. On the other hand, the Israeli Armoured Corps (IAC), upon which much depended, remained something of an unknown quantity and had still to win its spurs.

The IAC had played a very minor role in Israel's first war against her Arab neighbours, but it had

Above: Troops greet each other as an M3 half-track APC thunders by during Sharon's drive through the Sinai. Below: Tanks, closely followed by M3 half-tracks carrying supporting infantry, move through desert at speed during Israeli mechanised manoeuvres.

subsequently purchased a quantity of weaponless Shermans and fitted them with ancient 105mm howitzers, with far from satisfactory results. These highly unsuitable weapons had recently been replaced by 75mm high-velocity French tank guns, the turrets being modified with a counterweight to balance the longer barrel.

Israeli armoured strength now amounted to 100 of these upgunned Shermans, 100 recently arrived AMX13s, and 42 self-propelled guns of various types. Half-track APCs were available for some mechanised infantry units, but others travelled in

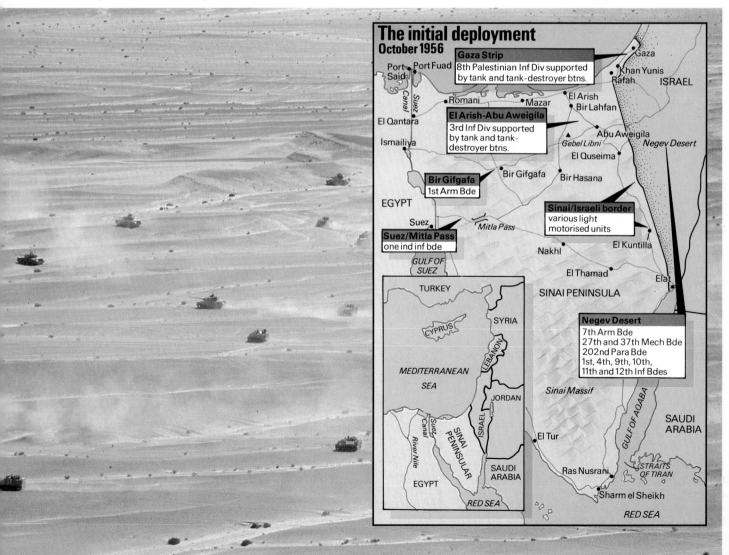

The initial deployment
October 1956

Gaza Strip
8th Palestinian Inf Div supported by tank and tank-destroyer btns.

El Arish-Abu Aweigila
3rd Inf Div supported by tank and tank-destroyer btns.

Bir Gifgafa
1st Arm Bde

Sinai/Israeli border
various light motorised units

Suez/Mitla Pass
one ind inf bde

Negev Desert
7th Arm Bde
27th and 37th Mech Bde
202nd Para Bde
1st, 4th, 9th, 10th, 11th and 12th Inf Bdes

Port Said · Port Fuad · Gaza · Khan Yunis · Rafah · ISRAEL
Suez Canal · Romani · Mazar · El Arish · Bir Lahfan
El Qantara · Abu Aweigila · Gebel Libni · Negev Desert
Ismailiya · El Quseima · Bir Gifgafa · Bir Hasana
EGYPT · Mitla Pass · Suez · Nakhl · El Kuntilla
GULF OF SUEZ · El Thamad · Elat
SINAI PENINSULA

TURKEY · SYRIA · CYPRUS · LEBANON · MEDITERRANEAN SEA · JORDAN · ISRAEL · Suez Canal · River Nile · SINAI PENINSULAR · EGYPT · SAUDI ARABIA · RED SEA

Sinai Massif · El Tur · GULF OF AQABA · SAUDI ARABIA · Ras Nusrani · STRAITS OF TIRAN · Sharm el Sheikh · RED SEA

commandeered civilian lorries and buses. The Israeli Air Force (IAF), flying Mystère IV, Ouragan and Vautour jet fighters, was some 60 per cent smaller than that of Egypt, but had the advantage of being able to deploy its entire strength over the combat zone.

Plan of attack

The Israeli attack was code-named Kadesh and was to be executed in phases, the first of which was designed to mislead the Egyptians as to Israeli intentions, and to prevent them from identifying the nature of the offensive in its early stages. This was achieved, first, by the initial deployment of units closer to the Jordanian than to the Egyptian frontier; secondly, by cutting the Egyptian command telephone network in Sinai, using F-51 Mustangs to fly *through* the overhead lines two hours before hostilities commenced; and, thirdly, by timing succeeding phases to give an impression of escalation following Egyptian reaction to the first Israeli incursion.

These operational phases are best summarised as follows: phase one was the seizure of the eastern end of the Mitla Pass, thus denying Egyptian reinforcements access to central Sinai; phase two was the elimination of the strong Egyptian position at Abu Aweigila, followed by an advance through central Sinai; phase three was the elimination of Egyptian forces in Rafah and the Gaza Strip, followed by an advance westwards along the coast road; and phase four was to be an advance to Sharm el Sheikh, intended to reopen the Straits of Tiran.

Phase one began at 1700 hours on 29 October, when one battalion of Colonel Ariel Sharon's 202nd Parachute Brigade dropped at the eastern end of the Mitla Pass, near the Parker Memorial. After a brief skirmish the battalion, commanded by Lieutenant-Colonel Rafael Eitan, dug in to await the remainder of the brigade. This, supported by an artillery battalion equipped with 25-pounder guns, a mortar battalion and a squadron of AMX13 tanks, had simultaneously begun an overland advance from the frontier.

Above: A Soviet-buit IS-3 heavy tank of the Egyptian Army on manoeuvres in the desert. The tank mounts a 122mm main armament with a 7.62mm co-axial machine gun and a 12.7mm anti-aircraft machine gun. Below: Israeli troops take advantage of a lull in the fighting to rearm and service their tanks.

The first obstacle encountered by the column was the garrison of El Kuntilla. Sharon circled the post and attacked from the west, using the setting sun to blind the defence, which quickly collapsed. Pressing on through the night, the column stormed El Thamad from the east at dawn on the 30th, using the rising sun to similar effect. The advance continued towards Nakhl, a fortified village and fedayeen base controlling a track junction. At 1700 hours the brigade deployed to attack, but the garrison fled before the assault could be launched, leaving behind a number of BTR152 APCs in working order. For Sharon the acquisition of these was most timely, as the civilian vehicles in the column had made heavy weather of the going and were falling steadily behind. By 2230 hours, however, the leading elements of the brigade had established contact with Eitan's battalion, having covered the 305km (190 miles) from their assembly area on the Jordanian border in 28 hours.

202 Parachute Brigade was now fulfilling its operational role, that of providing a cork which stopped the Mitla bottleneck. What followed next, unfortu-

nately, reflected the less attractive aspects of its commander's personality. Sharon was acknowledged to be a first class soldier, but was also known to be an ambitious and ungovernable subordinate. He requested Dayan's permission to send a patrol into the pass. Dayan, believing that Sharon was looking for ways in which to improve a less than ideal defensive position, sanctioned the patrol but specified that it was not to become embroiled in combat.

What Sharon actually intended was nothing less than the capture of the pass, and to that end he despatched a full battalion battlegroup. The Egyptians, however, had moved reinforcements into the pass during the night and these had taken up positions in the caves and sangars which dominated the narrow defile. The Israelis were quickly pinned down and a fierce and inconclusive fire-fight developed. At dusk on 31 October a volunteer deliberately sacrificed his life by driving through the pass in a jeep, drawing fire from the enemy's concealed positions. The location of these was noted and a second attack, delivered from the cliffs above, methodically wiped out the Egyptians, killing 200. The tragedy was that physical possession of the Mitla Pass had never formed part of the General Staff's plan, and yielded neither strategic nor tactical benefit. 202 Brigade's 38 dead and 120 wounded in this unnecessary engagement were bitterly resented by an army which strove to keep casualties to an absolute minimum, but somehow Sharon managed to survive all the criticism levelled at him.

Meanwhile, phase two of the offensive was already under way. The advance against the Abu Aweigila complex had begun during the night of 29/30 October and was made by a battlegroup designated as Task Force 38, commanded by Colonel Yehuda Wallach and consisting of the 7th Armoured Brigade, the 4th

Above: An Israeli soldier using a bazooka is given cover by a colleague while he engages, and destroys, an Egyptian tank.

and 10th Infantry Brigades, joined later by the 37th Mechanised Brigade. The Egyptian outpost at El Quseima was captured at dawn on the 30th by the 4th Infantry Brigade, which promptly despatched units southwards to establish contact with Sharon's paratroopers at Nakhl.

The 7th Armoured Brigade, commanded by Colonel Uri Ben-Ari, now closed up to the Abu Aweigila

An unnecessary battle

'This bloody capture of the Heitan defile at Mitla might have been justified if the task of the brigade was to reach Suez.... But in the present circumstances . . . there was no vital need to attack the Egyptian unit defending the approaches to the canal. The valour, daring and fighting spirit of the paratroop commanders are qual-ities which should be applauded and encouraged, but this battle was not essential. Moreover, after capturing the Pass, the paratroopers continued to base themselves near the Parker Memorial. The Pass was therefore attacked, captured and abandoned.'

General Moshe Dayan in Diary of the Sinai Campaign.

Sharon's drive through Sinai
29-31 Oct 1956

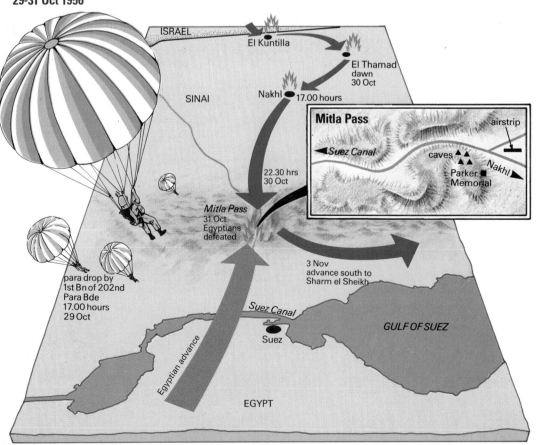

ISRAEL

El Kuntilla

El Thamad dawn 30 Oct

SINAI

Nakhl 17.00 hours

22.30 hrs 30 Oct

Mitla Pass 31 Oct Egyptians defeated

3 Nov advance south to Sharm el Sheikh

para drop by 1st Bn of 202nd Para Bde 17.00 hours 29 Oct

Egyptian advance

Suez Canal

Suez

GULF OF SUEZ

EGYPT

Mitla Pass

airstrip

Suez Canal

caves

Parker Memorial

Nakhl

complex, which consisted of several fortified zones surrounded by barbed wire, minefields and artillery killing grounds, and was defended by two Egyptian brigades, an artillery regiment and 23 Archer tank destroyers. Probing attacks against the eastern and southern faces of the complex were easily held, and the brigade's reconnaissance units began to search for a way round. This they found in the Wadi Daika, some way south of Abu Aweigila. The troops guarding this defile had been swept away by the tide of fugitives from El Quseima and, although they had destroyed a bridge, Israeli engineers quickly prepared a route for tracked vehicles.

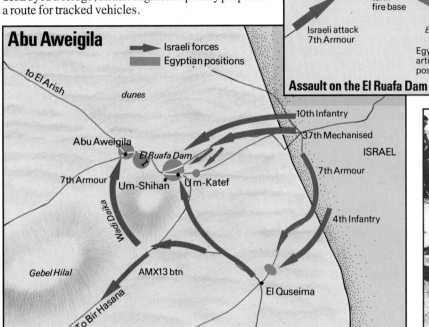

Assault on the El Ruafa Dam

Below: Death at Abu Aweigila. Press photographers record the scene after Israeli units, advancing across Sinai, successfully engaged and eliminated an Egyptian position. Bottom: Dusk descends on the desert as Israeli troops deploy from their half-track APCs ready for action.

Abu Aweigila

Attack on the El Ruafa Dam

'The attack started after sunset. In the dim, dust-laden twilight, the weary eyes of the tank crews could hardly see ahead. The Egyptians opened up their frontal fire with everything they had, and right away scored a direct hit on one of the half-tracks; all the men aboard became casualties. This stopped the rest of the half-tracks, but they recovered in a few minutes and continued their advance. Soon darkness fell, and all that lit the black night were the illuminated flight paths of the criss-crossing shells and the bursts of flame from exploding Egyptian ammunition stores that we had touched off. All the tanks of our assault unit were hit by anti-tank fire, but most of them managed to continue their advance. In the final stages of the battle, these tanks ran out of ammunition and their crews fought on with hand grenades and sub-machine guns. After clearing the Egyptian posts and their communications trenches from the last nests of resistance, the wounded were assembled and bandaged by the light of jeep headlamps.'

General Moshe Dayan in Diary of the Sinai Campaign.

A battlegroup consisting of a Sherman battalion and some mechanised infantry, commanded by Lieutenant-Colonel Avraham ('Bren') Adan, was passed through and by 0500 hours on 31 October had isolated the enemy complex from the west; by 0630 hours Abu Aweigila village had been taken and the outer shell of the defence had been cracked open. Ben-Ari had already deployed an AMX13 battalion on the Bir Hasana track to block a suspected counter-attack by Egyptian armour, but this threat proved to be illusory.

Adan, however, while preparing to deal with the next fortified zone, that surrounding the El Ruafa Dam, was compelled to deal simultaneously with a real counter-attack made by a formation of T34/85s from the direction of El Arish. The Egyptians, luckily for the Israelis, showed no inclination to close the range and their threat was contained by a combination of gunfire and air strikes. During the evening Adan succeeded in capturing the El Ruafa Dam in the teeth of fierce opposition which cost him 80 casualties, knocked out several tanks and damaged the remainder. His battlegroup had barely finished replenishing and carrying out essential repairs when the Egyptians attempted to recapture the position with a counter-attack from Um-Shihan, supported by fire from Um-Katef. This was defeated with a loss to the Egyptians of 37 killed and four Archers destroyed.

Death in the desert

The following day, 1 November, found Adan's force, now close to exhaustion, maintaining its blocking position to the west while the 10th Infantry and 37th Mechanised Brigades attempted unsuccessfully to storm the Um-Shihan and Um-Katef pockets, sustaining serious losses in the process. During the night, in response to orders from the Egyptian high command, the garrisons broke out in small groups and attempted to reach El Arish. Many of these brave men, who for three days had offered the most determined resistance, perished in the desert from heat exhaustion and thirst.

By now, the Israeli spearhead was already many miles to the west. Ben-Ari had been advised that the Egyptian 1st Armoured Brigade, believed to consist of two T34/85 battalions, an APC battalion and a company of SU100 tank destroyers, had left Bir Gifgafa and was about to intervene in the battle. Leaving Adan at the El Ruafa Dam, he assembled the remainder of the 7th Armoured Brigade and set off to intercept. No real contact was ever made, for the Egyptian column, which had already been subjected to air attack, had received orders to withdraw as quickly as possible across the canal. On his own initiative, Ben-Ari decided to follow and swept, almost unopposed, across central Sinai, halting his pursuit some 16km (10 miles) short of Ismailiya and the canal. His action was widely regarded as being both high-handed and risky, but was later defended by Dayan.

The rapid withdrawal of the 1st Armoured Brigade and the sudden disappearance of the Egyptian Air Force stemmed from indirect pressure applied by the Anglo-French task force which, from the evening of 31 October, had begun bombing Egyptian air bases.

In anticipation of the main Anglo-French landing Nasser decided to abandon Sinai, concentrate his air effort and preserve as much as possible of the 1st Armoured Brigade for future use. This, of course, left

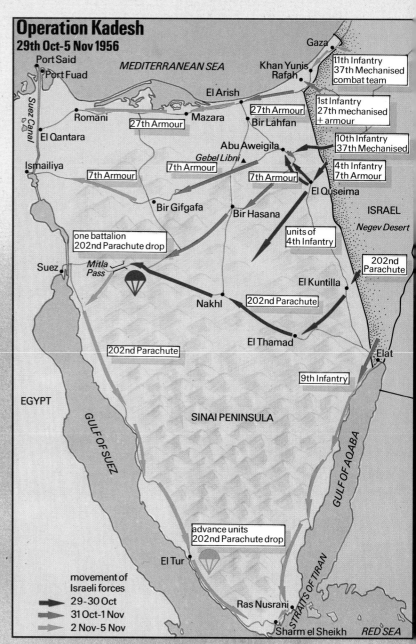

his troops in Sinai without air cover or an armoured reserve.

The third phase of the Israeli offensive, the elimination of those Egyptian forces occupying the Gaza Strip, was itself planned in two phases. In the first, commencing at midnight on 31 October, the 1st Infantry Brigade and the 27th Mechanised Brigade would strike into the base of the strip to seize Rafah, following which the latter would carry out an exploitation in the direction of El Arish. The second, beginning at 0600 hours on 2 November, would involve the 11th Infantry Brigade and part of the 37th Mechanised Brigade attacking Gaza itself.

The Rafah attack made slow progress at first, being held up by extensive minefields covered by enemy fire. At length the Egyptian positions were stormed after savage hand-to-hand fighting and the 27th Mechanised Brigade, commanded by General Chaim Bar-Lev, broke out onto the El Arish road. Some miles east of El Arish, however, lies the Jiradi defile, in which the coast road passes through an area of deep sand dunes. This was held by the Egyptians in strength and for a while they halted Bar-Lev's advance. An air strike was called down, and under cover of this he pushed an AMX13 battalion and a force of mechanised infantry into the dunes, from which they attacked and routed the defenders.

El Arish itself was entered on the morning of 2 November. Its garrison had consisted of one brigade of the embattled 3rd Infantry Division, but the 1st Mechanised Division, sent forward on the outbreak of hostilities, had just arrived after a difficult journey in which it had been subjected to air attack. Now the Egyptian high command ordered complete evacuation and withdrawal across the canal. There was little for Bar-Lev to do but follow up, and by dusk his brigade had passed through Romani and halted just short of the Anglo-French 16km (10-mile) zone, establishing contact with the 7th Armoured Brigade on its left.

Meanwhile, back in the Gaza Strip, the notorious Ali el Muntar ridge had soon been captured and the Egyptian governor of Gaza formally surrendered the town. The last pockets of resistance, centred on Khan Yunis, capitulated the same day.

The only remaining objective of the Israeli offensive was Sharm el Sheikh at the southern tip of the Sinai peninsula, but operations for its capture were already in progress. Colonel Avraham Yoffe's 9th Infantry Brigade had been moving steadily down the east coast of Sinai while the war continued, supplied by sea whenever possible. The going was difficult in the extreme and offered numerous natural defensive positions, of which the Egyptians failed to take full advantage. On 4 November the brigade reached Ras Nusrani, which had been turned into a veritable fortress, to find that it had been completely abandoned. This probably stemmed from the fact that Sharon's 202nd Parachute Brigade had been redeployed from the Mitla Pass and was driving down the west coast, having dropped an advance guard at El Tur. In consequence, the Egyptian commander decided to concentrate his troops inside Sharm el Sheikh. The decision availed him little for his men had no stomach for a fight, and Yoffe's brigade encountered only slight difficulty in breaking through his perimeter. By 0930 hours on 5 November Sharm el Sheikh was in Israeli hands and the Straits of Tiran were open.

Heavy Egyptian casualties

The end of the 1956 Sinai campaign coincided with the British and French parachute drops on, respectively, Port Said and Port Fuad. It had cost Israel 181 men killed, 25 tanks, two Mystères and nine piston-engined aircraft, the IAF's losses resulting primarily from concentrated ground fire. Approximately 2000 Egyptians were killed and 6000 taken prisoner. Captured equipment included 100 tanks and tank destroyers, a large quantity of artillery, and a useful number of APCs. In the short period prior to the withdrawal of the Egyptian Air Force, the IAF claimed the destruction of five MiGs and four Vampires. At sea the Egyptian destroyer *Ibrahim Awal* shelled Haifa on 31 October, but surrendered after a brief engagement with Israeli surface units, during which she also came under air attack.

Despite the stubborn resistance put up by the Abu Aweigila garrison, the Egyptian dispositions in Sinai were patently faulty and suffered from the lack of adequate reserves. The IDF, on the other hand, achieved complete surprise and retained the strategic initiative throughout. Much of the credit for this must go to the GOC Southern Command, Major-General Assaf Simhoni, who provided the intermediate link between his brigade commanders and Moshe Dayan. Simhoni, a former tank officer, had been determined from the outset that armour was to play the leading role in the campaign, and his concept had been fully vindicated. He was to die in an air crash just as the war ended, but from this time onwards the Armoured Corps was to be regarded as the cutting edge of the Israeli Army and was expanded accordingly.

In the opinion of the late Captain Sir Basil Liddell Hart the 1956 Sinai campaign was a brilliant application of the strategy of the 'indirect approach' which had rendered the Egyptian positions untenable from the beginning. The campaign, in his own words, had been 'a work of art'.

Bryan Perrett

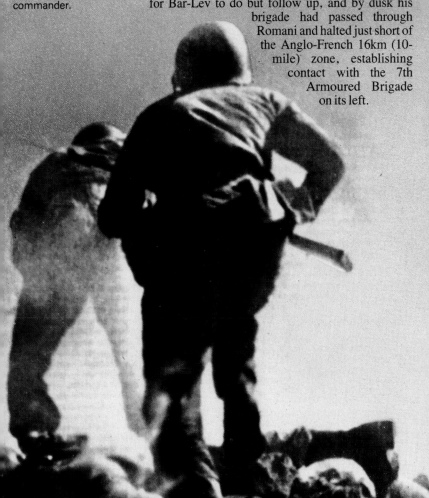

Below left: Two jeeps parked back to back form a podium from which the Israeli flag is raised after the successful capture, by Colonel Avraham Yoffe's 9th Infantry Brigade, of the fort at Sharm el Sheikh. Below: Members of an Egyptian commando patrol break forward in order to engage Israeli troops, stepping over the body of their dead commander.

Uniting for peace

How the UN brought an end to hostilities

Above: As the Israeli forces withdrew from Sinai, UN troops took up their positions. This Yugoslav soldier stands guard in the desert. Left: Under blazing sun, UN troops relax in Gaza.

The Israeli attack into Sinai on 29 October 1956 and the subsequent British and French military intervention at Suez provided the United Nations with a major challenge to which it responded by creating the first peacekeeping force in the history of the UN. The Security Council met on 30 October 1956 to consider a resolution censuring Israel and demanding the immediate withdrawal of Israeli armed forces; the resolution was defeated when it was vetoed by Britain and France.

The following day the British and French bombing began. This led to a Yugoslav resolution in the Security Council calling for a special emergency session of the General Assembly as provided for in the Uniting for Peace Resolution 377(v) adopted in November 1950 at the time of the Korean conflict. The Yugoslav resolution was a procedural one and so could not be vetoed. It was, therefore, passed, though Britain and France voted against. The Yugoslav delegate argued that since the Security Council was being prevented from exercising its primary responsibility for maintaining international peace and security because of the veto held by the permanent members, the matter should be considered by the General Assembly.

A hastily assembled meeting of the General Assembly then began on 1 November 1956, and early the following day the Assembly passed a United States resolution calling for an immediate ceasefire and the withdrawal of all forces from Egyptian territory. On 4 November a Canadian resolution was passed which called for the creation of a United Nations Emergency Force (UNEF) to be sent to the Middle East with the consent of the Egyptian government to supervise the ceasefire and withdrawal of the forces involved. Secretary-General Dag Hammarskjöld produced an outline plan within hours that was accepted by the General Assembly on 5 November, and more detailed arrangements were given approval on 7 November.

The aims of the peacekeeping force were to supervise the implementation of the ceasefire (which had been arranged on 7 November), take over the withdrawal arrangements, and assist pacification of the area by interposing itself between Egyptian and Israeli forces. In this way it was hoped that UNEF would contribute to peacemaking in the Middle East by creating a stable atmosphere in which negotiations for a long-term settlement could take place.

UNEF was composed of contingents from 10 member states: Brazil, Canada, Colombia, Den-

mark, Finland, India, Indonesia, Norway, Sweden and Yugoslavia, and totalled just over 6000 men at its peak in March 1957. It was commanded by a Canadian, Major-General E. L. M. Burns but was answerable ultimately to the General Assembly in New York through the secretary-general and a committee of seven of the contributing states which Hammarskjöld had appointed to assume political control of the operation. The 10 participating states in UNEF were chosen by the secretary-general and his committee from more than 20 states which had offered to contribute. Those chosen excluded the permanent members of the Security Council and came from states which were neutral and therefore impartial in the crisis, and were acceptable to the Egyptian government.

Above: UN troops patrol a desert area in a jeep which mounts a Browning 0.5in machine gun. Right: Armed with a Bren gun, a British soldier stands by as Norwegian troops are briefed.

Clearing the canal

UNEF was deployed entirely on Egyptian territory. The first troops landed in Egypt on 15 November 1956, wearing light-blue helmets and UN armbands but retaining the uniforms of their national forces. A temporary staging area had been established at Capodichino near Naples in Italy. The secretary-general himself flew to Egypt on 16 November for two days of talks with President Nasser and his foreign minister. Final details of the operation were arranged at this meeting, where a request was made by the Egyptian government for the UN to organise the clearing of the Suez Canal, which had been blocked during the fighting. The Egyptians also made clear their right under the UN Charter for the peacekeeping force to be withdrawn if Egypt so demanded.

A continuous shuttle then took place between Capodichino and Abu Suweir, with troops initially being flown to Egypt by Swissair and their equipment by the Italian Air Force, but from 26 November the Royal Canadian Air Force took over this role. General Burns set up his headquarters at El Ballah to the north of Ismailiya, and by mid-December UNEF totalled 5000 troops. The evacuation of the British and French forces was complete by 23 December and UNEF then took up its role as a buffer force between Egypt and Israel.

The UN troops were lightly armed, with rifles, machine guns, sub-machine guns, anti-tank rockets and some armoured cars, but force was only to be used

Above: Dag Hammarskjöld, Secretary-General of the United Nations, produced the outline plans for the provision of a UN Emergency Force to be sent in to Suez and the Sinai.

in self-defence and as a last resort. The operation was peaceful and successful, with the 10 different nationalities combining well and working with astonishing smoothness. By 23 January 1957 Israeli forces had withdrawn from Egyptian territory except for their positions at Sharm el Sheikh overlooking the Straits of Tiran at the entrance to the Gulf of Aqaba, and in Gaza. In the first week of March, the Israelis withdrew from these areas too, and UN troops then allowed Egyptian re-occupation. UNEF had completed its basic task by late March. The force, however, remained on the armistice lines for another 10 years with the intention of preventing another conflict between Egypt and Israel. The Suez Canal was also cleared, under the UN flag, by April 1957.

The cost of UNEF from 1956 to 1967 was $213 million. A special UN account was set up to meet these expenses and was funded by voluntary contributions and assessments on all UN members – though some states refused to contribute at all. The success of the operation was, in part, a result of the energy and resourcefulness of Dag Hammarskjöld himself. There is no doubt that the UN peacekeeping force – the first of its kind and created in just a few days – did play a central role in maintaining peace on the Egyptian-Israeli frontier in the subsequent years until it was withdrawn at the request of the Egyptian government in May 1967, just before the Six-Day War in June.

David Johnson

Mobility in battle

The development of mobile warfare since 1945

By 1945 the armoured fighting vehicle (AFV) had become the cornerstone of land warfare in all but the most difficult or most mountainous country. The success of the German Blitzkrieg during the years 1939 to 1941, the to-and-fro of the desert fighting in North Africa and the massive tank battles on the Eastern Front had all served to confirm this. All the major participants, apart from the Japanese, had built up large mechanised forces based on the tank, although the emphasis in organisation and handling was on combined arms. In other words, practice had shown that the tank on its own was vulnerable to anti-tank weapons and needed to cooperate intimately with infantry and artillery to be effective. And, as the Germans had demonstrated in northwest Europe in 1944-45, the tank itself could be a powerful defensive weapon, especially when Panthers and Tigers were dug in against the lighter Allied Shermans and Cromwells, and the attacking forces found themselves outgunned. The trend during World War II had been inexorably towards heavier and larger-gunned tanks.

With the coming of peace there was a drastic reduction in wartime armies and, at the same time, an appraisal of the experience gained. In the United States there was an influential body of opinion which believed that the power of the tank would now decline, especially after Hiroshima and Nagasaki had shown that strategic bombing was supreme, and by the beginning of 1946 only one out of a previous 16 armoured divisions had been retained. In Great Britain, although there was a broadly similar reduction in armour strength, condemnation of the tank was not so sweeping, while in the Soviet Union armoured forces

Below: A German Panzer Mark III acts as a protection against enemy fire for supporting infantry in Russia, 1942. Although later superseded, the Mark III was the spearhead of the first Blitzkriegs of World War II.

Principles of armoured warfare

'Everything is therefore dependent on this: to be able to move faster than has hitherto been done; to keep moving despite the enemy's defensive fire and thus to make it harder for him to build up fresh defensive positions; and finally to carry the attack deep into the enemy's defences. The proponents of tank warfare believe that, in favourable circumstances, they possess the means for achieving this.... We believe that by attacking with tanks we can achieve a higher rate of movement than has been hitherto obtainable, and – what is perhaps even more important – we can keep moving once a breakthrough has been made....

In any event, in land battles the tank possesses the unique quality of being able to bring its firepower to bear while actually advancing against the enemy, and it can do this even though all the defence's guns and machine guns have not been silenced.'

Heinz Guderian, writing in the Journal of the National Union of German Officers, *15 October 1937.*

remained of prime importance.

By the 1950s, when the Cold War was in full swing, the West looked again at its armoury and realised that Nato forces were greatly outnumbered in conventional land weapons. It soon became clear that should war break out once again in Europe the Russians would undertake a Blitzkrieg type offensive, relying heavily on large mechanised forces to penetrate the Nato defences, and keep driving until they reached the English Channel, something they would aim to achieve in a matter of days.

The Nato planners, conscious of their inferiority in conventional forces, saw tactical nuclear weapons as the only way of strengthening their defence. What conventional forces they had would be used to fight a delaying action back from the inner German border (IGB) to a main defensive position based on a natural obstacle, usually a river. Then the enemy would be canalised into what was called a nuclear killing zone (NKZ) in which he was to be subjected to nuclear attack. Should he choose to reply in kind, then the policy of massive retaliation would immediately be implemented.

Within the conventional-force aspects of this scenario, the tank was seen as the main anti-armour weapon, with infantry acting as an anchor, holding onto tactically vital ground. Although the Centurions, Pattons (and later M60s and Leopards) were clearly technically superior to the Soviet T34s, JS3s and T54/55s ranged against them, it was recognised that sheer weight of numbers would make the Russian breakthrough inevitable. There was, of course, an air of unreality about this theorising on the nature of a hypothetical battlefield; and yet it was hard for the planners to find realistic situations on which to base their opinions about the capabilities of more modern

Below left: The modern concept of mobile warfare includes not only tanks, but also both mechanised infantry and helicopter support. Below: Egyptian troops on manoeuvres with mechanised infantry vehicles. The move towards the mechanised infantry combat vehicle, which carries a substantial main armament, and away from the more lightly gunned armoured personnel carrier, is an attempt to deploy maximum firepower in the field.

tanks. Indeed, only in one part of the world, the Middle East, could armoured warfare be said to have burgeoned since 1945.

After the 1948-49 war, Israel had concluded that the only way to guarantee survival against her Arab neighbours in the future was by launching pre-emptive attacks against them should they threaten further invasions. The majority view within the command of the Israeli Defence Force (IDF) was that mechanised infantry should be the prime land weapon, because the armoured personnel carrier (APC) had more mobility than the Sherman tanks with which the Israelis were equipped, and that the latter should be used merely as fire support. Only a minority group, led by Colonel Uri Ben-Ari, argued that the tank must be the dominant weapon. Ben-Ari's views found little favour, especially as the few Israeli attempts to use tanks in 1948 had met with meagre success.

The APC lobby still held sway when Israel went to war again in 1956, but the Armoured Corps had been expanded to a certain extent and, in view of the fact that the Egyptians were relying on a static defence in Sinai, it was agreed that once the infantry had punched a hole in the defences, the armour would be allowed to pass through and exploit. In the event, Ben-Ari, now commanding the 7th Brigade, won a dazzling success at Abu Aweigila. Arriving ahead of the infantry he was supposed to support during the break-in operation, he smashed through the Egyptian defences and his tanks were the first Israeli units to arrive at the Suez Canal.

During the decade following 1956 the Israeli Armoured Corps (IAC) gradually got its view across that the tank was the decisive arm. General Israel Tal, its commander in the years leading up to 1967,

defined battlefield mobility as being not just cross-country agility, the term used by the mechanised infantry protagonists, but as the ability to move about the battlefield under fire. In this respect, the Pattons and Centurions with which Tal's forces began to be equipped in the 1960s were vastly superior to any APC available. Tal saw the tank as a 'mailed fist', carrying out not just the breakthrough but driving deep into the enemy's territory to carry out wholesale dislocation. Mechanised infantry would widen the breach and follow up behind the tanks as an insurance against counter-attack, while motorised infantry would be responsible for mopping up bypassed strongpoints.

Tal's theories were put to the test in 1967, and the results were awesome. Having broken through defences which some commentators compared to those of the Russians at Kursk in 1943, the Israelis cleared Sinai of Egyptian forces and reached the Suez Canal in four days. It was indeed a spectacular victory and seemed to confirm the primacy of the tank.

For the British, who, unlike most of their allies, believed in sacrificing speed for protection in their tank design, the Israeli successes were encouraging, but the problems facing Nato in Europe now looked overwhelming. To some observers there seemed no reason to believe that a pre-emptive strike covered by massive air power might not achieve a similar result for the Warsaw Pact forces on the north German plain.

Nato's problems were further aggravated in the late 1960s by the decision to adopt a policy of forward defence on the Central Front. This meant that the main defensive position was moved much closer to the IGB and there was now less room to delay the enemy and reduce his armour strength. Consequently, even more armour had to be deployed in exposed forward positions, leaving little for counter-attack. In other words, the armour was being tied down to a strictly defensive role without being allowed to make use of one of its prime characteristics, that of shock action. Another drawback was that because there was only a finite number of troops immediately available on the ground, the Nato defences were in danger of lacking sufficient depth to absorb Warsaw Pact incursions.

It began to seem that the tank was once again in the ascendant and power lay very much with the offensive by the late 1960s. But as usual in a technological race, other developments swung the pendulum back again. Defensive firepower had begun to improve in its turn.

Long-range firepower

The first of these new developments was the anti-tank guided weapon (ATGW). At the time, the maximum effective range of the tank gun, the main anti-armour weapon, was 2000m (2190 yards). ATGW had the ability to engage tanks at far greater ranges. Thus, intelligently positioned ATGW could begin engaging enemy armour further out, and achieve higher kill rates. The first ATGWs, the British Malkara and American Shillelagh, came into service in the early 1960s, and were quickly followed by others, including Soviet models.

Connected with ATGW was the increasing use of the helicopter. It was the Americans in Vietnam who developed the concept of the attack helicopter, and, in order to give it more 'teeth', it was decided to test it using ATGW. Experiments in the late 1960s, both in Europe and the United States, seemed to indicate that the helicopter's ability to hug the ground gave it great capacity for surprise and that it might well be an

Below: Israeli armour advances cautiously during the 1973 Yom Kippur War. In the foreground is one of the Israeli modifications of the Sherman chassis. Above right: An AMX10P MICV with crew and equipment. This vehicle mounts a 20mm M693 cannon and a 7.62mm machine gun which is co-axial with the main armament. It carries a total of 800 rounds of 20mm and 2000 rounds of 7.62mm ammunition. Below right: The MCV80 MICV which mounts a 30mm Rarden cannon and a 7.62mm co-axial machine gun. The MCV80 is expected to enter service with the British Army in 1985 or 1986.

effective antidote to the tank. Indeed, some enthusiasts began to believe that the attack helicopter would supersede the tank, a view reinforced by American successes during the North Vietnamese invasion of early 1972. Then, in 1973, came an even bigger shock to the 'tank school'.

The Six-Day War of 1967 had appeared to confirm General Tal's belief in the omnipotence of the tank, and so the Israelis increased the separation of their tanks from infantry. Indeed, the Israeli plans to safeguard the gains they had made in Sinai in 1967 relied largely on armoured forces. They had constructed the Bar-Lev Line on the eastern bank of the Suez Canal as a first line of defence. Should the Egyptians ever succeed in breaking through, the plan was to counter-attack with tanks and drive them back across the canal.

When, in October 1973, the Egyptians managed to cross the canal, catching the Israelis by surprise, the overconfident Israelis were thrown into confusion. For when they sent in their tanks to drive the Egyptians back, they discovered to their horror that they

Over page: Top left: An FV1620 Hornet mounting two Malkara missiles. The Malkara was replaced in the late 1960s by the BAC Swingfire mounted on the Ferret Mk5 (FV712) armoured car. Top right: A soldier prepares to fire the Franco-German anti-tank missile Milan. This weapon is normally used at platoon or company level and was designed as a medium-range light anti-armour weapon for use by infantry.

were an easy target for the Egyptians, who engaged them using Russian-made Sagger ATGW. Not until a complete Israeli tank brigade had been destroyed did they wake up to the fact that the only way to deal with the new weapon was to have infantry operating closely with the armour. It was an old lesson re-learnt the hard way.

In the aftermath of the Yom Kippur War, some theorists predicted the end of AFV primacy and claimed that the defensive was now all-powerful. But most Western commentators took a less extreme view, and realised that the right balance was what was required. The concept of the anti-armour 'family' was born. All anti-armour weapons, be they air or ground, guided missile, recoilless or tank gun, had their part to play on the battlefield, and it was a question of orchestrating them to make maximum use of their individual strengths. The tank would still remain an important member of the family, especially as improvements in fire control systems, gun ammunition and armoured protection during the 1970s meant that it could engage its opposite numbers further out with improved chance of a first round hit, as well as reducing its vulnerability. But another innovation also helped to restore the tank to its true role, especially within Nato. This was the advent of the mechanised infantry combat vehicle (MICV).

The first to appear on the scene was the Russian BMP of 1967, and this was followed shortly afterwards by the West German Marder. The advantage of the MICV over the APC lies in its increased armament, giving it an anti-armour capability which the latter does not have. The MICV can take its place in the firing line and can contribute significantly to the anti-armour battle, especially in engaging light armour. The result is that the Americans (M2 Bradley), the British (MCV80) and the French (AMX10P) are also introducing them.

There is a penalty to be paid, however. Their complexity means much higher costs, and it is unlikely that the Western democracies will be able to afford as many as they require. But at least the introduction of the MICV means that more tanks can be held back, to use shock action in what Nato commanders now term the counterstroke – that is, the use of armoured forces to hit an enemy in the flank when

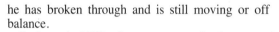

Below: The US guided projectile Copperhead. Bottom: A Copperhead about to hit an M47 medium tank.

he has broken through and is still moving or off balance.

In the early 1980s, there were two other important technical developments that made life more difficult for armour on the battlefield. The first was an improved precision guided munition (PGM). Using an observer with a laser designator, indirect fire weapons (those that cannot see their target) can now engage individual tanks. The first of these was the American Copperhead, an anti-armour round fired from conventional artillery guns, and developments are now taking place to apply this principle to the mortar. The mortar's high trajectory threatens the top of the tank, an area that in general has been only lightly protected. Secondly, armoured forces are now faced with the scatterable or remotely-delivered mine. Instead of having to pre-position minefields, with all the engineer effort that this requires, mines can now be fired directly into the path of an armoured advance.

All these technical innovations have undoubtedly made life very much more difficult for tanks and would appear to threaten mobility on the land battlefield. This is something which is of particular concern to the Warsaw Pact, reliant as it is on a strategy of a rapid, successful offensive.

Various solutions to breaking open the Nato defences are presumably under consideration. The first is probably an even greater emphasis on the power of artillery, something the Soviet Army has always set great store by, although it is interesting that it did not introduce self-propelled artillery until the early 1970s, 30 years after the West. Another is the concept of the operational manoeuvre group (OMG), a mechanised force which, accompanied by attack and troop-carrying helicopters, would penetrate the enemy defences prior to the main offensive and aim for tactical nuclear-weapon sites, headquarters and communication centres; dislocation would be the objective.

The questions posed by the new technology available on the battlefield have hardly begun to be answered, however. The Israeli advance into Lebanon in 1982 seemed to show that air superiority, using the latest electronic devices, could once again enable a ruthlessly executed armoured attack to be carried out and that modern battle tanks like the Merkava would, in the right hands, be able to spearhead ground forces; but the most recent anti-armour weapons were not present there. As so often since 1945, judgement has to be suspended.   **Charles Messenger**

Key Weapons

The M16 ASSAULT RIFLE

In the early 1950s, in the aftermath of the Korean War, the United States Infantry Board decided that a new, lightweight rifle was required, and in 1957 they published a requirement which asked for a weapon weighing not more than 2.72kg (6lb) when loaded, as accurate as the Garand M1 rifle at 460m (500yds) range, capable of automatic or single shot fire, and capable of penetrating a steel helmet or body armour at 460m (500yds).

Among the companies who took notice of this was the smallarms research company Armalite Incorporated of Costa Mesa, California. Their chief designer, Eugene Stoner, had already helped develop a modern gas-operated automatic rifle known as the AR-10, firing the 7.62mm Nato cartridge, but the weight requirement of the new weapon meant that a small high-velocity cartridge had to be used. The US Army and Air Force had been involved in an experimental programme which had led them to believe that the existing .222 Remington cartridge held promise, and Stoner began working on what was virtually a scaled-down AR-10 in .222 calibre.

Trials with the first prototype showed that the .222 cartridge was causing excessive chamber pressure, so the round was redesigned to have a slightly larger case, thus providing space to make adjustments to the propelling charge. This became the '.223 Remington' and has since been adopted world-wide as the

5.56×45mm cartridge. In March 1958, 10 test rifles were delivered to the US Army, and after extensive trials the new rifle, now known as the AR-15, was recommended as a possible replacement for the existing M14, though, generally, throughout the army there was strong opposition to the whole concept of small-calibre weapons. Subsequent tests led to some minor changes in the design, and in 1959 Armalite came to a business agreement with the major arms manufacturer Colt for the latter to manufacture the AR-15 in quantity.

The first large order for the AR-15 came from the

Previous page: An M16-armed Gurkha in Brunei. Above: The M16 in action with Marines in Vietnam. Below: An M16 with starlight night scope and XM148 grenade launcher. Opposite top: British and Gurkha troops in Hong Kong. Far right: An AR15 fitted with the Sopelem OB50 night sight. Right: South Vietnamese forces bring in a prisoner.

US Air Force, which required a light weapon for guard patrols on strategic bombers and airbases, and in 1962 8500 rifles were ordered. Then the Department of Defense ordered 1000; in 1963 a further 104,000 rifles were ordered for use by the air force and other categories of special service troops.

Many of the US Air Force weapons went to Vietnam, and these, together with the 1000 which had been sent to the US Military Assistance Group there, found immediate favour with the South Vietnamese who, being rather smaller than the average American soldier, found the light AR-15 a more convenient weapon. The Vietnamese requests for more AR-15s, combined with Defense Secretary Robert McNamara's enthusiasm for the rifle, led to the army taking rather more interest; they realised it would be a good weapon for the type of close-combat typical of the fighting in Vietnam, and by 1966 the army had bought more than 400,000 rifles. Shortly afterwards it was standardised as the M16 rifle.

Operational system

The M16 is gas operated, without the use of a conventional piston. When fired, a portion of the gas following the bullet is tapped off through a hole in the barrel and directed down a stainless steel tube back into the receiver where it is expelled into the hollow bolt carrier. The expanding gas forces the carrier back, and a cam slot in the carrier, working on a lug on the bolt, causes the bolt to be revolved to unlock from the chamber, and then be pulled back together with the carrier. As the bolt unit goes back so it re-cocks the hammer and compresses a return spring. At the end of its recoil stroke, the spring exerts itself and drives the bolt forward to collect another round from the magazine and drive it into the chamber. The bolt head comes to a stop on the cartridge but the bolt carrier continues forward for a short distance so that the cam slot turns the lug and locks the bolt. The firer then presses the trigger, the hammer is released to strike

M16 Assault Rifle

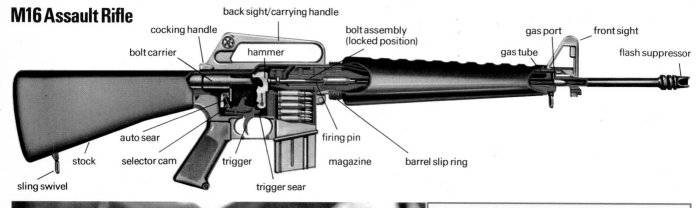

cocking handle
back sight/carrying handle
bolt assembly (locked position)
gas port
front sight
bolt carrier
hammer
gas tube
flash suppressor
auto sear
firing pin
selector cam
trigger
magazine
barrel slip ring
stock
sling swivel
trigger sear

M16 Assault Rifle

Calibre 5.56mm
Length 99cm (39in)
Weight (loaded with 30-round magazine) 3.82kg (8.42lb)
Rate of fire Cyclical 700-900rpm; practical automatic 150-200rpm; practical semi-automatic 45-65rpm
Maximum effective range 460m (500yds)
Magazine 20 or 30-round box
Cartridge M193 5.56×45mm round
Muzzle velocity 1000mps (3280 fps)

Left: Armed with an M16A1, one of Charlie Lademora's troops patrols the jungle area of the Tambis region of south Mindanao in the Philippines. Lademora, a former officer with the Philippine Army, set up a fighting force of army deserters and criminals in the mid-1970s to combat the threat of communist infiltration in the area. The M16 shown here mounts the standard US Army M203 grenade launcher, considerably increasing the firepower available to the unit, and is fitted with the later, curved, 30-round magazine.

Above: Equipped with M16A1s and the telescopic-stock variant, the M16A1 carbine, a unit of the 1st Air Cavalry Division (Airmobile) is deployed from a UH-1 against Viet Cong positions.

Below: US airborne troops capture a hilltop in Vietnam. Their M16s were a simple and effective weapon, particularly suited to the close-fire fighting typical of the war.

the firing pin, and the next shot is fired. On automatic fire, of course, the hammer rises as soon as the bolt is locked and fires the next round without the firer having to release and re-press the trigger.

When the M16 was introduced, much was made of the simplicity of the design and the fact that it required minimal maintenance and cleaning. Unfortunately, the troops in Vietnam took this to mean that it needed no cleaning at all, and this led to a spate of complaints about failure to eject and various other types of malfunction. A Congressional enquiry found that the type of powder used in the original 5.56mm cartridge had been changed to that used in the M14, a variety which generated much more fouling and carbon, and when deposited in the bolt mechanism it solidified to a rock-like hardness which could jam the weapon.

Some small changes were made to the rifle, notably the chroming of the chamber and later the whole barrel, thereby preventing the build-up of rust which had previously been a serious problem. A plunger was fitted, allowing the soldier to drive the bolt home if the cartridge was reluctant to enter a dirty chamber and the necessary cleaning equipment was issued. Alongside these improvements an education programme pointed out the need for basic standards of weapon care. After that the rifle was known as the M16A1 and thereafter worked effectively in the field.

During the 1960s much ill-informed comment was published about the lethal effect of the 5.56mm bullet fired from the M16 rifle. It is a light bullet which, in order to have the maximum possible target effect, has been closely matched to the rifling which spins it. So

Above: One of Lademora's cowboys cradles a Philippine version of the Colt carbine. Like the M16A1, the carbine is provided with a forward bolt assist directly below the cocking handle. The weapon shown here is fitted with the standard M16A1 closed flash suppressor and a 30-round magazine.

Below: The XM177E2. This later version of the Colt Commando was fitted with a 292mm (11.5in) barrel to permit grenade launching but retains the retractable butt and the 101mm (4in) flash suppressor of the E1.

long as the bullet is passing through the air it is stable and accurate, but as soon as it meets something thicker than air it will tumble over and deliver up all its energy in a massive blow. Thus, during the early stages of the Vietnam War, rumour circulated through the army about the explosive impact of the new small-calibre bullet. But while the M16 bullet was capable of inflicting severe damage to the human body the reports of Viet Cong being killed by shock from wounds in the hand were undoubtedly exaggerated. In addition, the latest 5.56mm bullets are somewhat heavier than the original American design and require a faster spin, so that they are now more stable and less devastating in their effect on the body.

During the Vietnam War a shorter and handier version of the M16 was issued to special forces units in the American armed forces. Initially designated the XM177E1 (XM177 for the air force) it became better known as the Colt Commando or CAR-15, and was highly regarded by the combat soldier in Vietnam. Although the firing mechanism is the same as that of

the M16, instead of the standard 533mm (21in) barrel the CAR-15 had a cut-down barrel only 254mm (10in) in length, and is provided with a telescopic butt which can be pulled out for firing from the shoulder.

Lacking the accuracy of the M16 at longer ranges, the CAR-15 was in effect a small-calibre submachine gun and as such proved ideal for the close-range jungle fighting that was characteristic of the war in Vietnam. Besides reducing long-range accuracy, the CAR-15's shorter barrel also had the effect of dramatically increasing muzzle flash so that a 101mm (4in) suppressor had to be attached to the end of the barrel, though a later model, the XM177E2, was fitted with a longer barrel which reduced the need for a flash hider. Although manufacture of the CAR-15 ceased in 1970 it remains a highly potent weapon.

In order to provide the infantry section with more punch, Colt developed the 40mm XM148 grenade-launcher which was designed to be attached to the underside of the M16 barrel. While popular with the GIs, the launcher was not considered sufficiently reliable and was replaced in the 1970s with the M203, also of 40mm calibre. Capable of delivering a rifle grenade to a distance of up to 500m (460yds) the M203 remains as the standard US Army launcher.

Since its standardisation with the US Army the M16 has been widely adopted in other countries; it is currently in use by the armies of Chile, the Dominican Republic, Haiti, Italy, Jordan, South Korea, Mexico, Nicaragua, Panama, the Philippines and Vietnam. More than 4 million M16 rifles have been manufactured in the USA and – under licence from Colt – Singapore, the Philippines and South Korea also produce the rifle. Numbers are also owned by other armies, including the British, who issue them to special forces, and used them in small numbers during the fighting in Borneo in the 1960s.

Greek, Turk or Cypriot?

The struggle for the future of Cyprus

As a result of an agreement in 1878 to protect Turkey against Russian invasion, the concession by Turkey of a British military presence in Cyprus, a strategically important island, was agreed – though Turkey was to retain sovereignty. When Turkey allied with Russia, however, in 1914, Britain renounced the 1878 agreement and annexed the island. This change of sovereignty was substantiated by both Greece and Turkey when they signed the Treaty of Lausanne in 1923, and two years later Cyprus became a British crown colony. But this sovereignty was seriously threatened between 1955 and 1959 by a campaign against the British presence waged by the Ethniki Organosis Kyprion Agoniston (EOKA, or the National Organisation of Cypriot Fighters).

Cyprus is the third largest island in the Mediterranean, 225km (140 miles) from east to west and 97km (60 miles) from north to south. It possesses few mineral resources and no natural deep-water harbours, but it offered a base from which influence could be spread over the eastern Mediterranean as various empires from the ancient Egyptian to the Ottoman had realised through the ages. In 1955 Cyprus had a population of 500,000, 78 per cent of Greek descent and 18 per cent of Turkish extraction. It

Inset: Archbishop Makarios (centre), who refused to condemn EOKA's acts of violence and blamed the uprising on the continued British presence. Below: A policeman stands by the burnt-out shell of the Lefkonika Post Office after it was set aflame by EOKA terrorists in reprisal for the arrest of seven of their members by security forces.

was a population divided not only by loyalty to two different states but divided also by language and religion and with a history of mutual hostility.

The aim of the Greek Cypriots was *enosis*, the union of Greece and Cyprus. The move for *enosis* had emerged in the mid-19th century, despite the fact that Cyprus had never actually been regarded as part of modern Greece. The Greek Orthodox Church in Cyprus favoured *enosis* especially after 1950 when a new leader was elected. This was Archbishop Makarios III who, at the age of 37, possessed a charismatic personality that was to bring him the leadership of the Greek Cypriot nationalist movement. His ideas were very popular among Greek Cypriots and Makarios rapidly acquired the loyalty of the Greek community. To the British his objectives and popularity were ominous, but for the Turkish Cypriots Makarios's preachings were outrageous.

Britain had to take account of these internal problems and attempt to balance them against British interests and policy towards the island. The pressures to end British rule in Cyprus built up only slowly before World War II but they accelerated afterwards and there were scenes of violence well before 1955. In 1931, for example, Greek Cypriots had burned down the governor's house in large-scale demonstrations.

In 1954 the British government announced that there could be no question of any change of sovereignty in Cyprus, arguing that Britain, as the

sovereign power, possessed absolute authority over the island and that this right had been recognised in the Treaty of Lausanne. Britain wanted to retain Cyprus as a base from which she could protect British interests in the eastern Mediterranean and the Middle East, especially since the impending withdrawal of Britain from Egypt had made it necessary to transfer the headquarters of British Middle East Command from Egypt to Cyprus in 1954. In addition the southeastern flank of Nato was considered to be a crucial region at a time when the Cold War was at its height. Britain also felt an obligation to protect Turkish Cypriots from the inherent dangers that were emerging in the *enosis* demands. Nevertheless, in recognition of the increasing domestic pressures in Cyprus, Britain did make proposals in 1954 for limited self-government over the island's internal affairs whilst intending to retain sovereignty. The Greek Cypriots, however, wanted more, and the Turkish Cypriots were alarmed at the proposals.

The Greek Cypriots adopted a two-pronged policy to further their ambitions. Internally they decided to try to raise the cost of the British presence through a campaign of insurrection with the intention of making it difficult, and ultimately impossible, for Britain to retain control of Cyprus. This they did by creating EOKA, the military wing of the movement for *enosis*, to carry out acts of violence against the authorities so as to force the British out.

EOKA was led by George Grivas, a Cypriot-born retired Greek Army officer who had visited Cyprus at Makarios's request in 1951 and returned in November 1954 under the *nom de guerre* 'Dighenis' – a legendary hero from Greek history. Grivas had begun to plan a guerrilla campaign in 1952 and it was he who led the Greek Cypriot extremists, whom the British

Above: Armed with a 9mm L2A1 sub-machine gun, a British soldier stands guard at a barbed-wire barricade separating Greek and Turkish quarters in Nicosia.

regarded as terrorists, into the insurgency campaign which lasted from 1955 until 1959.

The second avenue pursued by the Greek Cypriots was international, with the aim of using Greece to press for a settlement of the Cyprus problem. This the Greek government was certainly prepared to do since the Greek prime minister, Field-Marshal Alexandros Papagos, had been rebuffed by the British government when he had suggested discussions in 1953. Greece used the General Assembly of the United Nations to argue for national self-determination for Cyprus, through which the British assumed they hoped to achieve a Greek Cypriot government which would then be free to choose *enosis*.

The spark for revolt came in the autumn of 1954, when the General Assembly declined to take up the Greek cause. The UN decision prompted demonstrations in Nicosia in December 1954 and these were

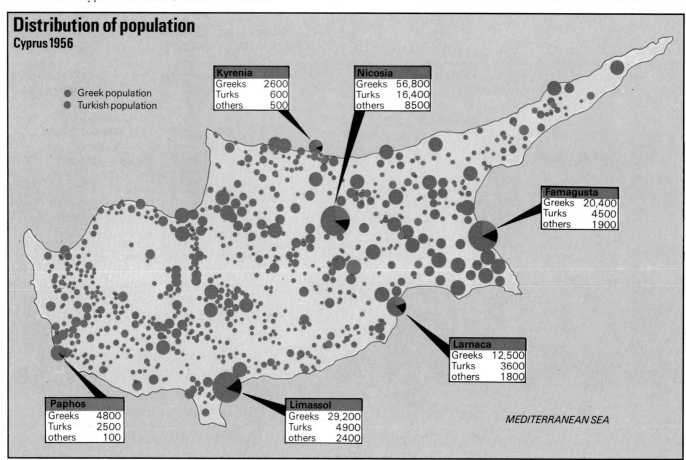

Distribution of population
Cyprus 1956

● Greek population
● Turkish population

Kyrenia	
Greeks	2600
Turks	600
others	500

Nicosia	
Greeks	56,800
Turks	16,400
others	8500

Famagusta	
Greeks	20,400
Turks	4500
others	1900

Larnaca	
Greeks	12,500
Turks	3600
others	1800

Paphos	
Greeks	4800
Turks	2500
others	100

Limassol	
Greeks	29,200
Turks	4900
others	2400

MEDITERRANEAN SEA

followed, in April 1955, by the first bomb attacks. Arms were being smuggled to the island from Greece and Archbishop Makarios, the champion of Cypriot nationalism, refused to condemn the violence, claiming that the responsibility for it lay with the British authorities. The EOKA campaign involved open violence, with murders committed in broad daylight, the targets often being the police. The campaign was vigorously denounced by the Turkish Cypriot community, which called for firm action to be taken by the British against terrorism.

The British government attempted to find a solution by inviting Greek and Turkish representatives to the London conference in August 1955, but the talks failed because of the opposing views of Greece and Turkey. The British prime minister, Anthony Eden, then appointed Field-Marshal John Harding, ex-Chief of the Imperial General Staff, as governor to Cyprus with the intention of taking a strong line against EOKA's terrorists so as to reduce Makarios's bargaining power. Harding took personal charge of the security situation and Britain declared a State of Emergency on 26 November 1955. This led to arrests, detentions, internment, deportations, curfews, and the introduction of the death penalty. The British had resorted to well-tried military tactics of counter-insurgency but the EOKA terrorists, despite being never more than a few hundred strong, tied down a British garrison of 25,000 men in 1956.

Combing the mountains

In March 1956 the British deported Makarios to the Seychelles, hoping that the removal of the head of the conspiracy would terminate the revolution but in fact it led to more murders and more executions. There were successes and failures for both sides; in particular Operation Pepperpot in June 1956 was a successful sweep against guerrillas in the Troodos mountains. EOKA never contemplated military victory over Britain, however; its aim was to make continued British control of Cyprus impossible. The British tried to produce a settlement with proposals for a more liberal constitution, but the Greek government rejected them

Right: The bloody result of the internecine Cypriot struggle between Greek and Turk. The photograph shows the scene after Turkish gunmen had fired on a group of Greeks in a cafe.

Below: After Greek orthodox thanksgiving services in October 1955, crowds of Greek youths flooded the streets of Nicosia. The situation quickly deteriorated into full scale rioting and troops and police intervened in strength.

In March 1957 Archbishop Makarios was released from detention and flew to Athens, where he once again sought support for *enosis*. The Turkish government then argued that self-determination would be acceptable to them if it applied to both Greek and Turkish communities separately, and so the spectre of partition emerged – but this proposal, too, was rejected by the Greeks and the Greek Cypriots. In October 1957 a new governor, Sir Hugh Foot (later Lord Caradon), arrived in Cyprus but the EOKA campaign continued with increased inter-communal violence, bringing with it the danger of civil war.

Towards the end of 1958, after a particularly heavy period of EOKA killings and amid accusations of British brutality, the Greeks and the Turks expressed willingness to negotiate a solution. On 31 December 1958, Grivas ordered a complete cessation of EOKA activities, when all the parties concerned, including Archbishop Makarios, accepted the compromise of independence for Cyprus. Greece and Turkey agreed to this outcome at Zurich on 11 February 1959, and this was followed by a conference in London on 19 February, when British, Greek Cypriot and Turkish Cypriot delegates reached an agreement on the form of independence to be given. Ultimately Britain retained sovereignty of two base areas at Akrotiri and Dhekelia, with the rest of Cyprus gaining independence under a new power-sharing constitution. Internally there was to be no *enosis* and no partition, and the settlement was to be guaranteed by Britain, Greece and Turkey.

So the new Republic of Cyprus was born after a war that had cost the lives of at least 90 guerrillas, 104 servicemen, 50 policemen and 238 civilians. Cyprus badly needed to settle down in peace and tranquility having achieved independence, but this was to prove impossible. Under Archbishop Makarios, who became president on 14 December 1959, the politics of the island were to lurch from crisis to crisis.

David Johnson

EOKA

Colonel Grivas and the terrorist campaign

From a Greek Cypriot and indeed Greek viewpoint, EOKA was a national liberation movement, but to the British it was a terrorist organisation. The Ethniki Organosis Kyprion Agoniston (EOKA or the National Organisation of Cypriot Fighters) was created in 1953 and was prepared to use armed force to achieve *enosis*, the union of Cyprus and Greece. EOKA was a fiercely nationalist movement which had the widespread support of the Greek Cypriot community in Cyprus and the approval of Greece.

The objective that EOKA set itself was to persuade the British to relinquish control over Cyprus, thereby freeing the Cypriots to decide their own future. EOKA therefore intended to adopt a guerrilla campaign directed primarily against the British in order to force Britain to leave the island. Simultaneously it sought to focus international public opinion on the future of Cyprus.

The aims of EOKA, and the conduct of its operations throughout the campaign, were masterminded by Colonel George Grivas, who was the unquestioned leader of the movement for four and a half years. Grivas had been born and raised in Cyprus but became a naturalised Greek and joined the Greek Army as a regular officer. It was his determined personality, ruthless leadership and fanatical belief in the cause of *enosis* which contributed so much to making EOKA an effective military organisation. Grivas was a traditional, conservative, military man who was brave and intelligent; he was also cunning, for he avoided detection on Cyprus throughout the campaign despite tremendous efforts to locate him. Grivas moved freely in the capital, Nicosia, at the start of the campaign and in the mountains to the south of Kyrenia, wearing a disguise of dark glasses and a moustache, but then set up his headquarters in the Troodos mountains before moving to a house in Limassol after Operation Pepperpot.

Grivas was very much an active military leader, supervising training, giving orders to group leaders, preparing propaganda leaflets, and encouraging morale through frequent visits to EOKA groups. His political leader was Archbishop Makarios, a man for whom he had immense respect. Makarios was less disposed to a military campaign than Grivas, and sometimes vetoed Grivas's plans when he considered them too extreme, but Grivas was in charge in the field.

Grivas set up the detailed organisation of EOKA on

Above: George Grivas addresses crowds in Athens after his return from Cyprus in 1959. Below: A security forces poster, describing EOKA as a destructive force.

Grivas's guerrilla tactics

'The British answer to our methods was to flood the island with troops. It was the wrong answer. Numbers have little meaning in guerrilla warfare. From the guerrillas' point of view, it is positively dangerous to increase the size of groups beyond a certain point. I call this the "saturation point". It is determined by the nature of the terrain, the skill of the fighters, their requirements in food and supplies, the tactics employed and the need to keep down casualties. Any given area can usefully absorb a certain number of men; in mountainous country, where peaks and ravines are dead ground, the figure is only a fraction of the numbers required elsewhere.'

General George Grivas, writing in his memoirs.

Below: Ex-EOKA men parade through Metaxas Square on the seventh anniversary of the independence of Cyprus and its declaration as a republic. Bottom: After the deportation of Archbishop Makarios a new wave of violence erupted. Here British and Cypriot police lie dead in the street.

classic guerrilla lines. When he had his headquarters in the caves of the Troodos mountains he was assisted by fewer than 20 close followers. The command structure then passed down to regional headquarters, sector headquarters and then to local commanders. At the height of the campaign in 1956, the active wing consisted of 7 mountain groups each of 5 to 15 men responsible for guerrilla attacks, raids and ambushes, and 50 town groups each of 4 or 5 men responsible for sabotage, shooting and bombing.

The largest number of groups operated in Nicosia, Famagusta and Limassol. For most of the campaign there were about 300 hard core, front-line guerrillas. These groups or cells would today be known as active service units (ASUs). In addition there was a passive wing of sympathisers who created village groups of a paramilitary nature. They numbered about 750 and were armed with shotguns collected from Greek Cypriot sympathisers and from raids. These special shotgun units also executed traitors.

The initial wave of terrorism, however, was launched by only 80 or so activists, organised into sabotage squads of 5 or 6 in the major towns. EOKA guerrillas tended to operate on the streets of towns at first, and then, when they became too well known, and therefore at risk, they moved up into the mountains. The Troodos range provided excellent bases for guerrilla operations, as well as providing good cover for training purposes. EOKA also made use of women and children as carriers of weapons on operations; the weapon would be given to the leader of the killer group, used, and returned to the carrier as quickly as possible. All EOKA supporters were bound together by taking a religious oath of allegiance to work for the liberation of Cyprus, not to reveal secrets of the organisation, and to be prepared to sacrifice their lives for the cause if necessary.

An explosive campaign

EOKA strategy was both military and political. The military campaign, which began in April 1955, was aimed at British government and military installations and property, and military and police personnel. EOKA indulged in sniping, street murder, arson, sabotage, mine-laying and bombing. The hit-and-run guerrilla tactic was particularly effective against isolated and vulnerable police posts and military patrols. A total of 1782 EOKA bombs exploded during the campaign, causing damage estimated at £10 million; many more EOKA bombs failed to explode or were discovered and defused. EOKA made use of home-made grenades and bombs. Grivas always claimed that the bombing was not random, but aimed at British servicemen and traitors. The first weapons used by EOKA came from Greece but, as the campaign developed, police armouries were raided and became a major source of supply.

On the political front, EOKA used propaganda skilfully. They issued leaflets to keep the issues in the headlines, and followed up with demonstrations, riots, boycotts and strikes. There was some intimidation too, but Grivas knew that he had to be careful not to alienate the population whose support EOKA needed. EOKA activity was often spasmodic, quiet periods occurring when truces were offered.

The use of force by EOKA prompted a violent response, with Britain taking every feasible measure to try to crush the organisation. Cyprus was flooded with British troops, who provided plentiful targets for EOKA gunmen and met with only limited success against acts of terrorism. EOKA tactics enabled just a few hundred terrorists to tie down 25,000 British troops. The EOKA campaign was successful in that it achieved some change in the British position over the future of Cyprus with the acceptance of independence. Militarily EOKA was most successful before 1957, after which more effort was devoted to producing a political solution.

The insurgents, then, were victorious in making the territory too costly for Britain to retain, but EOKA failed to achieve its ideal of *enosis*. The British, on the other hand, claimed to be content with the outcome of independence for Cyprus and retained two sovereign base areas on the island. Both sides in the conflict had been forced to compromise. When the EOKA campaign ended, Grivas returned to Athens to be welcomed as a hero and promoted to the rank of lieutenant-general in recognition of his achievement.

David Johnson

From mountain...

How the war for Cyprus was fought

The major handicap faced by British forces in Cyprus was a tendency to underestimate both the determination and ability of the Greek Cypriots to fight for *enosis* (union with Greece). The Special Branch, for example, became aware of Colonel George Grivas's presence soon after he secretly landed on the island in 1954, but the lackadaisical colonial administration made no attempt either to follow or arrest him. Similarly, the capture of the *Ayios Yeoryios* with its arms and explosives on the night of 25/26 January 1955 appears to have convinced the British they had

nipped the rebellion in the bud. In fact, explosives for the first bombing campaign were obtained from explosive stores in mines or from dumped British shells; later on, bombs were manufactured from easily obtained chemicals. Arms were subsequently posted to the island from abroad, there being no postal search. Vigilance was further reduced psychologically by the tendency of most Britons to believe that only a small minority of Greeks in Cyprus supported EOKA and that active demonstrations of support were induced exclusively by fear.

Above: A view of the Troodos mountains. It was from bases in these mountains that EOKA terrorists launched ambushes against British supply convoys, thus forcing the security forces to deploy considerable numbers of men away from the towns in order to pursue the guerrillas and protect the convoys.

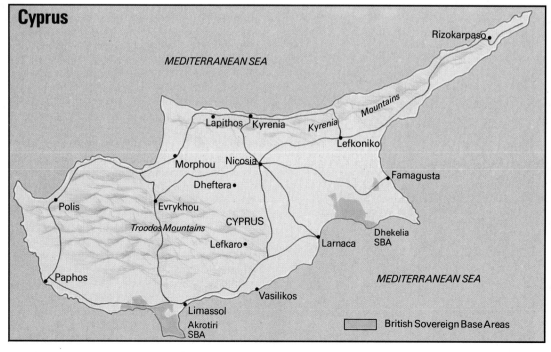

Cyprus

MEDITERRANEAN SEA

Rizokarpaso

Lapithos • Kyrenia *Kyrenia* Mountains

Lefkoniko

Morphou Nicosia

Dheftera •

Polis

Evrykhou

CYPRUS

Famagusta

Troodos Mountains

Dhekelia SBA

Lefkaro •

Larnaca

Paphos

MEDITERRANEAN SEA

Vasilikos

Limassol
Akrotiri SBA

British Sovereign Base Areas

... to market-place

To some degree, of course, this was correct. The Greek Cypriots universally supported *enosis*, and it was Grivas's intention to demonstrate this to the outside world. From early in the struggle his prime targets were neither the British nor the Turks but real, or imagined, traitors to the cause who were ruthlessly, sometimes callously, murdered. It was the predominantly Greek police force which became the first targets when EOKA resumed its campaign in June 1955 after an indifferent beginning in April. The police were 1700-strong but were poorly led and inadequately armed and equipped (some rural police stations did not have even a telephone). After a carefully orchestrated series of attacks and murders, those who did not resign were mostly willing to cooperate with EOKA, which also succeeded in infiltrating the Special Branch. The attacks not only deprived the security forces of sources of information, they also undermined operations by creating

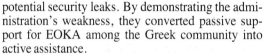

While civilian populations were constantly prone to sweep and search operations by security forces in the towns (above), Grivas and his men initially enjoyed a strong sense of security in their mountain headquarters (below).

potential security leaks. By demonstrating the administration's weakness, they converted passive support for EOKA among the Greek community into active assistance.

Cyprus District had some 4000 men organised into two infantry battalions and an artillery regiment plus support troops. Until the police came under attack, the army was not greatly involved apart from reinforcing police stations, guarding vulnerable points and patrolling. Reinforcements, including three brigade headquarters and four battalions, were brought in during June and some emergency regulations were introduced, but the army role remained basically defensive and there was little cooperation or coordination with the police.

Upon the arrival of Field-Marshal Sir John Harding as governor in October 1955 counter-insurgency took on a new vitality. An integrated, flexible framework was created and all intelligence efficiently collated and distributed. Operations were directed through, and coordinated by, a joint operations centre and executed by joint security committees involving the administration, police and troops in each of the seven administrative districts. Substantial reinforcements brought the garrison up to nine battalion equivalents (13,000 men) aided by 2000 police, the Greeks being replaced by 300 Britons and increasing numbers of Turks whose presence was bound to antagonise the Greeks.

The arrival of Harding coincided with Grivas's extension of the struggle to include attacks on British servicemen and installations, and in November a State of Emergency was declared. Some attacks were in urban areas; there were 21 shootings and bombings in Nicosia alone between November 1955 and March 1956. The British reacted with cordons and searches of both individuals and districts, although no permanent checkpoints or observation posts were established. A disturbing new feature the British had to

respond to was the development of guerrilla warfare in the Troodos mountains. Small parties of insurgents began ambushing convoys and attacking police stations in an effort to stretch the garrison further. The decision to move into the mountains played into British hands, however, for a good road system existed through the mountains which were, in any case, too small in area to provide adequate room for manoeuvre even for a force which numbered no more than 53.

Realising the guerrillas' vulnerability, Harding gave priority to the task of destroying them. For this purpose he used a mobile reserve force created early in 1956 of two, and later four, battalions. Preliminary operations began in April but it was not until June that a concerted operation, code-named Pepperpot, was launched. Areas around the Paphos Forest were cordoned off, and civilians were interrogated and their homes searched as patrols swept through the mountains. No attempt was made at preliminary reconnaissance; indeed, the Special Air Service was committed east of Suez throughout the Emergency, and the use of road transport compromised secrecy. Nevertheless, Pepperpot succeeded in eliminating half the guerrillas, Grivas himself narrowly escaping capture on three occasions despite warning of the operation. That he, and some of his comrades, were able to escape resulted from the inability of the British to assemble troops secretly and to the difficult nature of the terrain, both of which enabled the guerrillas to slip through the inadequately patrolled cordon.

The conscripts carrying out the operation displayed serious weaknesses. Many lacked basic skills, motivation and self-discipline. Marksmanship was poor and searches were often superficial. It is believed that a surreptitious cigarette started a blaze which killed or severely

Above: Field-Marshal Sir John Harding, Governor of Cyprus, who took personal charge of the security situation.

Below left: The British general issue booklet which listed the most wanted members of EOKA. Bottom right: British paratroops examine archaic pistols and swords found in a house during a search in Nicosia.

injured 40 troops. Although improvements did occur later, the uneven quality of the National Service army remained a problem throughout the Emergency.

Grivas had hoped the guerrilla campaign might lead to a national uprising, but Pepperpot and succeeding sweeps in the mountains thwarted this plan. The guerrillas were thereafter retained only for their nuisance value, the burden being borne by part-timers in the towns (220 strong in February 1956) and lowland rural areas (750 strong). Grivas himself moved to a Limassol hideout, and there followed a lull in violence until the autumn.

Arrest and detention

When the EOKA campaign resumed it coincided with the Suez operation, preparation for which hindered the British counter-insurgency campaign. During Black November 416 incidents occurred and more than 35 people were killed, but immediately afterwards EOKA came under massive pressure. The security forces had been steadily gathering information throughout the year. The wholesale arrest and detention of suspects who were then subjected to close interrogation proved valuable, the EOKA organisation was infiltrated by Q-patrols of defectors or pro-British Cypriots, and EOKA documents were discovered. Because of all this, a detailed picture of the organisation and its membership was built up, and from December 1956 to March 1957 EOKA was to suffer what Grivas later called 'hard blows'. Its urban and rural organisation was disrupted, 60 members facing capital charges while another 15 were killed including Gregoris Axfentiou, whom Grivas had been about to promote to assistant military commander. Grivas was forced to recognise that his organisation had grown too fast with too many unreliable members. Accordingly, from February 1957 he radically reorganised EOKA. There was a more rigorous selection of personnel, the adoption of a 'watertight' cell-structure and the creation of a security force. This work was undertaken during the first of a series of unilateral ceasefires in March 1957.

Despite the increased efficiency of the security forces a hard core of EOKA personnel always remained. Although EOKA's worst excesses could be restrained by a force whose minimum strength was

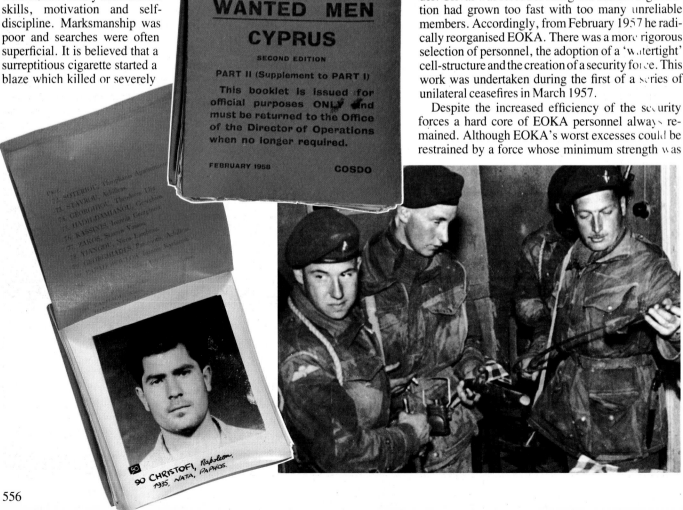

WANTED MEN
CYPRUS
SECOND EDITION
PART II (Supplement to PART I)
This booklet is issued for official purposes ONLY and must be returned to the Office of the Director of Operations when no longer required.
FEBRUARY 1958   COSDO

A false sense of security

'The airbase at Akrotiri was surrounded on three sides by water and its security was regarded as the strongest in the Middle East. It was decided to build a sergeants' mess and that local labour should be used. Accordingly, Greek and Turkish Cypriots were hired and were all but strip-searched before they were allowed on the base.

'Every day about noon we knocked off and went swimming at one of several beaches inside the base. One beach was particularly popular, and the officers suggested that a refreshment tent be provided. A Greek Cypriot was given the contract and he set up a large tent for the sale of Coca-cola staffed by two beautiful Greek girls. The girls proved very popular ... and the sale of Coke was brisk.

'After a few days of propositions and wolf whistles the girls decided to increase their earnings. So while one served Coca-cola at the front the other served favours at the back.

'At the same time, work proceeded on the mess and after nine months it was completed. Two hours after the last tile had been put in place, however, a loud explosion rocked the building. Where the new mess had stood there was now a large crater and a pile of rubble. It later transpired that while they had been constructing the building, the Cypriots had smuggled in plastic explosives disguised as filling in their sandwiches. So all the while the men were plotting to blow up the camp, the women were selling comforts in the tent.'

Leading Aircraftman Ralph Vernon, RAF Akrotiri, Cyprus, 1958-59.

20,000 troops and 4500 police, it was still capable of bombings and shootings and so a curious military impasse existed during the remaining months of the Emergency. In urban areas EOKA concentrated on sabotage, the best-known examples being the attempted assassination of Major-General D. A. Kendrew, commander of Cyprus District, on 26 September 1958 and the destruction of a Canberra bomber at Akrotiri airbase on 26 November the previous year. Assassination squads picked off individual members of the security forces and the Greek Cypriot community.

In rural areas stealth provided the key to successful countermeasures. More intensive patrolling was introduced, squads being dropped from trucks in concealed stretches of road, and counter-ambushes were set up with great success. Drivers of military vehicles were taught counter-ambush tactics as well as the development of counter-attacks, and the security forces set out to provoke ambushes on terms favourable to themselves.

EOKA's cell-structure and ruthless security kept it functioning despite the great pressure to which it was subjected. With the appointment of Sir Hugh Foot as governor in October 1957, operations by the security forces became secondary to political negotiation. Foot was more liberal in approach and wished to abandon politically counter-productive searches, detentions and curfews, but he did not shrink from taking hard, long-overdue decisions including the search of mail, a ban on the sale of chemicals (which could be used to make explosives), and curfews in towns and villages. These tactics were accompanied by such acts as the mass arrest of 2000 EOKA suspects in July 1958 and, later in the year, the dismissal of thousands of Greek civilian workers in British bases to prevent further acts of sabotage.

The declining effectiveness of the guerrillas during Foot's administration led Grivas, from March 1958, to concentrate on large-scale passive resistance. This period was marked by economic boycotts, demonstrations and widespread acts of minor sabotage broken by short ceasefires which were inevitably followed by flare-ups of violence aimed at thwarting

any political solution short of *enosis*. The rise and fall in tension during 1958 adversely affected army morale. There was talk at one point of forming unofficial revenge squads (which never materialised), and in a spectacular lapse of discipline in Famagusta on 3 October after a serviceman's wife was murdered, two units went on a rampage that resulted in three deaths (one a serviceman) and hundreds being injured. For the most part, however, the British Army endured its unhappy lot stoically.

The final ceasefire

During October Major-General Sir Kenneth Darling succeeded Kendrew and introduced a number of changes, overhauling his intelligence organisation and improving training for front and rear line troops. In urban areas covert patrolling was begun in an effort to improve efficiency; in rural areas military vehicles, which faced a steadily increasing threat from contact and controlled mines, were forbidden to travel at night while regular minehunting sweeps were conducted along the roads. Decoys were often used to trap the unwary and were employed extensively in the mountains, where sweeps were conducted during the winter of 1958-59, often with helicopter support, to eliminate the last few guerrillas in their hideouts. This was a convincing demonstration of security force effectiveness. The sustained pressure of the security forces may have been a major factor in Grivas's decision on Christmas Eve 1958 to announce his final ceasefire. By that time war weariness had set in, the Greeks acknowledging that *enosis* could not be achieved in the existing stalemate.

Had EOKA resumed its campaign in the face of efficient security force operations it might have been destroyed, but by the end of the struggle EOKA remained intact with a formidable armoury, although it had failed to secure its prime objective. The British forces, although failing to destroy EOKA, did restrict its activities with increasing success despite the fact that 80 per cent of the island population refused to support the authorities. Moreover, the British objective of retaining a military presence in Cyprus was achieved and, on these grounds alone, Cyprus may be counted a partial victory for counter-insurgency forces.
E. R. Hooton

Below: A British Army patrol on operations in the Troodos mountains. These operations were often difficult to coordinate as the terrain was not conducive to good radio communications. The elusive nature of the guerrilla bands meant that despite huge sweep operations in the mountain ranges, many insurgents were able to avoid capture.

Low-intensity c

The British Army's involvement in guerrilla warfare

There has been only one year since 1945 in which no British soldier has been killed in action. That year, ironically, was 1968, 'the year of revolution'. The irony is all the stronger because, in the years since World War II, British forces have been almost exclusively engaged in counter-revolutionary or anti-terrorist fighting – in other words, low-intensity operations.

The British experience has underlined three cardinal principles of low-intensity operations. First, the real battle is for public cooperation. Military actions can be judged successful only if, in the end, they contribute to that cooperation. As General (later Field-Marshal) Sir Gerald Templer put it in 1952: 'The answer lies not in pouring more troops into the jungle but in the hearts and minds of the people.' Secondly, these 'hearts and minds' are won not so much by providing roads and schools and clinics and water supplies (though these can help), as by instilling public confidence in government and, above all, in the government's ability to protect the security of ordinary families. Thirdly, consequent upon this cooperation comes the war-winning factor, intelligence.

At the end of World War II the British Army was well prepared for guerrilla and terrorist warfare. This was because of the sum of experience that had been built up participating with partisan and resistance movements against the Germans and Japanese in France, Norway, Italy, Greece, Yugoslavia and Malaya, and in the deep penetration operations of the Chindits, the Long Range Desert Group and the Special Air Service (SAS). There was a healthy sprinkling of people who knew what it was like to be a guerrilla, which helped when it came to fighting against them; people like John Davis, who fought with Malayan communist Chin Peng in the jungle from 1943 to 1945 and then led forces against him from 1948 to 1960.

This 40-year cavalcade led on from the postwar strains of Greece, Trieste and Iran, through Palestine and the 12-year Emergency in Malaya (by the end of which Kenya and Cyprus were in full flood), through Borneo, Aden, Oman and Northern Ireland – to name but a few of the bigger campaigns. In Palestine, as in India, the real slaughter began as the British withdrew. Preventing Arabs and Jews from killing each other in 1946-48 proved to be the early stage of a learning curve which led on to the Bogside, Springfield, the Ardoyne and the Lower Falls.

Malaya probably saw the steepest rise in the curve.

perations

There were two large rival communities (Malays 49 per cent and Chinese 38 per cent); an experienced guerrilla army; an ideally placed supporting organisation among the Chinese squatters on the jungle fringe who were remote and vulnerable to coercion; and ample stocks of arms in concealed dumps left over from the war. It was a guerrilla leader's dream, and Chin Peng was a proven leader.

24-hour protection

Success eluded the British until 1950, when the Briggs Plan was introduced to resettle half a million squatters into 480 new villages where they could be kept away from, or protected from, the guerrillas – whichever way they looked at it. For, whatever his loyalties, the isolated squatter had no option but to obey the man with the gun who came to his door for food. No-one was moved into a new village until *after* an adequate police post had been installed to give the people a reasonable prospect of protection, not only from the man with a gun from outside but also from the man with a knife prowling at night inside the village. This was a lesson which the Americans failed to learn when they tried to copy Malayan resettlement in Vietnam. In Vietnam, no 'strategic hamlet' had a resident army or police presence at night. As a result, no matter how much the government flew the flag during the day, the real control lay with the Viet Cong who meted out retribution during the night. This did not happen in Malaya. There were police on the beat in every village every night.

There is a well-worn myth that, in order to win, the government or the guerrillas need the full support of 'the people'. In fact, the overwhelming majority of the people, probably 80 or 90 per cent, do not wish to support either side; they want to keep out of it, so that they will not be either imprisoned or shot, so that they and their children can live secure. If they are confident that the government can and will maintain this security, they will accept the presence of the police and the army with secret relief, even if they think it necessary to display hostility. Some of them, provided that they can be sure of anonymity, will, one way or another, leak enough information into the ears of the security forces to get rid of the guerrillas; for once the guerrillas have gone the shooting will end. Even of those people who in principle sympathise with the guerrillas, most would in practice prefer them to go away and fight their war somewhere else.

So each side needs the active support of *some* of the people. The guerrillas need enough to provide them with food and other supplies, money and information. They also need a warning screen both in villages and at work to sound the alarm if army patrols appear. The people banging dustbin lids in Belfast are copying the Chinese in Malaya who banged latex tins in the new villages or among the rubber trees on the jungle fringe. Out of the two million Chinese in Malaya, the guerrillas at their peak relied on perhaps 50,000 active supporters in the new villages – 2 or 3 per cent of the Chinese population.

The government's main task was to reduce the number of supporters so that the guerrillas were starved of supplies, information and recruits – and to persuade enough of them to give intelligence information to enable the guerrillas to be found and their organisation broken up. If the majority of the population remains passive, the number of active supporters needed by a government is very small indeed.

British methods of counter-insurgency: information from police HQ (left) would be sent to patrols in the field (below), which would culminate in the capture of an insurgent (right).

There have been exceptions, both ways. In Germany in the 1970s, virtually the entire population supported the government against the Red Army Faction, so that the police were flooded with information. Similarly in Borneo (Sarawak) in 1962-66, any incursion by Indonesian guerrillas was at once reported to the police or the army. On the other hand, in some Latin American countries, the government security forces and 'death squads' are so brutal and oppressive that all the people, at least in some rural areas, support the guerrillas. This gives the guerrillas the status, as described by Mao Tse-tung, of 'fish in a friendly sea'. In these circumstances the support *is* complete because anyone who betrays the guerrillas to the government will be detected by his neighbours and retribution will follow. Neither of these situations, however, applied in Malaya, where the great majority, even of the Chinese, hoped above all to keep out of the war.

Another myth concerns the 'planting' of agents or informants in the ranks of the guerrillas or their supporters. This, too, is extremely rare, for clandestine movements, especially those with communist training, are acutely alive to the danger of infiltration and impose long probationary periods. Some movements (both criminal and political) trust no-one until he has personally 'killed a cop' and therefore burned his boats. The great majority of informers are recruited from people already *within* the movement. In Malaya these were usually people who had been terrorised into joining or supporting the guerrillas against their will.

The technique, therefore, was to work on the guerrillas' supporters in the villages, because they were easier to detect than the guerrillas in the jungle, and because they could lead the guerrillas into an ambush in more open ground (such as in a rubber estate) where there was a better chance of catching them. As operations developed, some of the guerrillas themselves would surrender or be captured and would be ready to cooperate in order to get off the hook. They were known as surrendered enemy per-

Above: Armed with the 7.62mm SLR, soldiers of the Royal Ulster Rifles move cautiously along a track in Sabah during operations in 1964.

Below: Moving in single file, a British Army unit patrols arid countryside in Aden.

sonnel (SEPs) and were the most fruitful informers of all, sometimes becoming what would now be known as 'supergrasses'.

The organisation from which most informers were recruited was the Min Yuen or Peoples' Organisation. The Malayan Communist Party (MCP) army of fighting guerrilla regiments and platoons was supported by small political and logistic guerrilla branches living just inside the jungle, each with the task of organising support from, say, 5 or 10 Chinese new villages. In each village there might be half a dozen 'masses executives' (MEs) who were hard core supporters, often blood relations of the guerrillas they supported. The MEs organised village sympathisers, willing or coerced, to smuggle supplies out of the

village when they went to work in the rubber estates. If the police Special Branch could spot some of these, it could give a lead to the MEs and thence to the guerrilla branch in the jungle. If someone in the chain – perhaps a coerced supplier who wanted to get off the hook – could be 'turned', that could be the start of what was known as contact intelligence.

By the last years of the Emergency the technique had been perfected in the Food Denial Operation. Having selected a guerrilla branch as a target, the security forces would impose tight food rationing so that it became difficult and dangerous to smuggle out food. This would deter some of the weaker suppliers, so that the number was narrowed down and surveillance became easier. As the food control tightened, those still smuggling were forced to take greater risks, so evidence of their activities was secretly recorded. When the time was ripe, Chinese Special Branch detectives would 'lift' selected MEs or suppliers and confront them with the evidence. This put them on the spot. The evidence would be sufficiently damning for them to realise that they faced the prospect of a long prison sentence. On the other hand, they feared that if they stopped the guerrillas would guess why and . . . dead men tell no tales.

The Special Branch detectives would hope to have picked someone who might be glad to get off the hook. They would remind him of the very generous rewards he would earn if he gave information leading to the capture or surrender of the guerrilla gang, so that he could get away from Malaya with his family to a safe country with enough money to start a new life. Once he had reached that frame of mind the informer usually went the whole way. The sooner all the guerrilla gang who knew him were behind bars the safer he and his family would feel.

So the guerrilla branch itself would come under pressure and suffer casualties. Within their ranks, too, were people who longed to get out. The government psychological warfare section (also run, of course, by Chinese, many of them ex-communists) was constantly working on them, through the radio,

Above: Major Frank Kitson, whose imaginative work in Kenya helped lead to the disintegration of the Mau Mau. Through the use of 'pseudo-gangs', much information was gleaned from Kikuyu villagers.

Above: A leaflet promising safe conduct to surrendered insurgents, distributed by the British security forces in Malaya. Even one rebel defection was valuable.

through loudspeaker aircraft and leaflets. The word spread through the jungle that they, too, would be enabled to get away and start a new life. The pincer movement of military and psychological pressure would eventually squeeze the first surrenders. The SEPs, even more than the village supporters, were aware that they would not be safe so long as their former gang was intact, and they were often ready to lead the soldiers straight back to attack their jungle camp. Once that phase had been reached, the crumble had begun.

The final guerrilla collapse in Malaya began in 1957 with the first 'supergrass' – a senior party official in Perak. He surrendered without his comrades realising it. Under police direction, but still in uniform, he went back into the jungle, visiting branch after branch in turn, telling them that party policy was now to come out of the jungle so that, after a period of rehabilitation, they would be free to pursue their politics outside. Within six months, the whole MCP organisation in South Perak had quietly melted away, without shooting and without casualties. The people were fed up with violence and glad to be rid of it.

If the key to success in Malaya was intelligence from informers and SEPs, it came only as a result of coordinated action by all government agencies: the local authorities (for resettlement and food rationing, for example); the uniformed police (village police posts); the Special Branch (intelligence); the psychological operations branch, and the army. This coordination was by State and District War Executive Committees, again able to call upon very experienced people. For example, the State Secretary who headed the committee for the final triumph in Johore was Chin Peng's old comrade from the war, John Davis. He knew the game.

The biggest single problem with the rural guerrilla is to find him. One of the most successful British officers in this respect was Major (now Lieutenant-General) Sir Frank Kitson. He had a genius for intelligence which he had earlier displayed in Kenya in 1954, where he organized former Mau-Mau terror-

ists into 'pseudo-gangs' which he (with blackened face) accompanied into Kikuyu villages. Here they asked for information of the whereabouts of other, real gangs. These pseudo-gangs were authentic Mau-Mau and were able to impress the villagers so much that the information would flow, leading (as in Malaya) to the discovery and elimination of the real gangs.

The learning curve is still climbing now in Northern Ireland. Once again, intelligence is the key. In 1972, the killing reached a peak of 467. By 1978 it had

Northern Ireland was the British Army's major anti-insurgent campaign of the 1970s and early 1980s. Below: Two soldiers protect a third firing CS gas. Bottom left: Troops prepare to move against rioters. Bottom right: Catholic women warn of British troops approaching.

been cut to 81 and it has remained around there ever since. This is lower than the killing rate from normal crime in many cities in terms of homicides per thousand. In these terms Belfast is now four times safer than Washington DC.

This has been achieved by successful cooperation between the army, the police (the Royal Ulster Constabulary or RUC) and the intelligence services. Once again, the task has been to stop people killing each other. In 1976 there were no fewer than 140 sectarian and factional murders by rival Protestants and Catholics. Through the formation of a special anti-terrorist force of RUC detectives, a larger number of murderers were arrested and so the sectarian murder rate fell. The average for the six years since 1976 has been about 30 per year, little more than one-fifth of its peak. At the same time there has been a continuous erosion in the ranks of the IRA, many more of whom are now in prison than out on the streets.

Secrecy and survival

The IRA themselves paid unwilling tribute to the success of RUC and army intelligence in 1978 when they disbanded their traditional semi-overt battalion and company organisation and reorganised on a basis of secret cells. This was because – as in the other cases quoted – too many of the people who lived in their traditional areas of support were getting disenchanted and giving information that was leading to the arrest and conviction of hard-core IRA men. The reorganisation improved IRA security but was a reverse step in terms of revolutionary theory because, instead of spreading out their organisation to the 'masses', they have had to pull back into clandestine cells.

Early in 1983 there was another development, again following the pattern of Malaya: the emergence of supergrasses. By the spring several mass trials were in progress – some of IRA and some of Protestant gangs – in which evidence was given by defectors from their own ranks. It is still too early to say whether this pattern will continue; but, if it does, it will be one more example of the learning curve in action, with the pincer movement of military and psychological pressure producing the secret of success – intelligence. **Richard Clutterbuck**

The KFIR

There can be few modern combat aircraft which have had a stranger developmental history than the Israel Aircraft Industries (IAI) Kfir – Lion Cub – multi-role fighter. First flown during 1972, the Kfir can trace its origins back to the Black Curtain project of four years earlier. During this time, Israel was making determined efforts to become at least partially self-sufficient in the production of combat aircraft. For an aviation industry the size of Israel's in the late 1960s, this was an extremely tall order. As a first step, it was decided to improve on existing hardware as a stepping stone towards the ultimate goal of an independently produced warplane.

American willingness to supply arms gave Israel access to the powerful US-built General Electric J79 turbojet (used in the F4 Phantom) and the Black Curtain programme aimed at combining this engine with the Mirage III airframe. The Mirage had formed the backbone of the Israeli Air Force's fighter arm since the early 1960s (proving itself in combat during the Six-Day War of June 1967) and the combination of engine and airframe, it was felt, would be a boost to the country's air force and a significant step on the road to self-sufficiency. Black Curtain reached fruition in September 1970 with the first flight of a J79-powered two-seat Mirage IIIBJ aircraft. Code-

Previous page: An underside view of an IAI Kfir C-2. Clearly visible are the 'canards' over the engine inlet ducts which serve to improve the Kfir's combat manoeuvrability, increasing its range of angles of attack, and which allow the aircraft to operate from shorter runways than the C-1.

Above: Ground crew arm a line of C-2s before a mission. The C-2 is provided with seven external weapon stations for a wide variety of stores including 'smart' weapons, rockets, AAMs and conventional bombs.
Below: A Kfir production line at Israel Aircraft Industries.

named Salvo, this aircraft was less than perfect, as was shown by defects in the engine installation and performance, but it gave the IAI a wealth of experience on fabricating parts for the Mirage airframe.

Whilst this programme was proceeding, the Israeli secret services had not been idle. In a remarkable example of industrial espionage, sets of manufacturer's drawings for the Mirage 5 and its engine the Atar 9C turbojet were obtained. Both airframe and engine were close relatives of equipment already in service with the Israeli Air Force. In view of this and the problems experienced with the Black Curtain/Salvo programme, it was decided to produce an Atar-powered aircraft based on the drawings.

Work proceeded apace, and the prototype Nesher – Eagle – flew in September 1969. The new type incorporated all the IAI's experience to date on the Mirage airframe and appeared in two versions optimised for interception (with licence-built Cyrano radar) or ground attack (with Aida II derived radar). The Israeli Air Force received the first aircraft of this type during 1972 and some 40 Neshers are believed to have taken part in the Yom Kippur War (October 1973).

Having built a complete airframe, plus a good deal of related avionic and ancillary equipment, the IAI returned to the idea of a J79-powered aircraft, the Kfir. The new aeroplane was again based on the Mirage 5 airframe but with a shorter, larger diameter rear fuselage to accommodate the American engine. Five air scoops (four on the fuselage sides and one at the base of the fin) were added to provide additional cooling for the J79 and its afterburner, and the lower forward fuselage was enlarged and flattened to provide room for the increased size of the intake ducts. This latter modification also resulted in a new nose profile with an almost triangular section and increased length. Other modifications included a revised cockpit layout, a new fuel system with greater capacity than that of the Mirage 5, strengthened, longer-stroke undercarriage members and a new avionics system mainly of Israeli origin.

The prototype Kfir flew during 1973 and, as the Kfir C-1, entered service with the Israeli Air Force in June 1975. The C-1 operated as both an air-superiority fighter and a ground-attack platform, for which roles it carried a fixed armament of two 30mm licence-built DEFA cannon mounted on the undersides of the engine air intakes and seven stores stations under the fuselage and wings for air-to-air missiles and a wide variety of air-to-ground munitions. At least two Israeli squadrons are believed to have been equipped with the type.

On 20 July 1976, a second model of the basic type, the Kfir C-2, was revealed. Actually in service since 1974, the C-2 exhibits a number of airframe developments aimed at optimising the type's performance. The most significant of these is the addition of non-retractable, swept-back foreplanes or 'canards' mounted above and behind the engine intakes. These units, combined with revised 'dog tooth' leading edges to the wings and small strakes on either side of the nose, are reported to have dramatically improved the Kfir's handling characteristics. In addition to the external modifications, the C-2 incorporates a number of systems improvements, including the installation of the advanced Elta EL/M-2021 or EL/M-2001B X-band air-to-air and air-to-surface target acquisition and tracking radar, in a slightly longer nose.

Like the preceding model, the C-2 carries a gun armament of two 30mm DEFA cannon, has the seven external stores stations, and is employed in the air-superiority and ground-attack roles. In the former role, the main armament is the Rafael Shafrir 2 air-to-air missile. The Shafrir is a relatively small – 2.6m (8ft 6in) long – infra-red homing weapon with an 11kg (24lb) high-explosive warhead, detonated by contact or proximity fuzing. Simplicity of design, handling and use have been major considerations in the weapon's design, a philosophy which seems to have paid off if the 75 per cent operational kill ratio quoted by official sources for the Shafrir is correct. In the ground-attack role, the Kfir C-2 can carry up to 4295kg (9469lb) of external stores made up of conventional 'iron' bombs, napalm, rocket pods, 'smart' weapons such as Maverick or Hobos, Shrike anti-

Above: A Kfir C-1 deploys its brake chute on landing. Amongst the Kfir's many structural alterations to the French Mirage design has been the strengthening of the main landing gear.

Below: A Kfir C-2 on display. Modifications to the original Kfir design include the addition of small strakes along the nose for improved manoeuvrability, while the nose itself has been extended to house improved target-acquisition radar. On the outer wing pylon is the Israeli-built Shafrir air-to-air missile, while the inner pylon mounts a 500-litre (110-gallon) drop tank.

radiation missiles, drop tanks and electronic countermeasures pods.

The latest Kfir sub-type to appear is a two-seat operational trainer version of the C-2, reportedly designated the TC-2, which was first flown in February 1981. The TC-2 features a new extended canopy and revised 'droop-snout' nose contours to improve forward vision from the rear seat. Surprisingly, installation of a second crew station has only increased overall length by 3.8cm (1½in). In all other respects, the type is similar to the C-2 and it is reported to have an equal performance to the single-seat version.

Informed sources quote 150 Kfir C-1 and C-2 aircraft having been built by the spring of 1979, with two or three airframes being constructed monthly. Latest estimates put the rate at 2.5 aircraft a month (C-2 and TC-2 models) with 200-plus Kfirs already in operational service. Alongside the newly constructed aircraft, a programme is in hand to bring the C-1s still in service up to approximate C-2 standard by the addition of up-dated avionics and the various aerodynamic modifications already described. As presently envisaged, the Kfir will remain in service until the 1990s when it will be replaced by the Lavi – Young Lion – which is currently in the design stage.

The appearance of the C-2 released a number of C-1s for potential export. Israel has been extremely active in trying to market a 'sanitised' Kfir – that is, one with the most security-sensitive and technologically-advanced equipment replaced by simpler units – especially to Third World countries. Potentially, there is a large market for the type, the more so when it is considered that a European equivalent could cost

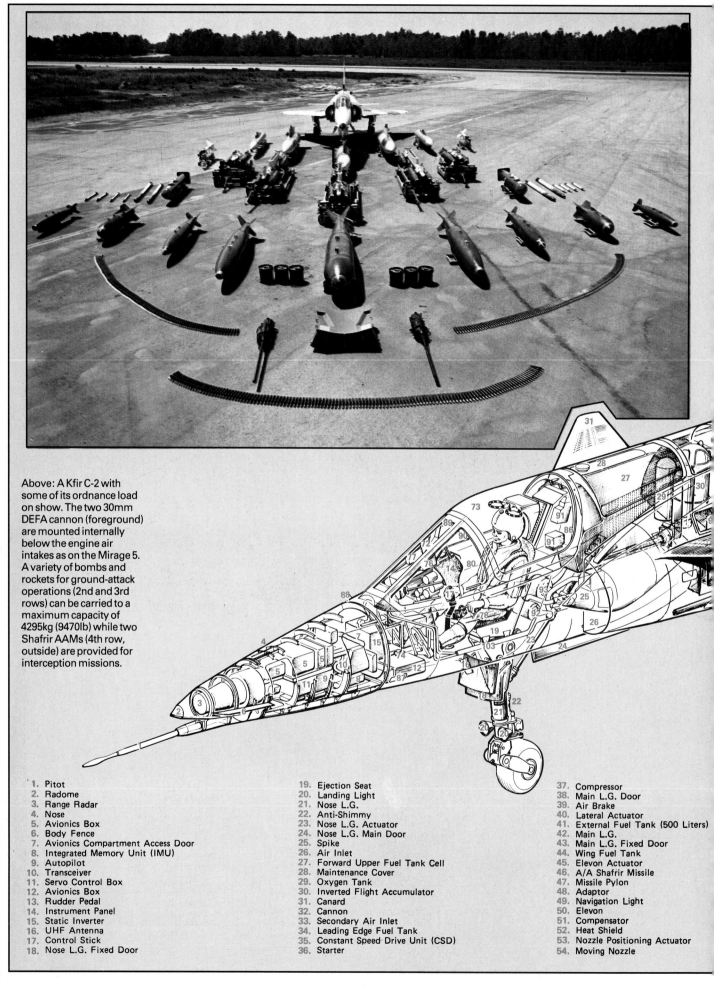

Above: A Kfir C-2 with some of its ordnance load on show. The two 30mm DEFA cannon (foreground) are mounted internally below the engine air intakes as on the Mirage 5. A variety of bombs and rockets for ground-attack operations (2nd and 3rd rows) can be carried to a maximum capacity of 4295kg (9470lb) while two Shafrir AAMs (4th row, outside) are provided for interception missions.

1. Pitot
2. Radome
3. Range Radar
4. Nose
5. Avionics Box
6. Body Fence
7. Avionics Compartment Access Door
8. Integrated Memory Unit (IMU)
9. Autopilot
10. Transceiver
11. Servo Control Box
12. Avionics Box
13. Rudder Pedal
14. Instrument Panel
15. Static Inverter
16. UHF Antenna
17. Control Stick
18. Nose L.G. Fixed Door

19. Ejection Seat
20. Landing Light
21. Nose L.G.
22. Anti-Shimmy
23. Nose L.G. Actuator
24. Nose L.G. Main Door
25. Spike
26. Air Inlet
27. Forward Upper Fuel Tank Cell
28. Maintenance Cover
29. Oxygen Tank
30. Inverted Flight Accumulator
31. Canard
32. Cannon
33. Secondary Air Inlet
34. Leading Edge Fuel Tank
35. Constant Speed Drive Unit (CSD)
36. Starter

37. Compressor
38. Main L.G. Door
39. Air Brake
40. Lateral Actuator
41. External Fuel Tank (500 Liters)
42. Main L.G.
43. Main L.G. Fixed Door
44. Wing Fuel Tank
45. Elevon Actuator
46. A/A Shafrir Missile
47. Missile Pylon
48. Adaptor
49. Navigation Light
50. Elevon
51. Compensator
52. Heat Shield
53. Nozzle Positioning Actuator
54. Moving Nozzle

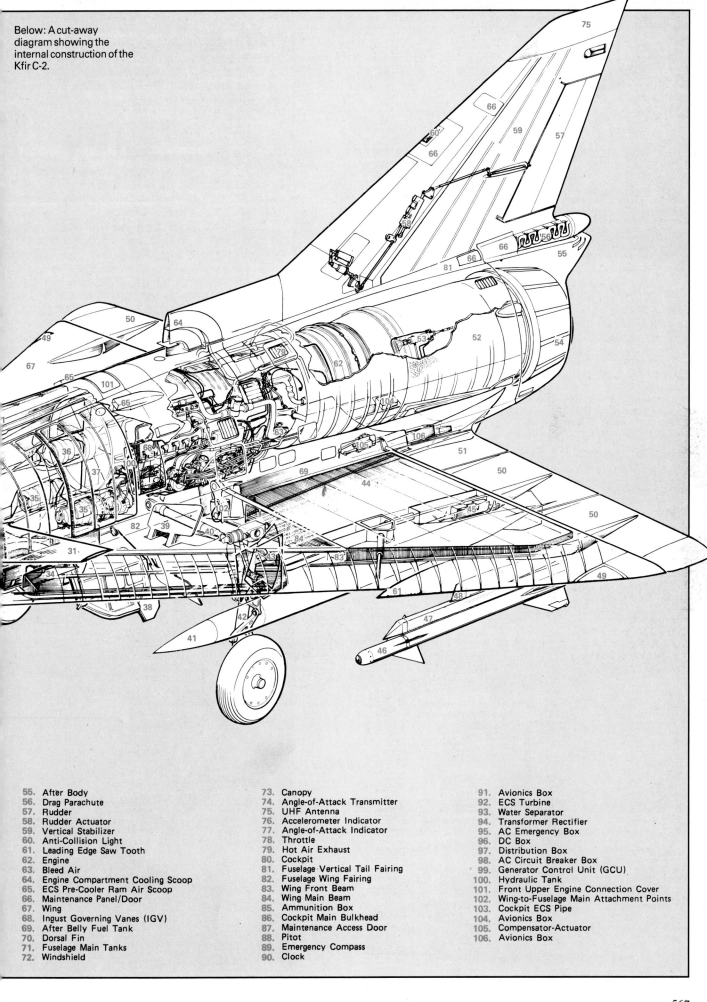

Below: A cut-away
diagram showing the
internal construction of the
Kfir C-2.

55. After Body	73. Canopy	91. Avionics Box
56. Drag Parachute	74. Angle-of-Attack Transmitter	92. ECS Turbine
57. Rudder	75. UHF Antenna	93. Water Separator
58. Rudder Actuator	76. Accelerometer Indicator	94. Transformer Rectifier
59. Vertical Stabilizer	77. Angle-of-Attack Indicator	95. AC Emergency Box
60. Anti-Collision Light	78. Throttle	96. DC Box
61. Leading Edge Saw Tooth	79. Hot Air Exhaust	97. Distribution Box
62. Engine	80. Cockpit	98. AC Circuit Breaker Box
63. Bleed Air	81. Fuselage Vertical Tail Fairing	99. Generator Control Unit (GCU)
64. Engine Compartment Cooling Scoop	82. Fuselage Wing Fairing	100. Hydraulic Tank
65. ECS Pre-Cooler Ram Air Scoop	83. Wing Front Beam	101. Front Upper Engine Connection Cover
66. Maintenance Panel/Door	84. Wing Main Beam	102. Wing-to-Fuselage Main Attachment Points
67. Wing	85. Ammunition Box	103. Cockpit ECS Pipe
68. Ingust Governing Vanes (IGV)	86. Cockpit Main Bulkhead	104. Avionics Box
69. After Belly Fuel Tank	87. Maintenance Access Door	105. Compensator-Actuator
70. Dorsal Fin	88. Pitot	106. Avionics Box
71. Fuselage Main Tanks	89. Emergency Compass	
72. Windshield	90. Clock	

several times the $5 million asking price of the Kfir. The main stumbling block to the type's success in the world's arms markets is its J79 engine, the licence for which forbids its resale to countries blacklisted by the American authorities. Because of this, the Kfir has so far only been sold to Colombia, which took delivery of 12 aircraft in 1982.

Israel has also marketed the Kfir's forerunner, the Nesher and, as the Dagger, 26 such aircraft were acquired by Argentina and played a part in the Falklands War of 1982. There is little doubt that in her current round of re-armament, Argentina would like to include the vastly more capable Kfir alongside the Mirages Israel is already supplying.

In service with the Israeli Air Force the Kfir has proved to be an efficient and effective warplane, especially in operations over Lebanon. The use of the J79 engine offers a vastly improved thrust-to-weight ratio over the Mirage aircraft, upon which the Kfir is based, with a consequent improvement in overall performance. The aerodynamic modifications incorporated in the C-2 model have also gone a long way to overcoming the inherent drawbacks of the delta wing, especially at low speeds and in combat manoeuvres. More importantly, the Kfir project has done much towards providing Israel with the skills and experience necessary for the production of a completely original warplane. Independence in arms manufacture could free Israel from the constraints imposed by her major weapons supplier, America, though the consequences such freedom might bring do not auger well for a long-term settlement to the problems of this strife-torn region.

Israel Aircraft Industries Kfir C-1, C-2 and TC-2

Type Multi-role fighter (C-1 and C-2); trainer (TC-2)
Dimensions Span 8.22m (26ft 11½in); length C-1 15.65m (51ft 4½in), C-2 16.45m (53ft 11¾in), TC-2 16.49m (54ft 1¼in); height 4.55m (14ft 11¼)
Weight Empty C-2 7285kg (16,060lb); combat-loaded C-2 interceptor 9390kg (20,700lb); C-2 ground-attack 14,670kg (32,340lb)
Powerplant One 8119kg (17,900lb) General Electric J79-J1E turbojet

Performance Maximum speed at sea level C-2 1389km/h (863mph), above 11,000m (36,090ft) C-2 Mach 2.3+ or 2440km/h (1516mph)
Range Tactical radius C-2 interceptor 346km (215 miles), C-2 ground-attack 768km (477 miles)
Ceiling C-2 17,680m (58,000ft)

Armament C-1, C-2 Two 30mm DEFA 552 cannon (140 rounds per gun); up to 4295kg (9469lb) stores including 227kg (500lb) bombs, 454kg (1000lb) bombs, Maverick and Hobos 'smart' weapons, Shafrir air-to-air missiles, napalm and electronic countermeasures pods

Above: An unarmed Kfir claws its way into the air from an Israeli airbase on a training mission. The final decision by Israeli planners to utilise the American J79 turbojet instead of the Atar powerplant, as fitted to the Mirage, gave the Kfir considerably greater thrust and a 20 per cent improvement on fuel consumption.

Below: The tactical camouflage configuration of an IAI Kfir C-2.

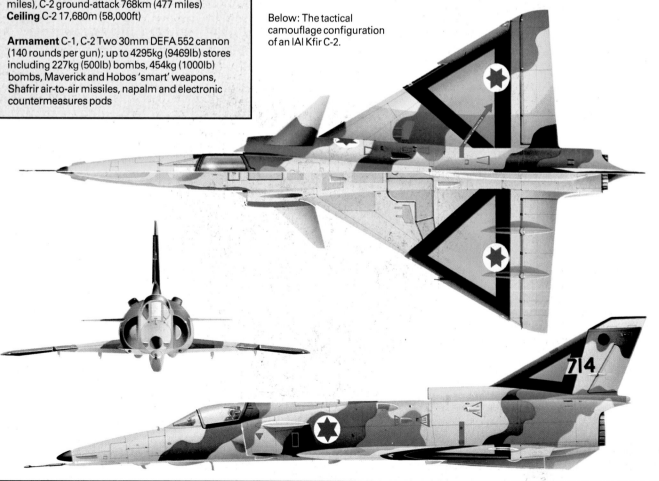

Send in the Marines!

Interventionary forces in the modern world

Nation states have been intervening by force in the affairs of other nation states since the beginning of recorded history. Sometimes they have been invited to intervene; on other occasions they have acted unilaterally. In Britain's heyday Lord Palmerston was in the habit of despatching a warship or two to the scene of action whenever he considered British interests were threatened. The outcome of this 'gunboat diplomacy', as it came to be called, was often the annexation of yet another stretch of desolate shore and seedy port to the Queen's dominions. High-handed action of this kind was taken very much for granted by self-confident colonial powers at a time when there was no world forum in which such unilateral action could be challenged, and when the industrial might of the West gave such interventions every chance of success.

The breakup of the former colonial empires after World War II has resulted in the creation of numerous small independent states, many of them inherently unstable and economically weak. The frontiers established by the former ruling powers are often bitterly disputed, as in the case of Somalia and Ethiopia where the Ogaden desert is claimed by both. Or a state's very right to exist may be resisted, as in the case of Israel where the Arab states are concerned. There have been fierce clashes between ideologies, as between the late Shah of Iran and the Muslim zealots, or between warring tribal factions, as in Uganda. It is certainly true that the world has become much more unstable since 1945.

Not only has the world state system become more unstable, however; it has also become, partly because of this instability, more interdependent. To a certain extent, the reasons for this are economic. What happens in the Persian Gulf affects the smooth running of the cities of the rest of the world; the Gulf War between Iran and Iraq threatened at first to cut supplies of the oil that is so essential to Europe and the Third World. Or again, there are regions of Africa, such as

Namibia, that are the main source of minerals crucial to certain areas of advanced technology. If such sources are threatened, dependent states may feel they have no alternative but to intervene to protect them.

Yet just as important as economic factors leading to military intervention are ideological ones. The weakness of most governments of the world means that events outside a state's borders may have important repercussions within. Muslim fundamentalism, as practised in Iran, for example, worried both the Iraqi and Soviet governments. The Soviet Union is gravely concerned by any liberalising of the regimes of its Warsaw Pact allies; the United States is terrified of left-wing governments in Latin America. In all such cases, the outside power may intervene with force to maintain or create a friendly government.

These two factors – the economic and the ideological - have added a much broader dimension to

Above: A young Marine mans a 7.62mm M60 machine gun in the Dominican Republic soon after the American intervention of 1965. The operation was carried out with overwhelming force, and little opposition was encountered.

Left: A sniper of the French paras during the Kolwezi operation of 1978. Kolwezi was an excellent example of the effectiveness of rapid deployment forces.

questions of intervention, but classic reasons – threats to the nationals of one nation marooned in another – still exist, of course. The Entebbe raid of July 1976 or America's attempt to rescue its hostages in Iran in April 1980 are prime examples. But often there is a confusion of motives. The French descent on Kolwezi in 1978, is an example: was it inspired by humanitarian concern for threatened European technicians, or by fears of the economic consequences for France should President Joseph Mobutu be replaced as ruler of mineral-rich Zaire, or by considerations of France's standing as a country willing to act quickly on behalf of its friends in black Africa? It was probably a mixture of all three.

If the motives for intervention are complex, then the moral issues raised are even more so. An event such as the Entebbe raid, in which threatened civilians are rescued in a lightning swoop, seems perfectly justified, but the Soviet move into Hungary in 1956, or the US landings in the Dominican Republic in 1965 are more difficult to view dispassionately, and reactions (of approval or disapproval) will probably depend upon the political standpoint of the observer.

With the world divided between the two mutually-antagonistic superpowers, each capable of destroying the other, and bearing in mind the virtual certainty of United Nations involvement of one kind or another, if intervention is to take place it must be both swift and effective. Long drawn-out debate, or hesitancy in the decision-making process, will compromise the entire operation. Intervention, if it is to be effective, must overwhelm the opposition, applying selective force to alter the situation to the benefit of the intervening power. Ideally, the force should be withdrawn after a short, sharp engagement to prevent escalation and embarrassing international ramifications.

Interventions since 1945 have varied greatly both in strength and in results. The Soviet intervention in Hungary in October and November 1956 resulted, according to some estimates, in 25,000 Hungarian dead; the Russians probably sustained 7000 casualties. On the other hand when they intervened in Czechoslovakia in 1968 the total casualties were 70 dead and 1000 injured. The ill-fated Anglo-French intervention at Suez in October and November 1956 resulted in 33 killed and 130 wounded for Britain and France; the Egyptian

casualties amounted to several thousand. More recently the Soviet intervention in Afghanistan is reported to have resulted in more than 10,000 Russian casualties; those suffered by the Mujahidin guerrillas probably add up to many thousands more.

It has to be said, however, that intervention in Suez, or Afghanistan was more properly akin to invasion than to intervention on the scale that took place, for example, in Jordan and Lebanon in July 1958 by British and American forces. There was, at the time, a fear that Brigadier Abdul Kassim's bloody revolution in Baghdad would be followed by takeovers in Amman and Beirut by the communists, supported by Egypt and Syria. On that occasion a British parachute brigade airlanded in Amman soon after a seaborne landing at Beirut by US Marines from the Sixth Fleet. Intervention was, in that instance, successful, probably saving King Hussein his throne and preventing (albeit temporarily) the collapse of Lebanon.

But where planning is faulty, where the intervening country has made a poor analysis of its opponent, or where there are divided

Above: Paratroops are the forces most likely to spearhead any interventionary operation. These members of the US 82nd Airborne Division relax before take off at Fort Bragg in North Carolina. In 1975, when this photograph was taken, events in the Middle East were causing concern and the division was on alert.

Below: The burnt-out shell of a helicopter bears witness to the disastrous attempt to rescue the American hostages from Iran in April 1980. Technical problems doomed the operation before it met any Iranian opposition.

counsels, then things can go badly wrong – as happened at the Bay of Pigs in April 1961. In this instance, undercover, confused attempts to bring down Fidel Castro by aiding a feeble invasion by Cuban exiles brought international opprobrium down on the United States.

The country intending to intervene, therefore, has to know exactly what it intends to do, and precisely the forces needed to achieve this objective. Then the decision can be made as to whether these forces can be assembled and brought into action in time. Often, inevitably, the answer can only be in the negative.

When Ian Smith made his unilateral declaration of independence in Rhodesia in November 1965, for example, there was an immediate clamour in the British press for him to be overthrown by force. It was argued that British forces had the measure of the Rhodesians. But this opinion failed to take into consideration the military facts. In the first place, intervention could only take place by air, but Rhodesia was surrounded by states over which the RAF had no flying rights. The nearest suitable airfield from which an airborne operation could be mounted was Nairobi in Kenya. This meant that transport aircraft, together with their escorting fighters, would be at the limit of their endurance by the time they reached Gwelo, the nearest suitable Rhodesian airfield. Moreover, it was highly unlikely that the efficient Rhodesian Army and Air Force would allow the operation to take place without resistance.

Secondly, the British government's economy measures had so emasculated the RAF's Transport Command that there was only sufficient lift for one parachute battalion, whereas the Rhodesians could deploy a brigade of infantry or more. The hard facts were that logistics made a nonsense of intervention, as the government had reluctantly to concede.

During the 1960s and 1970s, Western governments began to develop forces that would be able to intervene on a small scale, ready at any time to shore up a threatened friendly regime, to secure some vital

Above: The Turkish fleet at sea in 1974. Both Greece and Turkey had threatened to intervene in Cyprus at various times since the island's independence in August 1960, but in 1974 the Turks actually did so, their command of the sea providing the key to success.

economic point or to protect endangered nationals. Intervention forces need to be at instant readiness. This explains why, in so many instances, the troops employed have been units of paratroops, commandos and rangers. By the nature of their training these troops are expected to be fully professional, in a high state of physical fitness, accustomed to working in small parties and expert in weapon-handling and the operation of radios.

Since interventionary forces are likely to be flown in, a favourable air situation will be essential. The landing area may first be secured by parachute drop but the follow-up, including heavy weapons, will have to be air-landed. Fire support will be provided chiefly by machine guns and mortars, but light artillery may be landed. Ammunition re-supply will inevitably present a problem and conservation of ammunition must be impressed on all troops. Casualty evacuation will also be difficult until a civilian hospital becomes available. Mounting an operation of this kind involves meticulous preparation and a careful appreciation of the time and space factors involved, as the following example will show.

In 1978 there occurred an intervention by air over a great distance that turned out to be entirely successful. This was the Franco-Belgian intervention at Kolwezi in Zaire. It is likely to remain a classic example of bold planning and ruthless execution by highly trained airborne troops.

Kolwezi is the principal mining town in the copper-rich province of Shaba. As such its population included several thousand Europeans. These were

Left: American Marines in the Dominican Republic in 1965 supervise the distribution of food supplies to the civilian population.

Below: Glum looking Soviet soldiers in Afghanistan. For the troops of the USSR, a posting to this part of Asia is no passport to glory. The original massive intervention has become a holding operation in a vicious guerrilla war that shows no signs of ending.

mostly Belgians and French but included Americans and British. Shaba adjoins Angola, which was then in the throes of a struggle for independence. On 11/12 May 1978 a force of rebels, supported by Cuban troops, moved into Zaire and seized Kolwezi. The rebels, joined by members of the Zaire garrison, ran amok, in the course of which they killed 200 Europeans. The aim was to gain control of the mines and overthrow President Joseph Mobutu of Zaire.

On 16 May the US government alerted the 82nd Airborne Division and air transports with a view to evacuating European nationals; but on the following day the French president, Giscard d'Estaing, after consulting Belgium and the United States, decided to intervene. On 19 May the 2nd Parachute Battalion of the Foreign Legion emplaned in Corsica and flew to Kolwezi, seizing the airfield by parachute drop and air landing. They were followed later by Belgian paratroops, for whom there were insufficient aircraft to permit them to take part in the initial drop. Opposition was ill-coordinated and within a few days the situation had been restored. By 25 May, less than a week after their arrival, the French troops were withdrawn, having been relieved by the Zaire Army supported by a force of Moroccans.

Kolwezi is an excellent example of what can be achieved by highly trained troops when they are deployed by a government which knows its own mind and refuses to be deflected by debates in the United Nations or anywhere else for that matter. The French action undoubtedly saved many lives – as well as the political career of President Mobutu.

But there are other uses for such interventionary forces. A phenomenon of the 1970s was the rapid growth of international terrorism. One of the most

favoured actions was hijacking aircraft and holding passengers to ransom, either for money or in exchange for the release of political prisoners. Assassinations of important public figures or the kidnapping of others in return for ransom were the tactics of such groups as the Italian Red Brigade, the Baader-Meinhof gang in West Germany and the South Moluccans in Holland.

As international links grew between terrorist groups (often under the aegis of the Palestine Liberation Organisation), so specialised squads of police or soldiers were formed who were able to take their specialised skills anywhere in the world if need be. The West German IG9 successfully stormed a hijacked Lufthansa aircraft at Mogadishu in Somalia on 13 October 1977, while the assault on the Iranian embassy in London by the SAS on 5 May 1980 in order to release hostages is another example of the employment of special forces to counter terrorism.

Probably the counter-terrorist operation likely to live longest in the public's memory is the daring operation carried out by Israeli commandos at Entebbe airport in Uganda on 3 July 1976. Two German and two Palestinian terrorists had hijacked an Air France plane en route from Tel Aviv to Paris on 27 June. The aircraft had a crew of 12 and was carrying 256 passengers, many of them Israeli citizens. The plane was flown first to Benghazi, where Colonel Gaddafi made no attempt to detain it. It then flew on to Entebbe, where the passengers were incarcerated in the airport terminal, with the apparent connivance of President Idi Amin.

The terrorists demanded the release by the Israelis of 40 Palestinian terrorists in exchange for the safe delivery of the passengers but the Israeli government stood its ground. Meanwhile, it assembled a force of 200 commandos at Sharm el Sheikh at the tip of Sinai and flew them in three Hercules transport aircraft direct to Entebbe on 3 July. Landing just before midnight, the Israelis surrounded the airport terminal, overpowered the terrorists and released the hostages, who were then flown back to Tel Aviv on the Hercules. The aircraft refuelled at Nairobi before flying on, without which facility the operation would probably have been impossible to mount with any chance of success. After it was all over the Israelis paid tribute to the cooperation they had received from the Kenyan government. It is likely to remain for many years to come a copybook operation of its kind.

In the last third of the 20th century, it seems unlikely that the tendency by one state to meddle in the affairs of another, either for political or for ideological reasons, is going to diminish. There is, for example, growing discontent among the populations of the Soviet satellite countries; Latin America is in a state of ferment; the steady increase in influence of Islamic fundamentalism is a cause for concern in several Middle Eastern countries; independence does not appear to have solved underlying antagonisms in many African states; and southern Africa in particular seems far from stable.

Faced with such potential chaos, many states – fearful of economic, political or ideological threats to their traditional spheres of influence – continue to maintain specially-prepared forces capable of swift interventionary action should the need arise. In France, for example, Foreign Legion paras are earmarked for the role and are fully capable of carrying it

Above: A difficult moment in civil-military relations during the Tanzanian invasion of Uganda in January 1979. Although Tanzanian troops were ridding the country of the dictator Idi Amin, the relationship between intervening forces and civilian population was never easy, and in Uganda there were many unpleasant incidents.

Below: Kolwezi, 1978. The array of modern weaponry at the disposal of the rebel and invading troops was such that intervention in the mining town was a hazardous business, and the threat to the European technicians there was particularly severe.

out, as Kolwezi showed; in Britain, the 5th Infantry Brigade, with airborne capability, is kept available for operations outside the Nato area. The Americans have gone even further, creating in March 1980 a Rapid Deployment Joint Task Force (RDJTF) specifically for intervention in the Gulf states of the Middle East should they and their vital oil supplies be threatened by either internal or external attack.

The RDJTF – known officially since January 1983 as Central Command (CENTCOM) – is intended as a symbol of American support to friendly governments in a troubled region, but it has been fraught with problems. On the political side, there has been some difficulty in defining the exact circumstances in which intervention will take place: is it to be in response to a Soviet invasion of Iran, a spread of anti-Western Muslim fundamentalism, or an internal guerrilla campaign against an existing pro-Western government? In any event, the Americans would have to be invited in or face the prospects of international condemnation and escalating violence.

Even if this was all sorted out, military problems abound. The RDJTF was originally composed of a Marine Amphibious Force, three Army divisions (the 82nd Airborne, 101st Airmobile and 24th Mechanised) with full supporting units, about 500 tactical aircraft and an entire naval carrier battle group; during 1983 this was considerably increased. But the nearest American base is Diego Garcia in the Indian Ocean, over 3200km (2000 miles) from the Arabian Gulf, and the bulk of the force has, of necessity, to be kept back in the United States. Some staging and supply bases have been set up in Egypt, Somalia and Oman, and special transport ships have been prepositioned in the Indian Ocean, but CENTCOM clearly lacks both flexibility and speed of deployment.

Until such problems have been solved – either by the acquisition of more permanent base facilities actually in the Gulf area or by the development of yet more powerful air-transport capability – interventionary forces on such a scale would seem to be more of a deterrent symbol than a viable capability. As such, they undoubtedly have a value, but at the present time it is still the small, highly trained units, capable of short, sharp engagements designed to achieve a selected political aim, that are likely to succeed. Their record so far – from Jordan and Lebanon in 1958 to Kolwezi 20 years later – shows what they can achieve, and there is no reason to doubt that they will continue to be used. **James Lunt**

Lebanon and Jordan '58

Anglo-American operations in the Middle East

In July 1958 Britain and America intervened militarily in two Middle East states, Jordan and Lebanon respectively. These interventions, although distinct operations, were coordinated both militarily and politically. When the United States sent its Marines into Lebanon it did so in the knowledge that it had the political support of the British government, and when Britain sent its paratroopers into Jordan it did so in the knowledge that it had the political and military support of Washington. The Anglo-American special relationship, shattered by the Suez affair in 1956, seemed to have been completely revived.

That Britain and America could act in unison in July 1958 was due to the emergence of common views on two subjects: communism and Arab nationalism. Britain, for her part, did not actually change her views after 1956. For some years the British government had regarded both of these movements as twin threats to Britain's Middle East interests. The Soviet Union was seen as an expansionist power harbouring ambitions to take over the Middle East oilfields. The Egyptian leader, Gamal Abdel Nasser, was said to be paving the way for the Russians by undermining Western interests and promoting his pan-Arab nationalist ideas.

In order to deal with the first of these threats, Britain had sponsored the Baghdad Pact in 1955. This alliance, which also included Turkey, Iran, Iraq and Pakistan, was designed to act as a buffer against Soviet expansion. To deal with the second threat, Britain tried to appease and then to coerce Nasser.

On neither issue did Britain receive wholehearted American support. Despite her strong anti-communism, the United States declined to join the Baghdad Pact. And when Britain turned against Nasser in October 1956, America not only opposed Britain's Suez venture but forced the British government to call off the operation. Nevertheless, over the following 18 months, America gradually came to agree with Britain's assessment of both Soviet and Egyptian policies.

The first indication of this came in January 1957 when President Dwight D. Eisenhower announced a new policy towards the Middle East. The region, he said, represented a power vacuum which the Soviet Union was eager to fill. In order to prevent Soviet expansion, the US should give military assistance to any Middle East state which felt menaced by the USSR or its local allies. This proposal, subsequently known as the Eisenhower Doctrine, was approved by Congress and became law on 9 March 1957.

Although the doctrine was not invoked until July 1958, during 1957 and early 1958 trouble erupted in several Middle East countries, notably in Jordan, Syria, Saudi Arabia and Lebanon, and was regarded by America as a systematic attempt by Nasser and/or Russia to undermine Western influence. In Jordan, for example, a power struggle between pro-Nasser elements and King Hussein came to a head in April 1957. Hussein denounced the Soviet Union, Syria and Egypt for plotting to overthrow him. He exiled disloyal army officers, imposed martial law and

Right: A Lebanese Druze chieftain, festooned with ammunition. Walid Jumblatt's Druze Muslim followers have always been concerned to protect their interests against the rival Maronite Christians, and civil war remains a constant possibility in Lebanon.

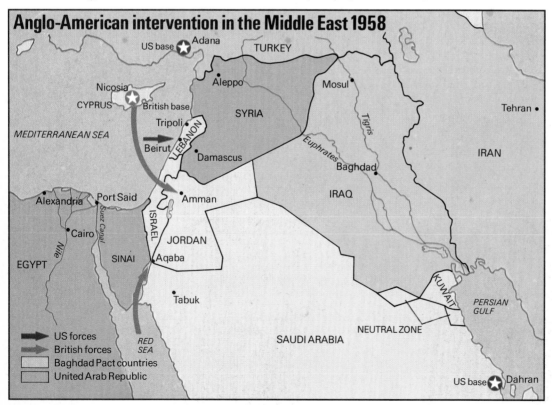

Anglo-American intervention in the Middle East 1958

TURKEY · US base Adana · Nicosia · CYPRUS · British base · MEDITERRANEAN SEA · Aleppo · Mosul · Tehran · Tripoli · LEBANON · SYRIA · Tigris · Beirut · Euphrates · Damascus · Baghdad · IRAN · Alexandria · Port Said · Amman · IRAQ · Cairo · Suez Canal · ISRAEL · Nile · JORDAN · Aqaba · SINAI · EGYPT · Tabuk · KUWAIT · PERSIAN GULF · NEUTRAL ZONE · SAUDI ARABIA · RED SEA · US base Dahran

US forces
British forces
Baghdad Pact countries
United Arab Republic

Below: Lebanese insurgents take cover as government forces open fire. The fighting in 1958 threatened to destroy the fragile balance of the Lebanese constitution.

rounded up dissidents. Hussein survived. The United States did not intervene, but she warned other powers to keep out of Jordan and, as a gesture of support, moved the Sixth Fleet into the eastern Mediterranean.

Increasing communist influence in Syria in late 1957 caused concern in the United States. The apprehension was intensified when Syria and Egypt announced on 1 February 1958 that they were merging to form the United Arab Republic (UAR). In Saudi Arabia shortly afterwards, on 24 March, the pro-Western King Saud was forced to transfer most of his powers to Crown Prince Faisal, said to be sympathetic to Nasser.

Further troubles, this time in Lebanon, brought America close to invoking the Eisenhower Doctrine. Lebanon, an ethnically divided state in which power was shared by Muslims and Christians, was verging on civil war by May 1958 as the pro-Western president, Camille Chamoun, faced an armed insurrection. The rebels, mostly Muslims, claimed that Chamoun was planning to cling to office after his term expired in September and called for his immediate resignation. Chamoun claimed that the rebellion had been incited by the UAR, which had sent men and arms across the border from Syria. He refused to resign and ordered the army to deal with the rebellion. The army, ethnically divided, seemed unable or unwilling to do so. Although the rebels were contained, they were not crushed and retained control of parts of Beirut, Sidon, Tripoli and almost all areas along the Syrian border. Chamoun appealed to the US for assistance, but America urged him to compromise. With the military situation stalemated, Chamoun took the matter to the United Nations, which sent a team to check on the allegations of UAR infiltration.

All these developments caused concern in Britain and America, but it took events in Iraq to trigger Western intervention. Iraq, which had united with its fellow Hashemite monarchy Jordan in February 1958 to form the Arab Federation, was regarded by the West as the pillar of the Baghdad Pact. On 14 July, however, the government of Nuri-as-Said was overthrown in a swift but savage military coup. Nuri, King Faisal II and Crown Prince Abdul Ilah were murdered and their bodies mutilated. In their stead a radical republican government sympathetic to Nasser and

hostile to Hussein was set up under Brigadier Abdul Kassim. This came as a devastating blow to the Western powers. The keystone of Western influence in northern Arabia had been removed.

The Iraqi coup led to swift American action. In accordance with the Eisenhower Doctrine, the US intervened only where it was asked to – and both Lebanon and Jordan requested help.

The first appeal came on 14 July from Camille Chamoun's embattled regime. Chamoun saw himself as next on the list of Nasser's victims. President Eisenhower, although not unmindful of the risks involved, especially the possibility of counter-measures by the UAR, Iraq or Russia, decided to respond positively. Discussions with Congressional leaders revealed that intervention was acceptable politically. Talks with military advisers indicated that intervention was militarily feasible. The mighty Sixth Fleet, comprising more than 70 warships, was already concentrated in the eastern Mediterranean. In less than 24 hours Eisenhower decided to accede to Chamoun's request. After consulting British Prime Minister Harold Macmillan, Eisenhower decided to send in troops.

The plan was for US troops aboard the Sixth Fleet's warships to disembark near Beirut, secure the capital and the immediate environs and so bolster Chamoun's regime. Americans were not, however, to get involved in the hinterland. The Sixth Fleet was ordered immediately to Lebanese waters and American units in the US and Europe were earmarked for rapid deployment to the Middle East.

The operation began on schedule on 15 July. Off the Lebanese coastline some 50 warships lay ready

Above: The Lebanese president, Camille Chamoun. After the short and savage coup in Iraq, Chamoun feared that he would become the next victim of revolutionary Arab nationalism and appealed to the United States for help.

Below: Under the protective umbrella of a US promise to provide material and moral support, British troops were flown into Jordan in response to King Hussein's appeal. Here a unit of Cameronians, heavily laden with kit, trek across the sun-scorched airport at Amman.

under the command of Vice-Admiral James Holloway. At 1500 hours Lebanese time, the first US troops landed – some 1700 men of the 2nd Battalion, 2nd Marine Regiment. They were joined the next day by another Marine battalion, the 3rd Battalion, 6th Marine Regiment, and on 18 July by the 1st Battalion, 8th Marine Regiment. These Marines waded ashore in combat formation in case of hostile fire from Lebanese units. In the event, such a precaution proved unnecessary. Large crowds of holiday-makers waved them ashore and with the full coopera-tion of the 9000-strong Lebanese Army the Marines moved off to secure key locations. Further soldiers were airlifted in so that by 20 July some 10,000 US troops were patrolling Beirut and its environs.

President Eisenhower also took wider precaution-ary measures in case of a military response from Iraq, the UAR or the Soviet Union. Tactical aircraft, notably F-100 Super Sabres, were flown into the US base at Adana in southern Turkey, as were several thousand US troops. The president also placed Strategic Air Command (SAC) on a heightened state of alert and ordered precautionary moves to protect the Persian Gulf area, if necessary by nuclear means.

Hussein under threat

In the meantime Britain was taking equally deci-sive, if less grandiose, action to defend Jordan. King Hussein's initial reaction to news of the murder of his kin in Iraq was that of outrage. He considered invad-ing Iraq and upholding the unity of the newly founded Arab Federation, but other issues had to take prece-dence. With Kassim and Nasser urging Jordanians to revolt, with UAR troops moving on his northern border and with pro-Nasser elements plotting within his own territory, Hussein's problems were grave, so he sought assistance from the USA and Britain.

America left the burden of this request to Britain, which placed Harold Macmillan in some difficulty. Two battalions of paratroopers were available in Cyprus, but intervention would not be without danger. Politically there was the risk of adverse reaction from some members of the Commonwealth as well as from within Britain itself. Intervention might also provoke Arab resentment, particularly against Hussein; after all, it was only a year since British forces had left Jordan. There were also risks on the military side. If Hussein fell, or if America decided upon a hasty departure from Lebanon, British troops would be exposed to disaster. Against this, non-intervention would almost certainly doom Jor-dan and its Hashemite dynasty to UAR control. Moreover, the United States had promised moral and material support. So, at 3 o'clock on the morning of 17 July, Macmillan decided in favour of intervention. British paras were to be flown from Cyprus to the Jordanian capital of Amman.

At dawn on the 17th, the first British troops – 200 men of the 2nd Battalion, The Parachute Regiment – touched down at Amman airfield. For several long hours it looked as if they would not be reinforced. The Israeli government had not been informed about the overflight of its territory and banned further flights. Later in the day, however, the Israelis relented. Further British flights over Israeli airspace took place that evening, with US fighters giving air cover. By 18 July the airlift was completed. Some 2200 men of the 16th Independent Parachute Brigade, along with sup-porting units of light artillery, had landed safely on

America intervenes

On 15 July 1958, President Dwight D. Eisenhower announced that US Marines were being landed in the Lebanon in response to an appeal from President Chamoun. 'Yesterday morning I received from President Chamoun an urgent plea that some US forces be stationed in Lebanon to help maintain security and to evidence the concern of the United States for the integrity and independence of Lebanon.... President Chamoun made clear that he considered an immediate US response imperative if Lebanon's independence, already menaced from without, were to be preserved in the face of the grave developments which occurred yesterday in Baghdad, whereby the lawful government was violently overthrown and many of its members martyred.

'In response to this appeal from the government of Lebanon the United States has despatched a contingent of US forces to Lebanon to protect American lives and by their presence there to encourage the Lebanese government in defence of Lebanese sovereignty and integrity. These forces have not been sent as any act of war.... There are in Lebanon about 2500 Americans and we cannot, consistently with our historic relations and with the principles of the United Nations, stand idly by when Lebanon appeals for evidence of our concern, and when Lebanon may not be able to preserve internal order and defend itself against indirect aggression.'

Above: The American response: US Marines leap ashore from their landing craft. Within five days there were some 10,000 US troops patrolling Beirut and its environs.

Jordanian territory. With the full cooperation of the Jordanian forces they proceeded, as planned, to secure key points in Amman.

For the British, like the Americans, these opening moves proved to be far less hazardous than had been expected. Resistance by local units did not eventuate. Military counter-moves by Iraq and the UAR, which again could not be completely discounted, failed to materialise. The Soviet Union held military manoeuvres along its borders with Turkey and Iran but did little else other than to protest loudly.

Both Britain and America sent in reinforcements but they were hardly needed. The situation

in Jordan had stabilised. King Hussein looked firmly entrenched and on 11 August received pledges of loyalty from Bedouin Arabs from throughout the kingdom. In Lebanon, too, order was returning. A new president, General Fuad Chehab, was elected on 31 July with support from both government and opposition leaders. Chehab succeeded Chamoun when the latter's term of office expired on 23 September. A new government, comprising Christians and Muslims, was formed on 15 October.

Meanwhile, the threat to Jordan and Lebanon from the UAR had receded and Iraq, after the initial excesses of the mob, seemed to pose no great threat. Furthermore, at the UN the Arab states had come to an agreement. They pledged not to interfere in each other's internal affairs and requested the UN Secretary-General to arrange for the withdrawal of Western forces. This resolution, sponsored by the Arab states, was adopted without dissension on 21 August.

The British and Americans willingly concurred. By 25 October 1958 the US had completed its withdrawal and by 2 November the last British troops had left Jordan. The British and Americans could claim that, without firing a shot in anger, they had saved two friendly regimes from immediate destruction.

Francis Toase

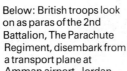

Below: British troops look on as paras of the 2nd Battalion, The Parachute Regiment, disembark from a transport plane at Amman airport, Jordan.

Nationalism and revolution
The Arab world in turmoil

The Middle East in the mid-1950s was a region in turmoil. Revolutionary nationalism tore through the Arab world, setting progressive against conservative, and produced an explosive mix which outside powers, especially Great Britain, the United States and the Soviet Union, hoped to manipulate. But the fissures and shifting alliances of the Arab states were to prove almost impossible to control, even for those politicians with the most prestige in the region.

Ever since the collapse of the Ottoman Empire at the end of World War I, three issues in particular have confronted the Arabs. The first is the problem of unity. The Arab world, though an ancient culture and civilisation, is a relatively young state system, and the Arab states only emerged in the 20th century. Their common ground is a fervent belief that the separate Arab states comprise one nation. This was the hope and aspiration behind the rebellion in 1916 against the Turks. This rebellion, against fellow Muslims and in alliance with the infidel, was the price the Arabs were prepared to pay for their independence. Instead all they achieved was a limited freedom, constrained by the introduction of new patrons and rulers, this time from the Western world.

The second issue has been the problem of their relationship with the Jews, first in British-mandated Palestine and later, after 1948, in the new garrison state of Israel. It was Arab failure to prevent the emergence of that state and the subsequent conflict with the Israelis, which has caused so much tumult, humiliation and division in the Arab world. Defeat in the first Arab-Israeli War of 1948-49 undermined practically all the Arab leaders of that generation. There was assassination and turmoil in Jordan, a military coup in Syria and finally the 'ancien régime' fell from power in Egypt. The military took over the reins of government and within a couple of years Colonel Gamal Abdel Nasser emerged as the strong man at the head of the state.

The third issue has been Arab relations with outside powers. The complications of this issue propelled Nasser onto a collision course with the West and with Britain in particular. It was Nasser's dream to see Egypt play its full part in international affairs and to become a leading power in the Middle East. Though he succeeded in securing a fairly amicable withdrawal of the British military presence, his nationalisation of the Suez Canal set in course a train of events which produced an alliance between France, Israel and Britain in 1956 and an invasion of his country.

Though the Egyptian forces were severely mauled in the 1956 war, and in military terms suffered a humiliating and ignominious defeat, Nasser emerged triumphant. The Anglo-French intervention on the side of Israel had transformed Nasser's personal position from being just another military ruler into that of national hero.

Failure on the part of Britain and France at Suez showed that the Arabs were no longer impotent and that even the mighty British could be humbled and humiliated. Iraq and Jordan, the two monarchies who were allied to Britain, were unable to resist the popular outcry of the Arab world and were obliged to join in the condemnation.

Nasser's reputation was so great that some leaders sought to join with him in creating a new pan-Arab world; others turned to Nasser to solve

Right: Pro-Nasser Syrians hold aloft a picture of their hero as they celebrate the revolutionary forces that were sweeping the Arab world in 1963.

Below: A sword-wielding Syrian enthuses a group of demonstrators awaiting the arrival of President Nasser at Damascus airport in 1963.

their own problems. Radicalism and revolution seemed the order of the day and a union of the 'progressive' forces within the Arab world a natural step forward. These feelings were particularly strong in Syria, where radicals of all persuasions were looking outside for help while engaging in bitter struggles with their rivals inside the country. The Sunna Muslims in southern Syria favoured union with Iraq while the communists looked to Moscow for an alliance, for the Russians were seeking clients in the Middle East.

In the end it was the recently-formed Ba'athist Party which led the initiative for a union between Syria and Egypt. Ba'athism, which means 'resurrection' or 'renaissance', was a political movement first formed in 1952 in Syria. It embraced the ideology of Arab nationalism together with some concepts of a French style of socialism. The Ba'athist appeal was something which Nasser found irresistible. Union with Syria gave Egypt an influence in the very heart of the 'fertile crescent', from where it could launch its offensive against the Hashemite kingdoms of Jordan and Iraq as well as Saudi Arabia. It helped resolve the dilemma of Egypt, a state which was Arab and so much stronger than other Arab states in human terms, yet isolated geographically and almost devoid of natural resources. Without material wealth Nasser could not sustain any drive for Arab leadership.

On 1 February 1958 Syria and Egypt joined in the United Arab Republic (UAR). The new capital was Cairo and Nasser its first head of state. Although the constitution allowed for two Syrian and two Egyptian vice-presidents, Field-Marshal Abdul Hakin Amer, a close personal friend and confidante, functioned as Nasser's 'viceroy' in Damascus.

Towards Arab unity

In 1962, the Egyptian newspaper *al-Ahram* expressed the ambitions of Egyptian revolutionary nationalism, the basic tenets of which were so worrying to more conservative Arab states.

'As a state, Egypt deals with all Arab governments, whatever their forms or systems. She takes her place beside them in the Arab League and at the United Nations and concludes defence, trade, cultural, and other agreements with them.... As a revolution, Egypt should deal only with the people. This does not imply interference on our part in the affairs of others, since the fundamental premise of our struggle is that the Arab people are a single nation. If Egypt as a state recognises frontiers in her dealings with governments, Egypt as a revolution should never hesitate or halt at frontiers, but should carry her message across them.... We have no right to separate ourselves from the struggle of other citizens of our nation. Egypt as a revolution will thus be not the Cairo government but a progressive party within the framework of the Arab nation. It should extend its hand to all progressive elements of the nation and openly stand beside them.'

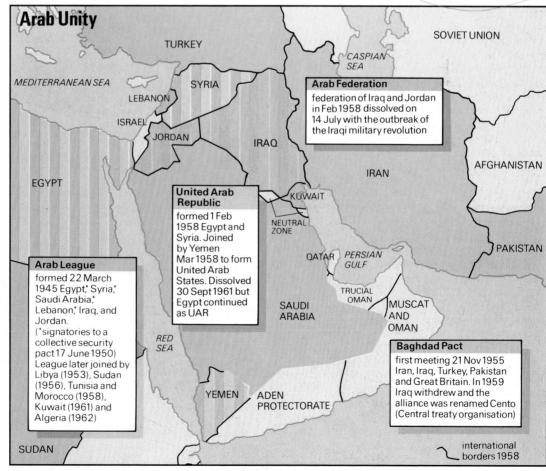

Arab Unity

SOVIET UNION

TURKEY

CASPIAN SEA

MEDITERRANEAN SEA

SYRIA

LEBANON

ISRAEL

JORDAN

IRAQ

IRAN

AFGHANISTAN

Arab Federation
federation of Iraq and Jordan in Feb 1958 dissolved on 14 July with the outbreak of the Iraqi military revolution

EGYPT

KUWAIT

NEUTRAL ZONE

United Arab Republic
formed 1 Feb 1958 Egypt and Syria. Joined by Yemen Mar 1958 to form United Arab States. Dissolved 30 Sept 1961 but Egypt continued as UAR

QATAR

PERSIAN GULF

PAKISTAN

TRUCIAL OMAN

MUSCAT AND OMAN

Arab League
formed 22 March 1945 Egypt,* Syria,* Saudi Arabia,* Lebanon,* Iraq, and Jordan. (*signatories to a collective security pact 17 June 1950) League later joined by Libya (1953), Sudan (1956), Tunisia and Morocco (1958), Kuwait (1961) and Algeria (1962)

SAUDI ARABIA

RED SEA

Baghdad Pact
first meeting 21 Nov 1955 Iran, Iraq, Turkey, Pakistan and Great Britain. In 1959 Iraq withdrew and the alliance was renamed Cento (Central treaty organisation)

YEMEN

ADEN PROTECTORATE

international borders 1958

SUDAN

The spectre of a union between two radical and hostile powers galvanised neighbouring Jordan and Iraq into action. The 22-year-old Hashemite cousins responded with their own union the same month which they called the Arab Federation. King Faisal II of Iraq became head of state and King Hussein of Jordan his deputy. The federation raised the banner flown by their great-grandfather, Sharif Husain, during the Arab revolt against the Turks.

On paper at least the union of these two countries presented a formidable alliance. They were geographically contiguous; Iraq was rich in oil and could use its wealth to fuel the economy of a resource-starved but militarily impressive Jordan.

The Arab Federation was short-lived, however. Its collapse was foreshadowed by the outbreak of civil war in Lebanon and the death of Faisal, his family and court in a bloody revolution that was soon to sweep Iraq.

Mounting turmoil

In Lebanon the delicate balance between Christian and Muslim was coming under threat. The Arab part of the population demanded that Lebanon should join with the UAR and their hero, Nasser, and to prove their commitment thousands flocked to Damascus to see him when he visited Syria. However the Christian president, Camille Chamoun, was coldly ambitious; not only was he set resolutely against such a move, he was also about to set aside the constitution to seek a second six-year term of office. There was considerable turmoil and civil disorder. Middle Eastern politics seemed set on a collision course between the UAR and the Arab Federation.

In Iraq the ageing prime minister, Nuri-as-Said, now made a fatal blunder. He ordered Iraqi divisions

under the command of Brigadier Abdul Kassim to march into Jordan; the intention was probably to invade Syria. But instead, Kassim and his subordinates marched their troops on Baghdad. As in Egypt, the army showed itself to be anti-monarchist, and on 14 July 1958, the young king, royal family and court were slaughtered. Kassim proclaimed a republic with himself as president. A single bloody blow had destroyed a bastion of support for the West in the 'fertile crescent' and the Arab world.

Meanwhile, violence in Beirut had flared into civil

Bloodshed in Baghdad

Mrs Carol Magee, wife of a British major, lived near the royal palace in Baghdad and has described how members of the Iraqi royal family were murdered in the coup of 14 July 1958. 'The rebels moved field artillery to bear on the royal palace and instructions were shouted from the leading rebel platoon for the king and his household to come out,' she told a correspondent of The Times. 'The king and members of his household, including the Crown Prince, emerged into the palace gardens. The platoon commander ordered the king to tell the entire party to go with him. The Crown Prince replied that they would not move, saying that the rebels had no authority. The Crown Prince then ordered an escort to open fire and the rebel commander was shot dead.' According to Mrs Magee, carnage followed and all 19 members of the royal party fell dead. 'Terrible things happened afterwards, including the mutilation of the Crown Prince's body and the hanging up of the corpse [right],' she said.

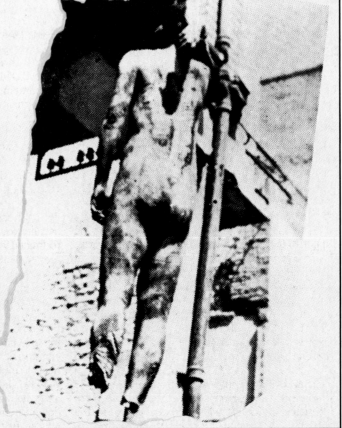

Left: Mohammed al-Badr who succeeded his father, Imam Ahmad of Yemen, in September 1961. An ensuing military coup forced Badr to flee to the mountains where he began to gather support among the hill tribes. It was not long before Saudi Arabia also gave him its support.

Left: Kurdish rebels march captured Iraqi soldiers to a prisoner of war camp. The Kurdish revolt was a problem, both practical and moral, for the Iraqi regime established after the coup of 1958. Below: Brigadier Abdul Kassim (centre), who led the bloody 1958 military coup in Iraq and became president of the new government.

war and the Lebanese government appealed to the United States for assistance. The US Sixth Fleet, undisputed masters of the eastern Mediterranean, sent its Marine Task Force ashore and rapidly restored order. At the same time King Hussein, desperate to contain the repercussions of the ill-fated Arab Federation, welcomed British paratroopers into Amman. The Anglo-American operations were textbook examples of successful military intervention in support of client regimes. Nasser's progress was halted and the Iraqi revolution contained.

Contrary to expectations at the time, Iraq did not join the UAR. Kassim was a nationalist first and a pan-Arabist second. And the force of the Iraqi revolution was also blunted by the Kurds, who chose this moment to start a war of insurgency for secession. The population of Iraq was just over 12 million. Political instability in the country derived in part from its sectarian diversity, with the Shi'ia Muslims providing the majority of the Arab population. The Kurds, who comprised at least 20 per cent, were not Arab but a pastoral tribal people with a national history predating Islam. They inhabited the largely inaccessible Zagros mountains astride southeastern Turkey, western Iran and northern Iraq. Although they accepted Islam, they were of the Sunna sect and never accepted Arab rule. Twice in the 20th century they had come close to achieving independence, and once again, in 1958, they raised their banner under the leadership of Mullah Mustafa Barzani and proceeded to tear the heart out of the Iraqi Army which tried to quell the rebellion.

In other affairs Kassim ruled the country with the support of the small but vociferous Communist Party, this in turn arousing the hostility of Egypt. Colonel Abdul Salam Aref, Kassim's associate, was a member of the Iraqi Ba'athist Party, and he too contested the pro-communism of his leader and was condemned to death for treason. Kassim commuted the sentence against his young subordinate in an act of clemency which he later came to regret.

Scarcely had the 'fertile crescent' begun to stabilise when events in southern Arabia caused the Arabs to concentrate on this hitherto rather quiet part of the Middle East. It was an area where the British were still entrenched militarily, and UK policy was to create a viable political structure to counter the threat from the

radical Arabs. Britain planned a federation based on the tribal sheikhs of the interior and the sultan of the Aden protectorate. This was vehemently opposed by the old reactionary Imam Ahmad, ruler in neighbouring Yemen. He 'associated' his realm with the UAR partly to protect his interests in the region and as insurance against the wrath of the radicals.

With Egyptian support the Yemen sponsored sabotage and terrorism among the disaffected and unruly tribes of the interior of the projected federation. Despite this campaign of intimidation six of the sheikhs later that year accepted the federation idea. London then attempted to find some means of associating the federation with Aden, though it had no intention of abandoning the excellent harbour and base facilities.

The early 1960s were to prove a turbulent time for Nasser. Despite the fanfares, there had been problems from the outset with Damascus. The Ba'athists had soon become disenchanted with Nasser's style of rule and moved into opposition. Neither did Egypt have the resources to bridge the geographical divide and the political experiment moved inevitably towards failure. In September 1961 a military coup brought a more nationalist-minded group of officers to power in Syria and the union was quietly dissolved.

Withdrawal and redeployment

The fragility of Arab unity was also exposed elsewhere in that year. Britain withdrew from Kuwait and this immediately was the signal for Kassim to claim the country for Iraq. Nasser could not allow a powerful, oil-rich, Soviet-backed Iraq to emerge in the Gulf any more than could conservative-minded Saudi Arabia, a state which increasingly saw itself as leader of the moderate Arabs. Both gave their tacit support to the redeployment of British troops to counter the Iraqi threat and later helped replace them with forces from the Arab League.

In September 1961 the ruthless Imam Ahmad of the Yemen died and was succeeded by his weaker son, Badr. A group of army officers led by Brigadier Abdullah al-Sallal rebelled and seized the main towns. Badr escaped into the country and rallied support among the hill tribes. The Yemeni republicans appealed to Nasser for military aid and assistance – which he was happy to provide; but what little unity that remained in the Arab world was further fragmented when Saudi Arabia gave its support to Badr and the royalist faction. The military presence of a radical Egypt in southern Arabia was viewed with the deepest misgivings by the Saudis.

In the years that followed, the Egyptian Expeditionary Force exceeded 50,000 men in a war which became known as Nasser's Vietnam. The Egyptians, ill-trained for a counter-insurgency war in strange and mountainous terrain, could make little progress against the royalist tribes. Pacification policies simply resulted in the wholesale destruction of villages and the alienation of the local population. The war was further complicated by the attitudes of the Arab Federation and Aden. The sheikhs supported the royalist cause, which in turn exposed them to republican attacks; the urbanised Adenis favoured the republican cause, hated the thought of a merger with the sheikhs who they saw as old-fashioned and reactionary, and wanted to be rid of the British. Student demonstrations escalated into riots and guerrilla attacks. Britain was determined to stay in Aden and so

reinforced the garrison, declared a State of Emergency in 1963 and entered into a full-scale counter-insurgency campaign.

There was little stability elsewhere in the Arab world. Kassim's Iraq seethed with discontent and, despite government repression, the Ba'athist movement gained ground. In February 1963 Aref and his Ba'athist allies launched a successful coup. Unlike his onetime leader, Aref showed no mercy. Kassim and many of his Marxist supporters were summarily executed.

A month later a coup in Damascus restored the Ba'athists to power. The movement looked to its pan-Arab heritage and a union between Egypt, Iraq and Syria. The Ba'athists, however, could not accept Nasser as their leader, and because there was no other candidate of comparable stature, the idea was still-born.

The Israeli challenge

By the mid-1960s the problem of Palestine forced Nasser and the other Arab leaders to resolve their differences and concentrate on the Israeli challenge. From January 1965 tension increased along the Arab borders of Israel. A Palestinian guerrilla group called Al-Fatah (meaning 'conquest') led by Yassir Arafat, a member of the politically extreme Muslim Brotherhood, had established its headquarters in Syria. Equipped with eastern bloc weapons, and funded by Egypt and Kuwait, it launched a series of raids from its guerrilla bases in Jordan and the Gaza Strip. The Israelis retaliated with conventional attacks and these in turn exposed weaknesses and shortcomings in the Arab armies.

Nasser realised that the Arabs were in no position to challenge the military might of the Israeli Defence Forces and sought to avoid a confrontation. However, Nasser was a prisoner of his own reputation and

The Arab world was united only in its opposition to the state of Israel, and during the 1960s, Palestinian organisations – such as Al-Fatah ('conquest') – became more active, with groups of Palestinian fedayeen (such as those being briefed on military techniques, above) stepping up raids on the Jewish state. In the search for support, even conservative heads of state were prepared to look for help from the communist world. Below: King Hussein of Jordan has talks with Nikita Khrushchev in Moscow in 1963.

events conspired against him, for there was no way he could abrogate his position as leader of the cause. In February 1966 yet another coup in Damascus removed the Ba'athists from power and this cleared the way for better relations with Cairo.

In November 1966, amidst rising tension along the borders, the Syrians persuaded Nasser to enter into a new defence pact. The Egyptian leader agreed against his better judgement; he was desperate to find some device which would allow him to control the impetuous and militarily foolhardy Syrians. A joint staff was established and the two states agreed to a single high command in time of war. However, the Syrians refused to accept Egyptian troops in their territory, which would have provided Nasser with the only effective constraint to their behaviour. It seemed that unity was only possible in the Arab world when conflict was looming with Israel; and as events were to show, such conflict would be militarily disastrous.

Eric Morris

Key Weapons

SOVIET APCs

part 1

During World War II the Soviet Union possessed few personnel carriers of any sort, and so tanks were used to carry infantry into battle. But infantrymen clinging to turrets were vulnerable to smallarms fire and air burst shells. As the tank has always been central to Soviet battlefield tactics it was logical that, when the war was over, armoured personnel carriers (APCs) should be introduced. The idea was that they should be capable of matching the speed of accompanying tanks while providing infantry in the assault with a measure of protection. As a result of this development, the entire infantry component of the Soviet Army is APC-borne.

Speed of advance is a prime consideration in present-day Soviet tactical thinking, and high mobility is therefore considered essential for APCs. The amphibious capability of current vehicles enables them to cross water obstacles and maintain momentum, and they are equipped to operate at night.

If, during a battalion advance, the lead reconnaissance element encounters resistance it is swiftly reinforced by an assault force of tanks and APCs, the latter moving a few hundred metres behind the tanks in pairs. The aim will be to outflank or envelop the opposition and continue the advance. Alternatively, surprise raids can be made deep into the enemy's rear. The highly mobile BMP is well suited to this task.

In a Soviet motor rifle regiment or battalion attack, APCs advance with the tank element across a broad frontage and in line abreast. When mounted, Soviet APCs and infantry are vulnerable to Nato anti-tank weapons, so the infantry often dismount and advance on foot while the APCs provide overhead fire support from some 400m (440yds) to the rear. When dismounted the infantry adopt extended-line formation on a 50m (55yd) frontage. APCs also have a part to play in defence, where the BMP's 73mm gun and low silhouette are particular assets.

The first echelon of a combined arms army – two motor rifle divisions plus one tank regiment – contains a high proportion of APCs. The second echelon

Previous page: The six-wheeled, open-topped BTR-152 APC which came into service with Soviet forces in the early 1950s. Above: Dismounted infantry advance under covering fire from tanks and the heavily armed BMP MICV.

Below: A BTR-40 captured by the Israelis. Like the BTR-152 it was based on an existing truck chassis and was open topped. Subsequent variants, however, incorporated overhead armour.

BTR-40 APC

Crew 2 plus 8
Dimensions Length 5m (16ft 5in); width 1.9m (6ft 3in); height 1.75m (5ft 9in)
Weight Combat loaded 5300kg (11,684lb)
Engine GAZ-40 6-cylinder, in-line, water-cooled petrol developing 80hp at 3400rpm

Performance Maximum road speed 80km/h (50mph); range (road) 285km (177 miles); vertical obstacle 0.47m (1ft 6in); trench 0.7m (2ft 3in); gradient 58 per cent; fording 0.8m (2ft 7in)

Armour 8-13mm (0.3-0.5in)
Armament One 7.62mm SGMB machine gun

Above: Israeli war booty. A captured Arab BTR-152 is pressed into service with the IDF. Left: An Egyptian BTR-50PK on the Suez Canal in 1973.

Below: The BTR-50PK, the first tracked and fully amphibious Soviet APC with overhead armour protection.

BTR-152 APC

Crew 2 plus 17
Dimensions Length 6.83m (22ft 5in); width 2.32m (7ft 7in); height 2.05m (6ft 9in)
Weight Combat loaded 8950kg (19,731lb)
Engine ZIL-123 6-cylinder, in-line, petrol developing 110hp at 3000rpm

Performance Maximum road speed 75km/h (47mph); range (road) 780km (485 miles); vertical obstacle 0.6m (1ft 11in); trench 0.69m (2ft); gradient 55 per cent; fording 0.8m (2ft 8in)

Armour 6-13.6mm (0.24-0.53in)
Armament One 7.62mm SGMB machine gun or one 12.7mm machine gun

Since the introduction of the BTR-50 series in the late 1950s, Soviet APCs have all been amphibious, which greatly improves their capability for maintaining momentum in an all-out advance. When negotiating water obstacles (above left) the BTR-50 is propelled by twin hydrojets mounted in the rear of the vehicle (above), and steering is controlled by opening and closing the exterior vents.

Left: A Soviet-built BTR-50PK with Finnish markings. Clearly visible in the front centre of the hull are the driver's vision block and three periscopes, while to the driver's right is the commander's cupola. Below: A command variant, the BTR-50PU on parade with the Egyptian Army. This vehicle is distinguishable from the rest of the series by the extra cupola on the hull front, additional antennae, and new ventilator arrangement.

BTR-50PK APC

Crew 2 plus 10
Dimensions Length 7.08m (23ft 3in); width 3.14m (10ft 4in); height 1.97m (6ft 6in)
Weight Combat loaded 14,500kg (31,967lb)
Engine V-6 6-cylinder, in-line, water-cooled diesel developing 240hp at 1800rpm

Performance Maximum road speed 44km/h (27 miles); maximum water speed 11km/h (6.8mph); range (road) 260km (161 miles); vertical obstacle 1.1m (3ft 4in); trench 2.8m (6ft 10in); gradient 70 per cent; fording amphibious. Propelled by two water jets in the rear of the vehicle

Armour 10mm (0.4in)
Armament One 7.62mm SGMB machine gun

contains a further motor rifle division along with the tank army's own motor rifle division. In the first echelon the bulk of the APCs would be BTR-60PBs; but BMPs – normally in the second echelon, from where they could be rapidly deployed on encirclement tasks – could be brought forward as reinforcements as required.

The Soviet Union's first practical design for an APC, the BTR-152, appeared in 1949 and entered service with the Soviet Army in 1950. This vehicle resembled the US M-3 half-track but was provided with six wheels, and early models were based on the ZIL-151 2½-tonne truck chassis. Subsequent models, however, incorporated the ZIL-157 chassis.

The BTR-152 weighed 9 tonnes and could carry 17 soldiers (half a platoon) in addition to the two-man crew. The rear compartment was open, however, and thus a prime requirement – overhead protection – was lacking for the mounted infantry. With side armour thickness of only 13.6mm (0.53in) the vehicle provided inadequate protection all round, although ports were provided through which troops could fire smallarms, and a pintle-mounted 7.62mm machine gun furnished additional firepower. In the BTR-152 the ZIL-123 engine was situated at the front under an armoured bonnet while the driver and commander occupied a side-by-side armoured cab. Subsequent

Above: An OT-62B (Model 2). This vehicle is the Czech equivalent of the Soviet BTR-50PK but incorporates the twin-cupola layout of the PU command vehicle. The cupola on the driver's right mounts a 7.62mm M59 machine gun.

Below left: A view of the OT-62B from the rear deck showing the two rectangular overhead hatches. Below right: A further Czech modification to the Soviet design included the provision of side doors in the troop compartment.

modification included the adoption of the now widely-used system of tyre pressure regulation which adapts tyre pressure to the terrain while the vehicle is on the move.

A number of variants of the BTR-152 have appeared. The BTR-152K introduced overhead armour while the BTR-152U is fitted with a higher roof of 2.72m (8ft 11in) and additional radio equipment to operate as a command vehicle. A BTR-152A with twin 14.5mm KPV machine guns in a powered mount has also been produced and is operated by a crew of four. Although the BTR-152 has been replaced in most Soviet units by the BTR-60P series of APCs, it is still operated in a secondary role by other Warsaw Pact countries; a great many of these APCs also remain in service with countries throughout the Middle East, Africa and the Far East where the basic vehicle is adapted to suit local requirements. A versatile vehicle, the BTR-152 can also be deployed beyond its role as an infantry carrier to transport mortar crews on the battlefield and to tow heavy equipment.

About the time the BTR-152 was coming into service, Soviet forces were provided with the smaller four-wheel BTR-40 APC based on the GAZ-63 truck chassis with two crewmen and the facility to carry eight soldiers. The basic vehicle has no roof armour

but has smallarms ports located in the side and rear of the vehicle. Further developments include the BTR-40K model which is fitted with overhead armour in the form of two sets of hinged doors, and the BTR-40A which deploys twin 14.5mm heavy machine guns for use in both an anti-aircraft role and against ground targets. Within the Warsaw Pact the East Germans have retrofitted some of their BTR-40s with AT-3 Sagger anti-tank missile launchers under a retractable roof.

A further model, designated the BTR-40kh has also been produced for deployment on the nuclear battlefield. This variant is fitted with monitoring equipment and an automatic marking pennant dispenser to designate clear and contaminated areas. None of the BTR-40 series of vehicles is provided with NBC fit and the crew have to rely solely on their NBC suits for protection.

Like the BTR-152, the BTR-40 has been phased out of front-line service although it was still in service with Soviet forces in Germany in the late 1970s and is also used extensively by the military police and a great many foreign operators outside the Warsaw Pact.

In 1957 the first tracked Soviet APC appeared. The 14.5 tonne BTR-50 was based on the PT76 light tank chassis and marked the introduction of amphibious APCs into Soviet service. The BTR-50 series is fully amphibious and, like the PT76, employs two water jets at the rear for propulsion when 'swimming'. The two crewmen are provided with periscopes, enabling them to operate when the vehicle is closed down; the

commander has a cupola situated on the left.

The first model to enter service was the BTR-50P which was an open-topped vehicle with the facility to mount anti-tank guns on the rear decking. The subsequent BTR-50PK, however, is provided with overhead armour protection, an NBC fit and is often seen with infra-red driving equipment and searchlight. While the open-topped model can carry up to 20 infantry, the PK variant normally only carries 10. A number of variants including specialised models have appeared. These include the BTR-50PU armoured command vehicle, an ambulance version, a mortar team transport and a mine clearance vehicle. Although the BTR-50 series has been replaced by the BMP MICV in Soviet front-line service, it is still deployed in a second-line capacity and in other Warsaw Pact armies.

The BTR-50PK provided the basis for the Czech OT-62 APC. The OT-62 has the more powerful PV-6 diesel engine than the Soviet V-6 in the BTR-50PK, and this Czech vehicle has also been fitted with an 82mm T-21 recoilless gun in addition to a 7.62mm machine gun. The OT-62C (Czech designated Topas ZAP) is the most advanced version and is armed with a 14.5mm and a 7.62mm machine gun. Also in service is an ambulance version, a command vehicle and the WPT-Topas armoured recovery vehicle.

Outside the Warsaw Pact the OT-62 is employed by Angola, India, Iraq, Israel (war booty), Morocco, Sudan, Libya. Like the BTR-50PK, it saw service with the Egyptians in 1967 and 1973.

Above: A Czech designed OT-62B (Model 2) APC. In addition to the M59 machine gun this vehicle is provided with an 82mm T-21 recoilless gun in a mount on the outside of the M59 turret. All models in the OT-62 series have an NBC system and the more powerful engine provides greater road and water speed than that possessed by their Soviet counterparts.

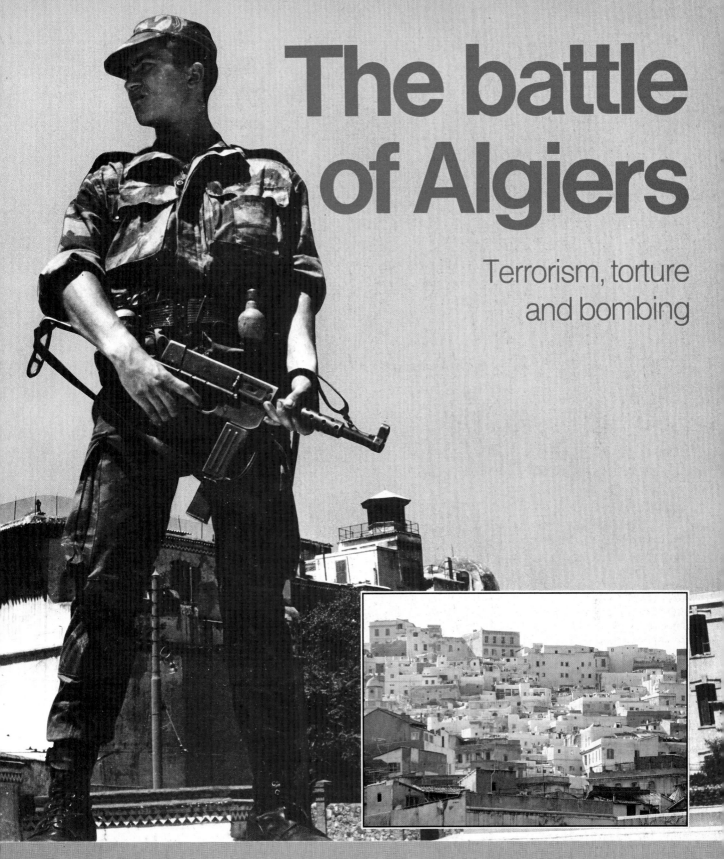

The battle of Algiers

Terrorism, torture and bombing

On the afternoon of 7 January 1957 Resident-Minister Robert Lacoste ordered General Jacques Massu, commander of the 10th Colonial Parachute Division, to assume full powers in the city of Algiers. In turning to Massu, Lacoste was underlining the civil power's inability to cope with a steadily worsening security situation. The immediate crisis had started in the summer of 1956 when, as a reprisal for the execution of two of its members, the National Liberation Front (FLN) began to carry out attacks on European male civilians in Algiers. In response to a wave of murders, European counter-terrorists blew up a house in the casbah, killing 70 Muslims. This encouraged Ramdane Abane, the 36-year-old FLN leader, to renew his demands for a campaign of terror against the French; and in September 1956 Ben M'hidi, political leader in the FLN's Algiers Autonomous Zone, and Saadi Yacef, his lieutenant, were ordered to prepare a large-scale campaign of indiscriminate terror.

The first bombs of this campaign, planted by

Above: One of Bigeard's paras of 3 RPC on watch in Algiers, armed with a 9mm M1949 sub-machine gun. Bigeard's troops were given the job of controlling the warren of the casbah (inset) where 62,000 Muslims provided the background for Ben M'hidi's terror campaign.

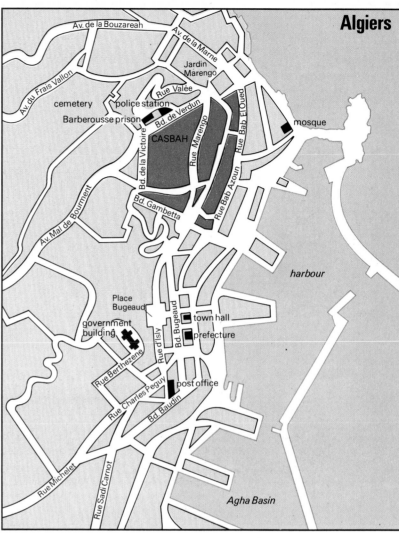

Above: Patrolling in the casbah. One of the main problems the French faced was to locate suspects before they were able to slip away; the interconnecting houses and alleys made surprise snatches difficult, but as French intelligence increased the FLN network was effectively penetrated so that Massu's paratroops were at last able to exert a stranglehold over the area.

female agents recruited by Yacef, exploded on 30 September, causing scores of casualties. By the end of 1956 bombings were an everyday occurrence. Moreover, French morale was depressed, and that of the FLN correspondingly boosted, by the ill-fated Suez operation. The already badly shaken *colons* (Europeans) were enraged still further when, on 28 December, Amédée Froger, mayor of Boufarik and a well-known conservative politician, was shot down at point-blank range by Ali la Pointe, a petty criminal who had become one of Yacef's most trusted agents. The discovery of a bomb in the cemetery at which Froger was to be buried provoked a savage anti-Muslim riot, polarising the European and Muslim communities to a greater extent than ever before and bringing Lacoste to the end of his tether. There was a danger that a full-scale civil war would erupt.

The crisis also had an international aspect. The Algerian issue was due to be debated before the General Assembly of the United Nations in 1957, and FLN successes in Algiers could be turned into powerful political capital. It was abundantly clear that the 1500 police in Algiers could not cope with the rising tide of violence, and so Lacoste turned to Massu and his paras.

Massu was a tough and experienced officer who had served in Africa, Europe and Indochina. Blunt and direct, he lacked subtlety and had no real interest in politics. His chief of staff, Colonel Yves Godard, was a rather different personality. Godard had fought

against the Germans and commanded a battalion in Indochina. But his formidable intellect and his knowledge of clandestine operations gave him a marked interest in the political dimension of revolutionary war, and he had an intense commitment to the concept of *Algérie française*.

Massu's division had taken part in the Suez operation and was, in consequence, somewhat embittered and frustrated: its new duties in Algiers gave it the opportunity of getting to grips with a task which would not be interrupted by political pressure. It set about that task with single-minded enthusiasm.

Massu's first step on moving his division into Algiers, was to divide the city into four areas, each controlled by one of his regiments. The rabbit-warren of the casbah, with its 74,000 inhabitants, 62,000 of them Muslims, was entrusted to Colonel Marcel Bigeard's 3rd Colonial Parachute Regiment (3 RPC), a formidable unit under a charismatic and forceful commander. Massu then procured the police files on all FLN suspects. The files were analysed by the division's staff and a large number of arrests were made – between 800 and 1200, according to Massu. All key points were secured by paras, movement within the city was tightly controlled, and house-to-house searches were carried out.

No sooner had the 10th Division moved into Algiers than it became involved in a major trial of strength with the FLN. In order to bring pressure to bear upon the United Nations, Ben M'hidi planned a

The acquisition and collation of intelligence was central to the French attempt to destroy the FLN in Algiers. Godard had supervised the construction of an *organigramme*, a blank order-of-battle chart into which names were inserted as they became known. The methods by which these names, and other information, were obtained from suspects became the most publicised aspect of the battle of Algiers and sharply divided opinion within France in general as well as in the army in particular. Among advocates of the doctrine of *guerre révolutionnaire* were some who believed that an insurgent enemy could only be defeated by temporarily abandoning the restraints imposed by a liberal democracy and using the harshest methods to crush the insurgents.

Intelligence and interrogation

The gathering of intelligence was aided by a body called the Dispositif de Protection Urbaine (DPU), headed by Colonel Roger Trinquier, another of the *guerre révolutionnaire* specialists. Algiers was divided into sectors, sub-sectors, blocks and buildings, and a senior inhabitant was made responsible for the activities of his area. Those arrested either because of information given by block-wardens, or for other reasons, totalled, according to one estimate, no less than 30 to 40 per cent of the entire male population of the casbah. Of course, not all were held for any length of time, but some underwent the full rigours of the interrogation process.

Massu was prepared to accept the harsh but not sadistic interrogation of captives. It was, unfortunately, impossible to establish where harshness ended and sadism began, and there is no doubt that, in many of their interrogations, French soldiers went well beyond the limits of humane conduct. One of the most common forms of interrogation was the use of the signals magneto, which was connected to the suspect by wire. Those subjected to this electric-shock treatment recalled it with horror. Various forms of water-torture, in which the victim was half-drowned and then revived, were also common. Massu argued vigorously that nothing his paras did compared with

general strike. Massu received orders to break it.

On the morning of Monday, 28 January, the strike appeared to be a complete success. Shops were shut, children stayed away from school, and public transport did not run. Massu's helicopters dropped leaflets ordering a return to work, and loudspeaker jeeps toured the streets, but without effect. Having failed with the velvet glove, Massu then applied the iron fist. Pickets were easily enough dealt with. Nobody, noted Massu, coveted martyrdom, and a robust order to 'push off' dispersed the pickets. Getting men back to work was only slightly more difficult. A list of workers in essential services had been compiled, and para patrols visited their homes and took them to work. Some shopkeepers were forced to open up by similar methods. If the shopkeeper could not be found, or had 'mislaid' the key to the iron grill in front of his shop, one of Massu's trucks simply pulled the shop-front down with a tow-rope.

Shortly before the strike, Yacef's bombers had carried out successful attacks on a bar, a students' cafeteria and the Coq Hardi brasserie, killing four people and wounding 50. Bigeard's men brought the casbah under close surveillance, paying particular attention to women, whose voluminous clothes could easily conceal weapons or explosives. Captured suspects were subjected to 'deep interrogation' and often gave useful information. By 19 February 3 RPC had seized a vast quantity of explosives and had captured many of Yacef's agents.

Above: Lieutenant Georges Grillot of 3 RPC, map under arm, in the Rue de la casbah. French paratroops were deployed in the casbah specifically to maintain a 'high profile' as a means of intimidating the Arab population.

Right: A French military policeman searches a woman for arms or bombs. The voluminous clothing of Arab women made terrorist weapons easy to conceal, and it was female guerrillas who planted the first bombs of the FLN's campaign of urban warfare.

the savage punishments inflicted by the FLN on pro-French Muslims – cutting off the nose and lips was a frequently-inflicted FLN penalty.

Some of the suspects endured worse than torture. Those who refused to talk, or who had been too brutally treated to survive, were disposed of, usually by being dumped at sea. The most widely-accepted figure for the 'missing' of the battle of Algiers is just over 3000, although the truth will never be known. If a detainee was too well-known to disappear without trace, he might either 'commit suicide' or be 'shot while trying to escape'.

The most spectacular victim was Ben M'hidi himself. In February, Ben M'hidi moved from place to place in an effort to keep ahead of the paras. He was reluctant to leave Algiers altogether, although the other members of the FLN's Coordination and Execution Committee who were also trapped in Algiers did depart for safer quarters. On 25 February Ben M'hidi was seized by paras in the Rue Claude Debussy, and on 6 March it was announced that he had hanged himself in prison with strips torn from his shirt.

His real fate is likely to remain shrouded in mystery. One version states that, after being interviewed

The question of torture

Colonel Yves Godard, General Massu's chief of staff during the battle of Algiers, left these reflections on the use of torture shortly before his death.

'Secrecy is the trump card, one might say the main weapon, of subversion. The terrorist who places a bomb in a bar is striking at innocent people. His action is, therefore, more obnoxious, more blameworthy, than that of the sharpshooter of previous times, who would only fire on enemy soldiers but who could expect to be shot without trial if caught. This, the first aspect of the problem, is in the realms of justice and morality.

'We who have the task of defeating terrorism are interested only in a second aspect, that of securing information – which is of the highest importance....So, should confessions be obtained by force? I would say no. Firstly, because such methods are contrary to the military tradition that forbids mistreatment of enemy prisoners.

'In addition to this principle, which should be sacrosanct, I have more down-to-earth reasons: obtaining confessions by physical suffering often results in invented statements which lead the security forces down false trails; and brutality gives ammunition to the enemy's propaganda machine, that can then exaggerate incidents and influence the opinion of many honest observers who are not natural allies of subversion.

'The use of brutality also allows those who confessed spontaneously to retract later, claiming they were tortured. And the number of suspects who confess voluntarily is much more than is generally known; I speak here from experience.

'We must not even use "limited torture", pleading that the individual will not suffer long-term damage. That is just playing with words, engaging in sophistry.'

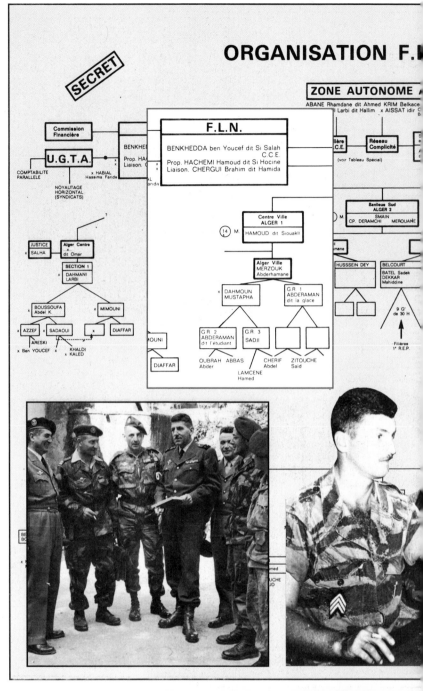

Top: The *organigramme* that was constructed to trace the structure of the FLN. Above inset: The crucial individuals: Godard (far left) who supervised the construction of the *organigramme,* Massu (fourth from left) who commanded the para division and Bigeard (on Massu's right) who commanded 3 RPC. Above inset right: Paratroops process police files. Right: The mass arrest of Algerians for interrogation.

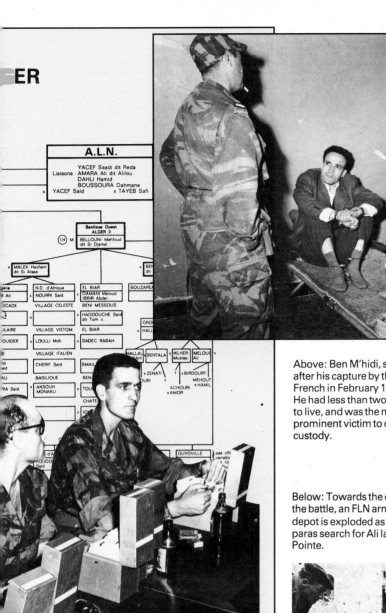

by Bigeard, he was shot by firing squad after receiving full military honours. Another suggests that Ben M'hidi was murdered by a special paratroop detachment, while Massu maintained that he had hanged himself with electric flex.

The fate of Ben M'hidi is an accurate index of the way the battle was going. Whatever the moral weaknesses of the paras' methods – and these remain a matter of intense debate – there is no doubting their success in extinguishing the flames of insurrection in Algiers. No bombs exploded in March, and it soon began to look as if Massu's mailed fist had indeed produced the desired result. At the end of the month, his division was withdrawn. The FLN made a brief comeback between April and June, but between July and October the French, having brought the paras back in, set the seal on their triumph by killing Ali la Pointe and, on 24 September, receiving the surrender of Yacef. By the middle of October the FLN Algiers Autonomous Zone had been effectively destroyed.

It seemed at the time that the battle of Algiers was a French victory. After all, Massu's men had brilliantly carried out their mission, defeating a determined and well-organised urban terrorist enemy. Indeed, many of the methods used by Massu's division may well be regarded as classical governmental responses to urban insurgency. But in the long term, the means used to achieve success did incalculable harm to France's international standing and to the French Army's position in French society, to say nothing of the psychological damage they inflicted on victims and torturers alike. Many Frenchmen came to believe that the war was simply not worth winning at such a cost. Paul Teitgen, secretary-general at the Algiers prefecture, who resigned over the question of torture, summed up the dilemma of the battle when he said: 'All right, Massu won the battle of Algiers; but that meant losing the war.' **Richard Holmes**

Above: Ben M'hidi, shortly after his capture by the French in February 1957. He had less than two weeks to live, and was the most prominent victim to die in custody.

Below: Towards the end of the battle, an FLN arms depot is exploded as the paras search for Ali la Pointe.

FLN

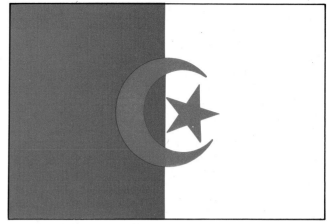

The fight for Algeria's independence

Urban terrorism – the bombing network

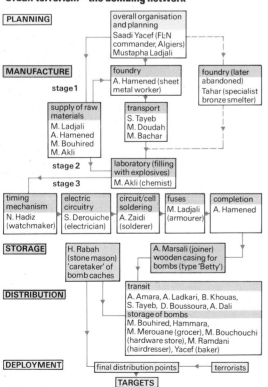

Above: The executive of the FLN in 1962, soon after the final negotiations with the French for Algeria's independence. The newly released Ben Bella is in profile in the centre. The FLN leaders were united by a fierce nationalism and a vague socialism; these proved no guarantee of stability once independence was granted, and the early years of the new state were to be marked by bloody internal disputes, culminating in the coup of 1965 that brought Houari Boumédienne to power.

During the years of the Algerian War the Front de Libération Nationale (National Liberation Front or FLN) managed to present a united, monolithic front to the world. In reality, however, it was riven with murderous disputes and its leaders changed constantly, either because they were killed or imprisoned by the French or because they were liquidated or betrayed by internal power struggles. It was a very difficult revolutionary body to characterise because it had no obvious leader and no clear political doctrine.

The origins of the FLN can be traced to July 1954 when nine hard-line opponents of the French presence in Algeria met secretly in France to form the Comité Révolutionnaire d'Unité et d'Action. None of the nine had had more than a basic education and many of them had served in the French Army as non-commissioned officers. Their revolutionary movement gained its title of FLN in October 1954 but it was, at first, short of lofty political ideals although it had established vital principles. The most important of these was that the revolt would continue until independence was achieved – however long that took.

At the start of the revolt many of the nine returned to Algeria to lead the fighting in the individual Wilayas or combat zones into which they had divided their country. Some of them, however, notably Ahmed Ben Bella, remained in other North African capitals to organise assistance for the fighters from friendly governments. Although Ben Bella soon became the

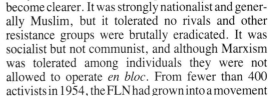

best known of the FLN leaders they were, in theory, all equal.

The shared leadership soon ran into trouble when a split developed between the 'externals' such as Ben Bella and the 'internals' such as Belkacem Krim who led the insurgents in Wilaya 3 (Kabylia). The revolt in Algeria was a desperate struggle against a very experienced enemy, and those doing the fighting blamed the externals for failing to supply them with arms and assistance. At first the externals did indeed fail to get much more than promises from allies such as Egypt's President Nasser, but they achieved a propaganda coup when they were invited to the Bandung Conference of 29 non-aligned nations in April 1955 and a resolution proclaiming Algeria's right to independence was passed.

Despite this, the internals made most of the political running with the emergence of Ramdane Abane. He was a political animal dedicated to terror as a weapon but with ideas of organising the FLN as a political party as well as an army. He set about organising a summit in the Soummam Valley in Kabylia in mid-1956 to which the externals were invited but craftily excluded by faulty travel arrangements. The summit marked the virtual eclipse of the externals.

Abane reorganised the FLN. Everything from military structure to tactics was overhauled, with the previously-dispersed guerrilla gangs brought under central control and formed into an Armée de Libération Nationale (ALN). Above all, Abane maintained that the political side of the revolt should be given greater importance than the military. It was to be run by a Comité de Coordination et d'Exécution (CCE) which included Abane and Krim. A clandestine newspaper was published and the Voice of Algeria radio set up, both of which were intended to politicise the Algerian people. In October 1956 Ben Bella and the externals were hijacked by the French secret service on a flight to Tripoli and imprisoned in

Below: An ALN unit on the watch for French patrols in the mountains. The troops are armed with a captured French M1924-29 light machine gun and an M1907 carbine. The 'internals', as the FLN commanders within Algeria were known, were constantly bemoaning the poor flow of weapons and supplies from the leadership in exile.

France. The internals were temporarily supreme.

By this time the FLN's political position had become clearer. It was strongly nationalist and generally Muslim, but it tolerated no rivals and other resistance groups were brutally eradicated. It was socialist but not communist, and although Marxism was tolerated among individuals they were not allowed to operate *en bloc*. From fewer than 400 activists in 1954, the FLN had grown into a movement with a well-organised army – the ALN – up to 20,000 strong, based in Tunisia.

As the battle of Algiers went against the FLN, its leaders were forced to flee the country and set up headquarters in neighbouring Tunisia. Abane's intolerance of opposition alienated the other revolutionaries to such a degree that he was liquidated in December 1957. But after his death the leaders in exile were no more effective in supplying the revolutionaries inside Algeria than Ben Bella had been. The war was going so badly, however, that it was clear that the French would never be militarily defeated, and so political efforts were given priority.

A political solution?

Sophisticated FLN representatives in New York cultivated American opinion and won over Senator John F. Kennedy, who made an important speech on their behalf in July 1957. The eastern bloc was a likely source of military supply so FLN representatives toured the Moscow-Peking circuit. Political backing was desperately needed to put pressure on France.

From 1958 to 1960 the military situation seemed hopeless, and a split developed between the CCE leadership and the army units outside Algeria. Lack of success began to make the ALN troops in Tunisia mutinous. The mutiny was coldly suppressed by a new strong man, Houari Boumédienne, who soon displaced Krim as leader of the ALN.

As it happened, the final negotiations were carried out in early 1962 by Krim and others of the moderate wing of the FLN. Remarkably enough they achieved a result close to the demands of the hard-liners, but the unity of the FLN dissolved with the coming of peace. When power-hungry externals returned to Algeria, violent and bloody clashes broke out with Wilaya commanders who felt ignored by them. The moderate wing of the FLN was largely eclipsed and the newly released Ben Bella was made president. Ben Bella's savage authoritarianism and excessive devotion to theoretical socialism led to growing chaos, however, and Boumédienne had the last word in the FLN's bloody feuding by arresting Ben Bella and becoming president himself in a bloodless coup in June 1965.

P.J. Banyard

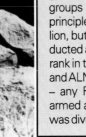
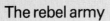

The rebel army

The ALN in 1956 was set up to organise the FLN's disparate guerrilla groups into a revolutionary army. In principle the largest unit was a battalion, but operations were mostly conducted at company level. The highest rank in the ALN was colonel. The FLN and ALN were often indistinguishable – any FLN member was ready for armed action. Like the FLN, the ALN was divided into 'internals' and 'externals'. The external ALN in Tunisia became a highly-politicised regular army, numbering some 20,000 men. Although officially integrated into the same organisation, the forces in Algeria were composed of small guerrilla groups supported by a much larger number of 'part-timers'. After independence the external ALN under Colonel Boumédienne proved a decisive force in the struggle for power.

Defence and counter-attack

The Morice Line and Challe's offensive

By the end of 1956 the French had cleared most of their colonial military entanglements out of the way and were able to make a major attempt to suppress the rebellion in Algeria. Yet there were certain geographical disadvantages now that they had been forced to abandon military control of Morocco and Tunisia, which bordered Algeria on the west and the east respectively. It was natural that Algerians fighting for their independence should find help and support from nations that had so recently won their own freedom from the French.

These links were essential to the revolutionaries, who were always hampered by lack of arms and the pressure of French military superiority. Morocco was always useful, but its border was less rugged and more easily policed than the border with Tunisia. In addition to this, the National Liberation Front (FLN) were more in sympathy with the regime of President Habib Bourguiba than with Morocco's constitutional monarchy, so Tunisia became their preferred base and military springboard.

The French responded to this danger by constructing a static fortification to seal off the Tunisian border. It was called the Morice Line and was named after the current minister of defence. The barrier ran south from the Mediterranean through the mountains and forest for 320km (200 miles) and into the wastes of the Sahara. It was completed in September 1957 and was remarkably successful.

At the centre of the Morice Line was a high fence electrified with 5000 volts. On either side of the fence was a 45m (50 yard) wide killing ground scattered with anti-personnel mines and cordoned off with barbed wire entanglements. Behind the fortifications was a cleared track used by French patrols. It was an unpleasant obstacle but hardly one which would have daunted well-equipped soldiers from making a night crossing if it had not been for one technical sophistication: electronic devices warned the French precisely when and where a raiding party had cut the wire.

In response to this warning a number of unpleasant things began to happen. Batteries of automatically ranged and sighted 105mm howitzers were brought to bear on the spot immediately, garrison troops raced to make contact, backed up by mechanised and armoured units, and four highly mobile parachute regiments with helicopter transport stood ready to hunt down any soldier who got through the screen. A successful crossing would have to be made by night, and the French reckoned they could destroy the crossing force by the evening of the following day before its members could disperse into the interior.

In the early months of 1958 the Line demonstrated its effectiveness. In February the 9th Chasseurs Parachute Regiment recorded killing 137 rebels. By the end of April the French reckoned that they had killed

Opposite: The grim effectiveness of the French frontier defence: another infiltration attempt fails as an FLN guerrilla dies from electrocution. The Morice Line was one of the best defensive systems of modern times, and by sealing off the Tunisian frontier it enabled the French forces in Algeria to grind down the insurgent forces in the mountains of the interior. Below: A French observation post above the Line.

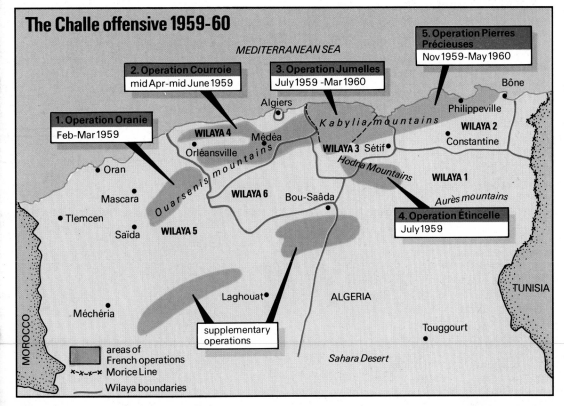

The Challe offensive 1959-60

5. Operation Pierres Précieuses
Nov 1959–May 1960

2. Operation Courroie
mid Apr–mid June 1959

3. Operation Jumelles
July 1959 –Mar 1960

MEDITERRANEAN SEA

Bône

Algiers

Philippeville

Kabylia mountains

WILAYA 2

1. Operation Oranie
Feb–Mar 1959

WILAYA 4

Médéa

Constantine

Orléansville

WILAYA 3 Sétif

Hodna Mountains

Oran

Ouarsenis mountains

WILAYA 1

Mascara

WILAYA 6

Bou-Saâda

Aurès mountains

Tlemcen

4. Operation Étincelle
July 1959

Saïda

WILAYA 5

MOROCCO

Laghouat

ALGERIA

Méchéria

TUNISIA

Touggourt

supplementary operations

areas of French operations
×-×-×-× Morice Line
Wilaya boundaries

Sahara Desert

Above: General Maurice Challe. Although initially many observers were worried about his lack of experience, Challe masterminded a series of operations, known collectively as the Challe offensive, which forced the FLN onto the defensive and broke their capacity for sustained warfare.

or turned back 80 per cent of attempted ALN (the FLN's National Liberation Army) infiltrators. It was far too costly for the ALN to continue in this vein so they limited their Tunisian ventures to occasional attacks and ambushes on the garrison troops to pin them down. Crossing the Morice Line became rare and largely restricted to vital couriers.

This meant that the revolt in the six Wilayas within Algeria was starved of reinforcements and supplies but, because 80,000 French troops were busy defending the Line, military pressure on the FLN/ALN was lessened. So the internal revolt flickered on, defying French control, until President Charles de Gaulle established the Fifth Republic at the end of May 1958 and began to look for a new military commander for Algeria. By the end of the year he had chosen Air Force General Maurice Challe and ordered him to mount a crushing offensive against the ALN. It did not at first seem an inspired choice. Challe, the epitome of calm imperturbability, faced some opposition from his senior officers when he arrived to take up his duties in December. They doubted that a mere airman could master the intricacies of land warfare but he was, in the event, to prove himself the ablest of all the French commanders against the ALN.

Taking the initiative

Challe found that the French Army in Algeria was spread thinly over the whole vast area of the interior in its attempt to smother the revolt, and that the mobile forces which backed up the scattered garrisons were rushed in penny packets to the scene of major outbreaks. As a result the initiative lay with the rebels, who were fairly secure in the *djebel* (mountain areas) or when operating under the cloak of darkness. Challe's slogan was that 'Neither the *djebel* nor the night must be left to the FLN'.

The essence of the Challe plan was that the country should be combed through, area by area, with overwhelming force. Each area would first be infiltrated by hardy units of *commandos de chasse* (fast pursuit groups) guided by special tracker units (*harkis*) composed of pro-French Muslims. These mixed forces would stealthily seek out the companies of rebel soldiers and pin them down before the entire mobile reserve of elite French units arrived to wipe them out. The French troops would not immediately leave after the battle, but would stay to pursue the broken rebel forces for weeks until they were virtually eliminated.

So much for the ground plan. What gave Challe's ideas their cutting edge was that he also thought in

another dimension; he knew the difference that aircraft could make to counter-insurgency warfare. He made sure that his soldiers were supplied with enough big, American-built helicopters to move two battalions into position in a few minutes. For air strikes he organised more than 300 antiquated Harvard T-6 trainers. The Harvard could do little over 320km/h (200mph) at top speed, but its slow passes over ALN positions enabled it to deliver a strafing from its four machine guns and two rocket pods with much greater accuracy than would have been possible with supersonic jets.

One after the other the ALN strongholds were cleared out by the newly adapted French forces under their brilliant commander. The eastern Ouarsenis and Wilaya 4 were subjected to two months of intensive operations from 18 April in Operation Courroie. Next, Challe intended to turn on Kabylia – the most impregnable stronghold of the ALN and the stamping ground of many of its greatest leaders – but by the middle of July intelligence reported a concentration of rebel troops in the Hodna mountains which link Kabylia with the Aurès. Despite his almost placid exterior, Challe was a commander who moved with speed and flexibility. He swiftly changed his orders and moved with force into the Hodna, severely damaging the ALN there. He then turned on Kabylia. Code-named Operation Jumelles, this offensive was a striking success. By late October the French claimed to have inflicted 3746 casualties on the ALN in Kabylia and smashed their organisation. In November Wilaya 2 was under attack in the mountains north of Constantine.

By the end of 1959 ALN troops remained active only in the Aurès, and Challe had made his plans for that area. Before he could embark on this final mopping up operation, however, he lost the political confidence of de Gaulle for not dealing firmly with the Europeans in Algiers during the troubles of 'Barricades Week' in January 1960. Three months later Challe was recalled and he handed over to General Crépin, who declined to undertake the action against the Aurès because he felt that it was too complicated for a man fresh to his command. Nevertheless, FLN/ALN activity there was reduced to a low ebb for,

Above left: Colonel Bigeard of 3 RPC directing operations in the hinterland after his success in the battle of Algiers. The French forces had to be able to adapt to varieties of terrain, whether advancing among the rocks of the Kabylia mountains (above) where sudden ambush was a constant possibility, or returning fire in the open Sahara (below), where the lack of cover could make a patrol vulnerable to a well-sited enemy unit. Right: Pushing forward around Timmoun in the Sahara, paratroops examine the body of a dead guerrilla.

parallel to Challe's operation, the FLN as a whole had been badly affected both by the lack of reinforcement resulting from the success of the Morice Line and also by the terror unleashed by the subtle warfare of the secret agents employed by the French Groupement de Renseignement et d'Exploitation (GRE).

By August 1957 the leaders of the Algiers FLN had been captured and the man who was nominated as leader in their stead was a shadowy French double agent known by the alias of Safy le Pur. He succeeded in making contact with Wilaya 3 (Kabylia) which was commanded by Amirouche (real name Ait Hamouda), a fine, determined soldier greatly feared by colleagues for his wild and excessive cruelty. Once Safy le Pur had succeeded in betraying a number of Amirouche's commanders, it dawned on that ferocious man that the Algiers organisation had been 'turned' and his own was suspect. As a result Amirouche launched a cruel and self-perpetuating purge in which many genuine revolutionaries were liquidated wholesale.

Wilaya 3 may have lost as many as 3000 operatives by this terrible internal butchery and things were hardly better elsewhere before Amirouche and the commander of Wilaya 6 were killed in March 1959. They had quite possibly been betrayed by subordinates terrified by the purges. The commander of Wilaya 4 disappeared two months later, probably for the same reason. To add to the uncertainty the GRE kept up their work in the areas being swept by Challe's offensives so that villagers who would normally supply the ALN with food and support were reluctant to do so because they never knew where the double agents would be operating.

As the Challe offensive gathered momentum the ALN soldiers were starved as well as hunted and weighed down with suspicion of each other. More than half their organised companies within Algeria had been destroyed by Challe's offensives and, most significantly, more and more of them were surrendering rather than fighting with their usual fierce determination when trapped by the French. For those who remained in the mountains the privations were extraordinary. They were often forced to live on grass and roots, unable to light a fire for days on end for fear of the prowling *harkis* and commandos.

There is no doubt that Challe had won a major victory for the French despite his untimely recall, but was it total? The danger that the rebels would regroup and reorganise once the military pressure slackened was ever present. Yet the scale of demoralisation in the Wilayas was so great that the first signs of total success became visible in the summer of 1959.

At that time the French began to monitor radio signals from Si Salah (real name Mohamed Zamoun), a respected veteran and now commander of Wilaya 4, accusing the leaders in Tunisia of neglectful arrogance and threatening to make his own peace with the French. Over the ensuing months Si Salah entered into negotiations with the French, accompanied by all the senior political and military officers of his Wilaya. By June 1960 he had had a secret, personal audience with de Gaulle during which he made it plain that he accepted the French terms for making peace and offered to make contact with the leaders of other Wilayas to persuade them to follow his course. At last Challe's offensive had achieved political as well as military victory over the rebels of the Algerian interior. It was de Gaulle who abandoned this prize – the bird in the hand – in favour of negotiations with the external FLN in Tripoli. Si Salah and his accomplices were liquidated by agents of the external FLN and the French military success was converted into political defeat.

P.J. Banyard

Ends and means

The ethics of modern warfare

Above: British troops in Northern Ireland, where the limitations on military conduct are strict.

'All's fair in love and war,' runs the saying. This is possibly so in affairs of the heart, but nothing could be further from the truth where military matters are concerned. Mankind may be naturally violent or human violence may be a cultural imposition (depending on which of many theories one cares to believe), but there can be no doubt that war is one of the most sophisticated and carefully constructed of human activities; and as such it has almost always been hedged in by restraints, growing out of the morality and the politics of the societies within which, or between which, conflicts have taken place. Rules of war, however defined, have helped draw the lines within which warfare could take place.

It is undeniable, of course, that many of these limitations are occasioned by self-interest rather than by sheer principle; but these restrictions – whether they be the limits placed on indiscriminate use of firearms by British soldiers in Northern Ireland, or the international agreements on the non-use of toxic agents or the non-pollution of water supplies – are perceived to have a moral, ethical, basis. And it is the strength of this moral imperative that makes it possible to describe many of the most obvious examples of savagery and slaughter that have occurred in recorded history as 'atrocities'.

The problem of the ethics of war has become extremely complicated since 1945, in spite of the fact that during the 20th century the Hague and Geneva Conventions have seemed to place the conduct of war within very strict limits. Five often interlocking factors combine to present moral problems far more complex than those of previous ages.

The first factor lies in the technological advances of modern weapons. The ability to inflict great losses on an adversary from extreme range has developed to an unprecedented degree. At the very summit of modern weaponry, of course, nuclear weapons pose a particular dilemma. The slaughter of whole civilian populations would have seemed a horrifyingly immoral act before 1939 – it is still questionable whether the mass bombings of German and Japanese cities in World War II that inaugurated the new age were justified in strictly military terms – and it is possible to argue that

the disappearance of so basic a rule of war as the safety of civilian populations has had repercussions all along the line.

On a practical level, however, nuclear weapons are the major illustration of the fact that one human being can destroy hundreds or even thousands merely by flicking a switch. We tend to think of atrocities as occurring where people are killed or tortured by others on the spot, at close quarters; but nowadays there is no absolute reason why this should be so. Take the case of a US Marine in Vietnam, who in the heat of battle kills a peasant family; is he more or less guilty of immoral conduct than the pilot who drops napalm on a village, or the helicopter gunner who arbitrarily rakes a paddyfield with fire? The temptation to see the Marine as the more culpable is strong, but his action may have resulted in less suffering. Similarly, in the Middle East, is the Palestinian terrorist who plants bombs or shoots at Israeli civilians more immoral than the Israeli artilleryman who bombards a Palestinian refugee camp?

Too often, the answer to such questions comes out of political prejudice. For the second factor affecting the ethics of modern warfare concerns the intense polarisation of world politics, and the confusion of such polarisation with concepts of the 'just war'.

All politicians claim their wars are justified, but few could claim it with as much conviction as the Allied leaders of World War II. No modern commentators argue that a Nazi-dominated Europe would have been desirable. Since 1945, the idea of the 'just war' has lingered on and become interwoven with the tissue of propaganda surrounding most conflicts. For in addition, many wars involve the future direction of a society – whether it should be independent of another state, whether it should be a Marxist state or whatever. Where these large-scale questions are concerned, the combatants exude an often-terrifying moral fervour; to reach a goal that is felt to be crucial, any methods will do. Such politicians also tend to regard their enemies as the incarnation of oppression and evil – the 'great satan' as the Ayatollah Khomeini described some of his foes. Such attitudes naturally bring in their train disregard for many of the formal

Vietnam posed the most severe moral problems for the USA. Not only were there many examples of atrocities against civilians – the most notorious being the My Lai massacre for which Lieutenant James Calley (below) was court-martialled – but the war brought home many of the dilemmas of modern war. The bombing of villages or areas of jungle (right and right inset) appeared a fairly straightforward military activity. But such bombing inevitably resulted in horror and terror for civilians, and photographs of the effects of bombing (right) caused widespread condemnation around the world.

conventions regarding military behaviour.

The third factor lies in the growth of publicity. Wherever Western forces fight, cameramen and reporters are always at or near the scene of fighting; Vietnam was known as the first 'television war'. The world's press also makes great efforts to report conflicts from all over the globe. Given the political capital that some countries wish to make out of such situations, and the hunger of the Western press for a newsworthy incident, emphasis is placed on the shocking story. Apart from affecting our perception of military conduct, press concentration on warfare may, of course, prevent excesses; but to judge from some of the more disgraceful episodes of recent times – Indonesian Army activities in Timor or the Sabra and Chatila massacres in Lebanon – it has hardly had this effect. It may merely have publicised atrocities in such a way as to brutalise the public while trivialising the issues.

The fourth factor is that many wars have been fought between peoples of widely differing cultures. People who look or behave very differently are easy to describe and treat as sub-human; to shoot them out of hand or torture them seems less reprehensible. It is unlikely, for example, that the French or the Americans would have treated Europeans as they treated, respectively, Algerians and the Vietnamese.

The fifth factor is that, since 1945, guerrilla warfare has spread all over the world. This factor is by far the most important, for it brings together all the other four, and magnifies moral problems.

Before 1939, the major powers had refused to include irregular or guerrilla forces within the Hague or Geneva Conventions. The majority of governments and their security forces regarded guerrillas as terrorists or bandits because they had no recognisable authority, refused to wear uniforms or carry their arms openly, and by the very nature of their organisation resorted to ambush, assassination and unconventional methods. Therefore, guerrilla forces had no rights in national or international law, and governments and their security forces did not feel restrained by ethical considerations when combatting them. So guerrilla warfare was characterised by brutalities and atrocities on both sides.

Before 1945 the European colonial powers had fought nationalist guerrillas who believed that their countries were under foreign occupation. But these guerrilla movements were generally unsuccessful and the European powers were able to maintain their authority. After 1945, nationalist guerrillas adopting revolutionary guerrilla warfare with its ideology, organisation and external support created a far greater challenge to the European powers. Both governments and guerrillas found that they were fighting to 'win the hearts and minds' of the local indigenous population as well as the home population of the European power. Ethical considerations concerning the conduct of the war and its effect upon civilians became an important factor, not least in terms of propaganda and public relations.

Mao Tse-tung had advised guerrillas to maintain good relations with the local population and not to abuse them by stealing their crops and damaging their property. In practice, the Chinese communists and other guerrillas were quite prepared to resort to force to gain popular support, food, intelligence and manpower. Terror became a weapon of guerrillas which was not solely used against those members of the population who were insufficiently active supporters of the guerrillas. Barbaric acts could be carried out in the name of freedom and national liberation, on the basis of the end justifying the means.

Frequently, guerrillas carried out acts of terror against the security forces in the hope of provoking them into committing indiscriminate retaliation. All too often they were successful, with local security forces burning villages and executing local civilians as a reprisal for an attack that in all probability they neither knew about nor supported. Sometimes it has been impossible to distinguish between a guerrilla and an innocent civilian. For the soldier or policeman on the ground it was tempting to be safe rather than sorry.

Ethical considerations in counter-insurgency were probably most openly discussed during the battle of Algiers in 1957. The men of General Jacques Massu's 10th Colonial Parachute Division believed that the FLN, by its indiscriminate bombings and murders, had lost any rights it might have claimed to protection under international law. To break the power of the FLN and to discover the individual cells of its organisation in Algiers meant obtaining detailed information about the Muslim population. Much of this

Right: A masked guerrilla in Lebanon. Guerrilla war raises many ethical problems. Should guerrillas who break many of the accepted rules of war be treated as regular soldiers or as common criminals? Is counter-terror justified against terrorists?

information could be provided from police dossiers, government departments and through informers, but much had to come from interrogation of suspects.

During the battle of Algiers 30 to 40 per cent of the male population of the casbah were arrested at one time or another; and torture became institutionalised as an interrogation technique. This could take the form of the *gégène*, which meant that the suspect would have electrodes fastened to various parts of his body which could then be activated from a field telephone. The water torture included having the head frequently immersed in water until the suspect was half drowned, or having the lungs and belly filled with cold water from a hose-pipe inserted in the mouth.

General Massu later claimed that the end had justified the means because the French had won and had thus halted the FLN-imposed terror and indiscriminate killing and maiming of both Europeans and Muslims. Many French officials believed that their actions had not been indiscriminate, and that the paras could not be compared with the Nazis as they had resorted neither to taking hostages nor extermination.

Yet the use of torture in Algiers provoked a storm of criticism. The FLN used the issue as an effective propaganda weapon in the United Nations and among non-aligned countries. It also provoked strong reactions among French officials, some of whom requested a posting back to France and later publicised their opposition to such methods in the press.

The most formidable argument used against torture by critics was the effect it had on the practitioners. It brutalised many soldiers and policemen and gave others a lingering neurosis and guilt complex. It also contradicted their claim that they were fighting against an evil that the FLN represented. If the counter-insurgents claimed to be defending certain values such as the rights of the individual, freedom of the press and democracy then they had to operate within certain ethical restraints. In those circumstances the end could not justify the means.

Where war can be limited to conventional forces fighting against each other for a tangible gain – as in the Falklands – then it can be relatively clean (although debate continues about the sinking of the *General Belgrano*). But where guerrillas are fighting for the hazy moral imperatives of national identity and political freedom, then ethics become a propaganda weapon rather than a guide to conduct. **Ashley Brown**

Below: The massacres of Palestinian refugees in the Sabra and Chatila camps in 1982 after the Israeli invasion of Lebanon shocked world opinion, and were an especial cause for concern within Israel itself, for the excuses the Israeli Army gave for not having protected refugees from the Phalangist militia who entered the camps were uncomfortably reminiscent of the comments of the World War II German Wehrmacht about the massacres of Jews on the Eastern Front.

Key Weapons

SOVIET APCs

part 2

From BTR-60 to BMD

In November 1961 a new vehicle appeared which represented a considerable advance on previous Soviet APCs. The BTR-60, a 10-tonne vehicle, has eight powered wheels with power-assisted steering on the front four and two 90hp petrol engines that provide a road speed of 80km/h (50mph). It is fully amphibious with a single hydrojet for propulsion and two smaller jets for steering and is capable of a water speed of 10km/h (6mph). The boat-shaped welded steel hull has a good ballistic shape and 'swimming' characteristics, while torsion bar suspension with hydraulic shock absorbers endow it with a high degree of cross-country mobility.

The original BTR-60P model was open-topped, but overhead protection and an NBC system were introduced in the BTR-60PA variant. The most common version, the BTR-60PB, incorporated a small machine gun turret housing a 14.5mm KPV heavy machine gun and a secondary 7.62mm PKT co-axial machine gun. The driver is seated front left with the vehicle commander on his right, and both are provided with direct vision windscreens protected by steel hatches that can be raised and infra-red driving lights and searchlight for night operations.

The BTR-60PB can carry up to 14 infantry in addition to the two crew members. One of the main disadvantages of its design, however, is that it has no rear exit doors. Mounted troops have to climb out of

Previous page: A battle-scarred BTR-60PB lies abandoned after action in Golan during the 1973 Middle East war. Right: Infantry dismount from the early model BTR-60P while one of the vehicle's SGMB 7.62mm machine guns provides covering fire. This open-topped model was soon replaced by the PB variant which provided overhead armour, but dismounting through roof hatches still remained hazardous.

Below: A column of Soviet naval infantry BTR-60s rolls ashore from a landing ship. The lead vehicle is a BTR-60PB which mounts the distinctive small conical turret housing the 14.5mm HMG main armament. Clearly visible on the hull side are the numerous hand and footholds which allow the infantry complement to mount and dismount from the vehicle.

BTR-60PB APC

Crew 2 plus 14
Dimensions Length 7.56m (24ft 10in); width 2.83m (9ft 3in); height 2.31m (7ft 7in)
Weight 10,300kg (22,707lb)
Engines Two GAZ-49B six-cylinder, in-line, water-cooled petrol developing 90hp at 3400rpm

Performance Maximum road speed 80km/h (50mph); range (road) 500km (310 miles); vertical obstacle 0.4m (1ft 4in); trench 2m (6ft 7in); gradient 60 per cent; fording fully amphibious; water speed 10km/h (6.2mph)

Armour 9mm (0.35in)
Armament One 14.5mm KPV heavy machine gun; one 7.62mm machine gun

Right: A BTR-70, the modified version of the 60PB, on display. While retaining the basic layout and armament of the PB, the 70 is provided with larger troop compartment hatches and improved service access to the two diesel engines. Other modifications include a redesigned wheelbase with larger tyres and a flatter shaped hull.

Below: With trim vane extended and hydrojet vent casing fully open, a BTR-60PB demonstrates its amphibious capability. Below inset: Afghan guerrillas in characteristic victory posture pose for photographers on a captured Soviet BTR-60.

the two small roof hatches and jump over the side of the vehicle, a hazardous operation while under heavy fire in close support operations. The BTR-60PB also has a volatile fuel system making it liable to 'brew up' if hit.

Despite its age and design inadequacies the BTR-60 still equips the majority of front line Soviet Army troops, as well as the Soviet naval infantry, and is a reliable and versatile vehicle. Further variants include the BTR-60PU command model and the BTR-60PK long-range communications vehicle. The BTR-60 equips a number of countries outside the Warsaw Pact and it was the main APC of the Arab armies in the Yom Kippur War of October 1973. It has also seen action with the North Vietnamese Army in Vietnam, with the Ethiopians in the Ogaden War (1977-78), and in Angola. In 1978 an improved version known as the BTR-70 made its appearance. It is thought to be powered by two diesel engines (reducing the fire risk) and to have an improved troop compartment hatch arrangement.

When the BMP mechanised infantry combat vehicle (MICV) first appeared in 1967 it aroused considerable interest among Western analysts. It mounts a 73mm gun with a co-axial 7.62mm PKT machine gun and is provided with an AT-3 Sagger anti-tank guided weapon (ATGW) launcher with one missile mounted on the launch rail and four further rounds carried inside the vehicle. The combination of these weapons provides considerable firepower for the eight-man infantry section. The 73mm 2A20 smooth-bore main gun is not stabilised and is fed by a semi-automatic loading system. A major disadvantage is the tendency for this system to feed the loader's arm, instead of the shell, into the breech. Its slow rate of fire, eight rounds per minute, is largely attributable to the design which automatically elevates the gun during the reloading cycle.

The BMP carries 40 HEAT and HE rounds. The PG-9 fin-stabilised projectile, which resembles that of the RPG-7, is vulnerable to deflection by crosswinds. If the gunner is to have any real prospect of hitting his target the vehicle must be halted. Even so

BMP-1 MICV

Crew 3 plus 8
Dimensions Length 6.74m (22ft 1in); width 2.94m (9ft 8in); height 2.15m (7ft 1in)
Weight Combat loaded 13,500kg (29,762lb)
Engine One V-6 six-cylinder diesel developing 290hp at 2000rpm

Performance Maximum road speed 80km/h (50mph); range (road) 500km (310 miles); vertical obstacle 0.8m (2ft 7in); trench 2m (6ft 7in); gradient 60 per cent; fording fully amphibious; water speed 8km/h (5mph)

Armour 23mm (0.9in)
Armament One 73mm gun; one 7.62mm machine gun co-axial with main armament; one launcher rail for AT-3 Sagger ATGW

Right: Since the early 1950s Soviet APC design has placed increased emphasis on weight of armament. While early vehicles such as the BTR-152 carried light support machine guns, later generations were upgunned to provide heavier covering fire and attack capability. Armament on the BMP MICV shown here includes both a 73mm main gun with a co-axially mounted 7.62mm machine gun and the AT-3 Sagger ATGW system.

he is at some disadvantage since there is a blind spot caused by the infamous raised projection on the turret ring which automatically elevates the gun barrel to prevent it striking the commander's infra-red searchlight. For targets over 800m (875 yards), the Sagger missile is selected, but much dexterity is required to load, launch and hold the wire-guided missile on course. The maximum range of the Sagger system is 3000m (1.8 miles).

The vehicle's driver is seated front left with the commander behind him, while the infantry complement occupy the troop compartment to the rear. Infantry enter and exit through two doors in the rear of the hull and are also provided with four hatches and periscopes in the roof. Smallarms firing ports are located in the hull sides.

One of the main considerations in the BMP's design was mobility, allowing the vehicle to travel fast in an advance across an NBC-contaminated

Below: A formation of Soviet BMP-1s on exercise. While most Soviet-built APCs have a crew of two, the BMP's heavier armament necessitates the inclusion of a gunner in addition to the vehicle's driver and commander. The driver's position is situated at the front of the hull with the commander behind him while the gunner occupies the one-man turret. Both driver and gunner wear overalls and are armed with pistols while the commander wears battledress and carries an assault rifle.

battlefield. This 14-tonne tracked APC is powered by a six-cylinder diesel engine and has a road speed of 80km/h (50mph). Like the BTR-60 it is fully amphibious, using its tracks for propulsion, and is fitted with an NBC defence system. Vulnerability is still a problem, however, due to its relatively thin armour. Experience in the Middle East wars has highlighted the risk of incineration of the crew should the fuel cells in the rear doors and passenger compartment or ammunition stowage be hit. Yet, used aggressively and in strength, the low-silhouetted vehicle poses a serious threat on the battlefield.

The BMP series also includes the BMP-2, which appeared in late 1982. This variant carries a 30mm machine cannon and the AT-5 Spandrel anti-tank missile system. Other variants are the BMP-R reconnaissance vehicle and the BMP-U command vehicle; and in 1980 Soviet forces in Germany received the BMP-80, which is reportedly armed with a 30mm

Left: Smallarms firing ports and individual infantry periscopes on the hull of the BMP.

Right: Two views showing details of the interior arrangement of the BMP; the driver's position with T steering bar (left) and a section of the troop compartment (right). Mounted infantry are seated on benches facing outwards and are provided with twin rear doors for entry and exit from the vehicle.

Left: Rather than risk the possibility of incineration, an Iraqi crew beats a hasty retreat from their BMP during an Iranian air attack.

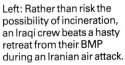

cannon and co-axial 7.62mm machine gun and features a power-operated ramp at the rear for the entry and exit of infantry.

The BMD, which first appeared in 1973, is an APC designed for deployment with the Soviet airborne forces. Based on the BMP, but a much lighter vehicle, it can be air-dropped and carries a crew of three with six airborne infantry occupying open seats at the rear. The BMD is powered by a 280hp diesel engine and has a road speed of 80km/h (50mph). It is a fully amphibious vehicle, propelled by two hydrojets, and is provided with NBC fit and night-vision equipment. Armament consists of a 73mm gun, two 7.62mm machine guns in the bow, one co-axial with the main

Right: A captured BMP-1 on exhibition in Israel. Several Middle East Arab armies are equipped with this vehicle. In combat these BMPs have not always been deployed to their best tactical advantage and the 1973 war saw the Golan Heights littered with knocked-out Syrian APCs.

gun and the AT-3 Sagger ATGW system. Like so many Soviet APCs, the BMD has seen action in the Ogaden as well as being extensively deployed in Afghanistan.

A further addition to the Soviet APC inventory is the MT-LB multi-purpose tracked vehicle. It was originally designed as an artillery tractor but its role has been extended to include cargo transport, APC, command, communications and prime mover deployments. Like all later generation Soviet APCs it is fully amphibious and NBC protected, although it is only lightly armed with a 7.62mm machine gun.

Soviet tactical thinking places a great deal of emphasis on the deployment of APCs, which have a considerable role to play in both first and second echelon assaults. Crew and infantry protection, however, has not been the prime design consideration; and although the Soviet APCs achieve high cross-country mobility, they are very vulnerable to modern anti-armour battlefield weapons systems in the hands of highly-skilled operators.

Above left: Soviet motorised infantry disembark through the rear doors of a BMP. Above right: The smaller BMD which equips the Soviet airborne forces. In an assault without tank support, the BMD normally precedes the dismounted infantry and is provided with two bow-mounted machine guns for extra frontal firepower.

Below: Capable of being dropped by parachute, the BMD provides important battlefield and cross-country mobility for accompanying airborne troops.

BMD Airborne Infantry Combat Vehicle

Crew 3 plus 6
Dimensions Length 5.3m (17ft 5in); width 2.65m (8ft 8in); height 1.85m (6ft 1in)
Weight Combat loaded 9000kg (19,840lb)
Engine One V-6 water-cooled diesel developing 280hp

Performance Maximum road speed 80km/h (50mph); range (road) 320km (200 miles); vertical obstacle 0.8m (2ft 7in); trench 1.6m (5ft 3in); gradient 60 per cent; fording fully amphibious; water speed 10km/h (6.2mph)

Armour 6mm-25mm (0.2in-1in)
Armament One 73mm gun; two 7.62mm machine guns in bow; one 7.62mm machine gun co-axial with main armament; one launcher rail for AT-3 Sagger ATGW

Index